D1202174

I SHOP IN MOSCOW

I SHOP IN MOSCOW

ADVERTISING AND THE CREATION OF

Consumer Culture

IN LATE TSARIST RUSSIA

Sally West

NORTHERN ILLINOIS UNIVERSITY PRESS / *DeKalb*

© 2011 by Northern Illinois University Press

Published by the Northern Illinois University Press, DeKalb, Illinois 60115

Manufactured in the United States using postconsumer-recycled, acid-free paper.

All Rights Reserved

Design by Julia Fauci

Library of Congress Cataloging-in-Publication Data

West, Sally, 1958–

I shop in Moscow : advertising and the creation of consumer culture in late tsarist Russia /
Sally West.

    p.   cm.

Includes bibliographical references and index.

ISBN 978-0-87580-648-8 (clothbound : acid-free paper)

1. Advertising—Social aspects—Russia—History—19th century. 2. Consumption (Economics)—
Social aspects—Russia—History—19th century. 3. Advertising—Social aspects—Russia—History—
20th century. 4. Consumption (Economics)—Social aspects—Russia—History—20th century.
5. Consumers—Russia—History. 6. Popular culture—Russia—History. 7. City and town life—
Russia—History. 8. Russia—Economic conditions—1861-1917. 9. Russia—Social life and customs.
10. Russia—Politics and government—1801-1917. I. Title.

HF5813.R9W47 2011

659.10947'09034—dc22

2011001147

CONTENTS

LIST OF ILLUSTRATIONS

LIST OF TABLES

ACKNOWLEDGMENTS

This book has been a long time in the making, and I wish to thank the many people who have given helpful feedback at all stages from dissertation, to conference papers, articles, and manuscript drafts. Although the list would be too extensive to name them all, there are those without whom the project would not have seen the light of day. I thank first my dissertation advisor, Andy Verner. It was he who suggested looking at the advertising pages of prerevolutionary newspapers, which everyone else at the time ignored, to "see what you find." His support throughout graduate school modeled what a good advisor should be. I also thank Diane Koenker for her consistent encouragement and helpful comments at the dissertation stage. In addition, Louise McReynolds and Linda Scott provided valuable feedback at that time. The staff of the Slavic library at the University of Illinois, Urbana-Champaign, helped tremendously in finding elusive sources, and their friendly faces and cheerful support brought relief to my countless hours of poring over microfilm newspaper collections. I would like to take this opportunity to thank the University of Illinois, especially its history department and library, for being such a wonderful place to study Russian history.

For supporting my research in Russia, I gratefully thank the International Research and Exchanges Board (IREX), which funded ten months' archival study in 1992–1993. Thanks also to the American Council for Teachers of Russian (ACTR) and to Truman State University for funding subsequent summers in Russia. The Social Sciences Research Council provided a grant to support the last year of dissertation writing. My Russian advisor, Professor Boris Vasile'vich Anan'ich, was unfailingly kind and supportive as he introduced me to scholars and archivists in St. Petersburg. I know he expected to see this book a long time ago, so I hope it does not disappoint now.

I have received ongoing encouragement from my fellow Russian historians and dear friends, Tom Trice and Roshanna Sylvester. Since a semester sabbatical in 2006 gave me the luxury of time to become reenergized about this project, they have given generously of their valued skills to critique drafts of each chapter. Knowing the challenges of combining a committed and busy teaching schedule with research, they always believed I would finish, and their excitement about this book speaks of their friendship as much as, if not more than, of their interest in the topic.

I have also been very fortunate in my friends and colleagues at Truman State University. I am especially grateful to my research and writing group made up of scholars in art history, English, rhetoric, and anthropology—Julia DeLancey, Sara Orel, Christine Harker, Cole Woodcox, Janet Davis, and Amber Johnson—whose careful readings and interdisciplinary perspectives brought refreshing new insights to my writing and thought. Thanks also to Torbjörn Wandel for his own work and comments on the introduction. Among my students and student assistants at Truman, Jeff Luttrell and Erica Flanagan's ever upbeat and nudging question, "How's the book coming?" provided more impetus than they realize. I am also grateful to Jeff Naylor, Sherry Dare, and the student assistants at the Pickler Library media lab for helping me to digitize the images.

The participants of the 2006 Midwest Russian History Workshop at Indiana University read chapter 5, and I especially thank Christine Ruane and Charles Halperin for their valuable and extensive feedback at that conference. Parts of chapters 3 and 5 were first published elsewhere in modified form and are reprinted here with permission: "The Material Promised Land: Advertising's Modern Agenda in Late Imperial Russia," *Russian Review* 57, no. 3 (July 1998), and "Smokescreens: Tobacco Manufacturers' Projections of Class and Gender in Late Imperial Russian Advertising," in *Tobacco in Russian History and Culture: From the Seventeenth Century to the Present,* edited by Matthew P. Romaniello and Tricia Starks (New York: Routledge, 2009). My thanks to *Russian Review* and Routledge.

I dedicate this book to my mother, who is too modest to realize how much and in how many ways her life has inspired her children and all who know her. She revived her desire to write and illustrate children's books in her retirement and, after a hiatus of forty-five years, began publishing again at the age of eighty-six.

Note

DATES—Unless otherwise stipulated with the notation N.S. (New Style), all dates are in the Julian calendar (Old Style), which was twelve days behind the western (Gregorian) calendar in the nineteenth century and thirteen days behind in the twentieth.

TRANSLITERATION—The Library of Congress standard of transliteration is used except in the case of names with widely accepted English spelling, such as "Tolstoy" and "Tsar Nicholas."

All translations are mine unless otherwise stated.

I SHOP IN MOSCOW

INTRODUCTION

The sudden deluge of commercial advertising that flooded the city centers of Moscow and Leningrad/St. Petersburg in the early 1990s seemed to most Russians to be an invasion of foreign culture. Where so recently buildings had been topped only by iron communist slogans, where the the occasional sidewalk display case had touted heroes of socialist labor rather than goods, now the Marlboro man towered over city traffic and Pepsi signs covered street kiosks full of Snickers bars and an amazingly eclectic assortment of imported commodities. The content of this onslaught of commerce was indeed predominantly foreign, but few realized at the time that the pervasiveness of advertising brought Russia's streets closer to their own pre-Soviet existence. The commercial cityscape of the 1990s had more in common with that of the 1910s than of the 1980s.

The cities of late tsarist Russia were replete with advertising. Shop signs covered façades along major streets, and advertising columns stood sentinel along the sidewalk. Brand names traveled thoroughfares on the sides of buses and trams, plastered shop windows and streetlights, and even decorated theater curtains during intermissions. Outside stores, pedestrians would be handed leaflets promoting sales; at home and in taverns and teahouses, readers found newspaper pages so full of advertisements that sometimes it was difficult to distinguish news stories from commodity promotions. Brand packaging found its way into the personal details of daily life: soap at washstands, tea in cupboards, cigarettes in pockets.

Advertising did not end with the Bolshevik Revolution, although the economic devastations of the First World War and the Civil War dealt incapacitating blows to all aspects of commerce. In the 1920s under the New Economic Policy (NEP), advertising made a comeback, and not just in the famous constructivist partnership of poet Vladimir Maiakovskii and graphic designer Aleksandr Rodchenko.[1] Constructivist advertising was memorable, but the modest newspaper ads of private enterprise were more pervasive. Even after Stalin put an end to the mixed economy of NEP, advertising did not entirely disappear. Yet throughout the rest of the Soviet period it served a governing ideology rather than the market. It no longer represented the multiplicity of commercial needs or that experimental quality of consumer culture that, in its continuous need for reinvention, was so linked to the modern experience in the late nineteenth and early twentieth centuries.

The purpose of this book is to explore advertising's role in the emergence of Russian consumer culture in the late imperial era up to World War I. Consumer culture constituted one of the many forces unsettling tsarist society in its last decades, as social mobility and industrialization remade many people's life experiences and expectations.[2] I argue that advertising exemplified and amplified the tensions and ambiguities of modernity in Russia; it consciously promoted a modern agenda by encouraging a consumerist ethic at odds with autocratic society, yet it spoke in the language of both tradition and change, simultaneously perpetuating and undermining the values of Russian cultural heritage.

The term "modernity" has been criticized in recent scholarship as an overly used analytical category that often sinks beneath the weight of all it is intended to signify. Rather than imposing our own interpretive notions of modernity on the past, Frederick Cooper cogently argues for a more nuanced investigation of ways in which this concept was used by historical agents themselves.[3] This study seeks to do just that, as advertisers in late imperial Russia expressly saw themselves as facilitating the modern, in terms of both trade practices and broader social change. Analyzing their words and images, this book examines the sometimes conflicted projections of what modern consumer culture meant to those who were promoting it.

I adhere to the tripartite distinction between "modernization," which includes such broad developments as industrialization, urbanization, and technological innovation; "modernism," as in artistic and literary movements; and "modernity," meaning ways of experiencing and responding to the transformations of modern life occurring in the nineteenth and twentieth centuries.[4] In this framework of experiencing the modern, which necessarily includes how people processed modernization, Russia was as much a participant as any of the countries we more readily associate with modernity. The emergence of a thriving Russian consumer society by the late nineteenth century significantly mitigates axiomatic assumptions about Russia's overall backwardness in comparison with the West. It should bring into question the solidity of the East/West dichotomy that too often relegates Russia to a liminal status in European history.

While the processes of modernization in Russia were similar to those in Western societies, the belated and sudden onset of Russian industrialization beginning in the 1880s meant that the culture shocks and changes in self-perception that accompanied the transitions to modern life were more intense. Britain's industrialization, for instance, began almost a century before the mass production of consumer goods in the last half of the 1800s. Even in Germany, which experienced later and speedier industrialization than Britain, the trappings of consumer culture, such as department stores, emerged about two decades after the country entered the industrial age.[5] In Russia's trajectory, however, mass consumption and the social effects of industrial production developed more or less in tandem.

The compression of events in Russia, which for many Westerners had been separated by decades, only heightened the impact of change for those caught up in it. The infamous working and living conditions of laborers in Britain's early factories were already improving by the time that consumer culture came into full swing. But in Russia large numbers of peasants flocked into the burgeoning cities for work only in the last two decades of the nineteenth century, to be thrust into conditions just as vile and danger-ous as those immortalized by Engels in his description of early industrial Manchester.[6] At the same time as they were confronting the servile condi-tions of industrial labor, Russian workers were being exhorted to find self-fulfillment and liberation in a particular brand of liquor or tobacco. They had to learn to be industrial producers and consumers at the same time, thus intensifying their experience of modernity's apparent contradictions.

Contradictions connecting the impact of modernity and consumption are highlighted below in four major paradoxes; they link the Russian and Western experiences but also indicate the distinctive challenges posed by circumstances of late tsarist Russia. Such paradoxes, which have long been noted by social commentators, remain central to understanding the significance of early consumer culture.

1—INDIVIDUALITY AND CONFORMITY   Inherent in both the politics and consumerism of modern times is the possibility for increased indi-vidual choice as well as mass manipulation. Modern polities demand the participation of their people. On the emancipatory side, this is seen in the shift from individuals' self-perception as traditional subjects with-out rights to that of citizens with a sense of civil liberties and political representation. Such transitions were belatedly touching all segments of Russian society by the turn of the twentieth century, as evidenced by increasing pressure for political concessions from the tsarist regime. In the modern marketplace consumer culture also demanded participation, promoting the transformation of self-identification from passive subject, accepting the lot ascribed by traditional state and society, to individual consumer, aspiring for personal fulfillment and choice through the acquisition of goods.

On the repressive side both modern politics and consumption can seek to impose conformity, manipulating opinions and tastes.[7] Modern advertisers everywhere have promoted heightened individual identification while also encouraging people to think of themselves as members of a community of consumers, in which certain tastes are obligatory for acceptance. For Russians in the imperial period, however, both concepts—the consuming individual and the community of consumption—presented new prospects in a country where individualism had been traditionally minimized and community had been largely tied to social estate.[8]

2—TEMPORAL PARADOXES   Modernity is never complete. The old coexists with the new, especially since the "new" in modern life is always changing and is not a fixed end goal. In the transition to modernity, the whole of Russia was in many ways a series of anachronistic contradictions: a peasant society swiftly becoming a world industrial power; a modernizing economy under a stubborn autocracy that still believed in the divinely ordained role of monarchy; a population becoming consumers and citizens, but still subjects of the tsar.

The advertising industry in late imperial Russia was itself a temporal paradox, an agent of change, yet rooted in the past. Still in its infancy, it was hardly an industry in the current sense of professionally trained men and women working creatively in large companies with market research and multimillion-dollar budgets. Only semi-industrialized itself, advertising's media were nonetheless industrial (most prominently, the mass-circulation press), and its messages sounded the values of the modern marketplace, even if some of its writers might better fit a Gogol' short story. "Advertisers," as I use the term in this context, thus implies an ad hoc assortment of business owners and the writers and artists they hired to create their publicity. In the development of content, the advertisers were not the advertising agents, who simply placed already composed ads in various media. Early advertising was the voice of the businesses themselves.

In their borrowing and mixing of traditional and modern themes, advertisers became cultural producers, but not yet mass producers. The definition of mass culture depends upon whether one emphasizes production or consumption. On the consumption side, mass culture is that which is made for the masses, usually for profit; this would include prerevolutionary advertising. As regards production, however, the concept of mass culture (and indeed the coining of the term itself) belongs to the interwar years, with the rise of the entertainment industry in the United States. This became an industry in the literal sense, with "regularized products" that were "capital-intensive and assembled according to complex divisions of labor."[9] In contrast, tsarist Russia's eclectic collection of copywriters and artists was more cottage industry than slick professionalism. While Russian advertising was certainly on the cutting edge of mass consumption, in terms of mass production, it straddled old and new. Advertising was mass-distributed promotion of mass-produced goods for a mass audience, but the messages themselves were not yet produced by advertising professionals. This serves to make them that much more interesting; they were closer to the businesses they represented.

3—The shock of the new—continuity within discontinuity
Discontinuity and its resulting disorientation are a large part of the experience of modernity. And yet theorists of modernity going back to Charles Baudelaire (who first analyzed the concept), Georg Simmel, and Walter Benjamin have noted that the emphasis on newness—the "ever-new"—is so inherent and continuous that it becomes a recurring cycle of the "ever-same."[10] The consumer ethic of modern life fully embodies this principle.

First, the messages of consumption offer novelty so frequently as to become repetitive, masking the unchanging "fetish character of the commodity."[11] Second, in appealing to people to consume, advertisers explicitly draw on novelty and tradition. Modernity is not a clear-cut "sloughing off" of the unenlightened past in favor of a more rational present. To see it as such is to ignore the cultural context that brought about the forces of change, as Charles Taylor argues.[12] Modernity is rather "the new in the context of what has always been there."[13] Even periods of the most radical change carry elements of continuity.[14]

Thus, although Russian advertisers wanted to create a modern consumer society for purposes of increasing demand for their goods and promoting what they saw as the civilizing process of greater consumption, they sought to do this within the anchored stability of notions of traditional culture.[15] For Russians, especially urban residents seeing their environment radically and rapidly altered, the process of modernization was a shock to the system. No wonder, then, that advertisers attempted to inculcate the values of consumption through both traditional and modern idioms. The speed of industrial progress sharpened the contradictions within imperial society. While touting that progress, its commercial sponsors sought also to reassure their audience that change was not a threat to Russian cultural identity. In the process of appropriating traditional themes, however, they played with them and changed them, ultimately commodifying the "eternal" values they seemed to laud. Intentionally or not, even when they honored cultural heritage, advertisers subverted it in the service of modern commerce. Simply by virtue of promoting the modern consumer ethic—the belief that goods offer solutions to life's problems, that consumption is the means to satisfaction and to creation of self-identification—advertising could not help but be a force for change in tsarist Russia, both socially and culturally.

4—THE SIMULTANEITY OF HOPE AND FEAR IN MODERN LIFE.[16] Then as now, advertising appealed to both fear and hope, another coupling that became a central characteristic of modernity. To be modern, writes Marshall Berman, is "to live a life of paradox and contradiction." It is "to find ourselves in an environment that promises us adventure, power, joy, growth, transformation of ourselves and the world—and, at the same time, that threatens to destroy everything we have, everything we know, everything we are."[17] It would be difficult to find lines that better sum up advertising's promises for modern life, as well as the problems to which it proffered solutions for the inhabitants of the modernizing Russian city in the last years of imperial rule.

Fear and hope coexisted not just as deliberate manipulations of the public but also for the modernizers themselves. Those business people who adopted modern advertising in Russia did so in the face of resistance from both fellow tradespeople and some in society who saw such practices as part of the incursion of foreign commercial influences, along with department stores and fixed prices instead of haggling. Advertisers in Russia had to prove to themselves and others that their innovations would pay off and that advertising did not threaten the Russianness of the nation's commercial culture.

A greater internal ambivalence about espousing the modern agenda through advertising emerged in relation to manufacturers targeting a class-segmented audience; in some cases, industrialists' social interests of maintaining a compliant workforce conflicted with their market interests of creating working-class consumers. In these instances, advertisers betrayed anxiety over the very forces they were helping to unleash. This class anxiety, I would argue, was more acute in the context of Russian consumer culture, given the mounting political polarization that the 1905 revolution ultimately did little to assuage.

ADVERTISING AND CONSUMER CULTURE IN RUSSIAN HISTORY

The draconian impact of war and revolution cut off the development of consumer culture in Russia midstream; however, there is ample evidence that prior to this a consumer culture was spreading in both urban and rural

Russia by the turn of the twentieth century. The works of Jeffrey Burds and Barbara Engel, among others, have clearly shown the impact of consumption on peasant communities as a result of out-migration for work in the cities; Jeffrey Brooks has demonstrated the urban and rural spread of commercial print culture; Louise McReynolds's studies have highlighted the commercialization of leisure and the press; Christine Ruane has explored the spread of fashion and, along with Marjorie Hilton, discussed the rise of department stores and the modernization of Russian retailing.[18] Although there is little evidence to show how contemporaries reacted to particular ads, there is no doubt that the overall message of consumption was getting through.

Lori Anne Loeb, in her work on British advertising, defines consumer culture as "a social movement from an ethos of production to an ethos of consumption, from a cultural emphasis on work, sacrifice, and saving to a cultural emphasis on leisure, self-gratification, and self-realization."[19] This bourgeois ethos of production and thrift is problematic for the Russian context, where the bourgeoisie was still only a nascent minority. The Protestant ethic of sacrifice and saving did not apply widely in a Russia in which the nobility was notoriously profligate and the peasants fatalistic to the point of seeing saving as a sin.[20] The connection between piety and profit can be found in certain strains of Russian thought going back to the Muscovite era and expressing itself clearly in the late imperial business practice of holding Orthodox blessing ceremonies for the openings of new stores.[21] But in general, rather than an ethos of consumption replacing one of production, both characteristics of modern industry and commerce were being simultaneously promoted from a variety of state, manufacturing, and trade quarters.

In the broader context, advertising facilitated (and complicated) several central developments associated with the modernization of Russian society. First, essential to the transition from estate structure (*soslovie*) to class was the notion of social mobility and a more fluid definition of personal status. In those campaigns for which advertising segmented its audience, it mainly addressed the working class and the well-to-do bourgeoisie, the two groups that embody class as occupationally and economically defined social categories, rather than estates based on birth. However, in many cases advertising ignored class altogether by encouraging the notion of individual or shared fulfillment across the socioeconomic spectrum. The promise of consumer culture included possibilities for self-definition that do not easily fit the standard historiographic emphasis on class as the central category of analysis for Russia during the revolutionary era.[22] Advertisers disregarded class distinctions as often as they reified them.

A second, crucial development in imperial Russia's modern transformation is the emergence of civil society, in the sense of institutions, groups, and cultural spaces existing autonomously in a traditionally state-created social structure. Advertising facilitated the development of civil society, both functionally by funding the mass-circulation, nongovernmental press born out of the Great Reforms of the 1860s and substantively by voicing private industry's messages of opportunity and choice. However elusive the material reality, both advertising's promise of intentional self-fashioning (grow taller or shapelier; overcome weakness; become attractive through the right choice of cigarettes; throw off peasant identity by adopting urban dress), as well as its proffered choice of community through shared pleasure in consuming selected brands, created at least the notion of voluntary identification and association. In this sense advertising contributed to the loosening of prescribed status and the impetus toward independence from an authoritarian regime.

Thirdly, advertising was a natural component of the economic transition to industrial capitalism. Advertising was the messenger of mass consumption, characterized in Rosalind Williams's words by "the prevalence of standardized merchandise sold in large volume, the ceaseless introduction of new products, widespread reliance on money and credit, and ubiquitous publicity."[23] The ultimate demise of market enterprise with the Bolshevik takeover in 1917 has made it too easy to dismiss the vitality of capitalism's beginnings in Russia. The growing advertising industry created a very public platform for commerce that often stayed a step ahead of officialdom and developed independently of the bureaucratic government. Then, as again today, Russian soil proved as fertile for consumer culture as that of the West.

HISTORIOGRAPHY AND METHODOLOGY

During the Soviet period, few historians addressed prerevolutionary advertising, and those who did so were Soviet scholars interested in advertising's negative, capitalist influence on the press. Aleksandr Bokhanov's 1984 monograph, for example, explores advertising at some length, but solely from the financial and political point of view.[24] While scholars in the West have long studied the varied meanings of advertising in their national histories, no one in the Soviet period considered advertising as a viable source for Russian cultural history.[25]

With the revival of advertising in the transition from communism, there has been an understandable surge of interest among Russians about their own advertising history. Since the 1990s several publications (some available in English) have reproduced the colorful posters and shop signs of the late nineteenth and early twentieth centuries, reacquainting Russians with this vibrant aspect of the country's commercial past.[26] Over the last decade, the literature in Russian has greatly expanded, including V.V. Uchevona and N.V. Starykh's two-volume survey of Russian advertising in the context of Western advertising since ancient times.[27] The majority of recent works, however, are concerned with the practice of present-day business. Nevertheless, the post-Soviet emergence of culture studies (*kul'torologiia*) has included advertising among its themes, and more scholars are recognizing the rich analytical potential of past, as well as present, advertising.[28] In the words of philologist Elena Karmalova, "It is precisely addressing advertising's history, its sources, that convinces us that it is genetically linked to the soil of culture, to its archaic forms, by ritual and myth, with socio-cultural phenomena, inherent in each epoch."[29] The excavation of these cultural roots is just beginning in Russia.

In Western scholarship, many books over the last two decades have discussed the significance of late tsarist commercial culture, but none has focused on advertising as its main topic.[30] The present study is the first attempt to combine an in-depth reconstruction of advertising's development as an industry in prerevolutionary Russia with an analysis of the themes and messages in advertising's most prevalent medium, the mass-circulation press.[31] As such, it offers new avenues into several fields of historical scholarship, including cultural, business, and gender history. Where works such as those of Jeffrey Burds and Barbara Alpern Engel have shown the impact on peasant life of urban consumer culture, a focus on advertising looks at the other side of the process—the messages attempting to draw the populace into consumption.[32] It also adds significantly to the current interest in visual culture in historical scholarship generally.[33] In their recent anthology, *Picturing Russia*, which advocates further exploration of images in Russian studies, editors Valerie Kivelson and Joan Neuberger note Russia's historical tendency to turn to the visual "in order to summon a new reality into being."[34] Advertising was (and is) as much a part of those deliberate efforts to turn "seeing into being" as were early modern religious imagery and Stalinist socialist realism.

In the realm of popular culture, the study of advertising complements works such as those of Richard Stites and Louise McReynolds, who show elements of play in people's daily lives.[35] Not everything seemed inexorably destined toward suffering in the experience of late imperial Russians, as the usual emphasis on class, politics, and intelligentsia despair suggests. The humor in many advertisements speaks to a lively sense of fun that businesspeople expected to resonate easily with the general population.

The messages and images selected by advertisers also tell us much about popular culture by showing which icons of Russian cultural heritage were thought to carry meaning for the public at large. Playing with unfamiliar references would hardly have served advertisers' purpose of reaching a broad contemporary audience.

In the field of commerce, this book adds to our understanding of the broader culture of trade, that which lay between the famous entrepreneurs who left philanthropic legacies and the literary stereotypes of petty cheats such as feature in the plays of Aleksandr Ostrovskii. Marjorie Hilton's work on commercial culture is an important contribution to filling this gap, showing the changing image of commerce as modernizers within the business community pushed for reform of trade practices and venues.[36] The study of advertising offers a different lens into the world of trade and manufacturing by looking at ways in which businesspeople addressed their potential customers, as well as ways in which they saw their own role in civilizing society through consumption. The very vitality of commerce in the last years of the tsarist regime constitutes an argument against the inevitability of decline in early twentieth-century Russia. These points about popular and commercial culture are not intended to argue for unbounded optimism for the potential of late imperial Russia, but rather to suggest that, for many people living their daily lives, enjoyment in the present and hope for the future were not deadened by foreknowledge of catastrophes to come.

Nor was opportunity universally thwarted by the tsarist regime. As a new industry advertising was often one step ahead of regulations, and some enterprising individuals took advantage of open doors to find a new source of livelihood, whether running an advertising agency, composing advertisements, or publishing advertising sheets. This included women, who sometimes found advertising opportunities more open to them than might have been expected in more established industries.

However, this book contests the assertion common in both Western and Russian historiography that early consumer culture was targeted primarily at women. By broadening the focus out from fashion and by looking at the mass-circulation press, my findings place male consumers front and center, alongside women. A gendered analysis of Russian advertising not only restores men to the arena of consumption but also contributes to growing scholarship on masculinity in Russian history.[37]

As noted, the primary focus of this book is on advertising in the mass-circulation press, in particular the daily newspapers of Moscow and St. Petersburg. Although analysis of some commercial posters is included, the majority of advertisements discussed are taken from the press.[38] There are several reasons for the emphasis on newspapers, the most obvious being that many have been preserved in libraries in both Russia and abroad, making the mass-circulation press the most accessible medium for a study of Russian advertising. More importantly, however, newspapers present the best opportunity to assess the size and nature of the intended audience, as well as the frequency—and thus representativeness—of specific advertisements and advertising approaches over time. Many of the newspaper ads discussed would appear repeatedly over time and often in multiple periodicals. We also know a fair amount about newspapers' circulation, including that they spread well beyond the cities in which they were published.[39]

In contrast, it is often difficult to know when posters were published or where they were placed, who saw them, how long they stayed posted, or how often they were changed. Thus, while posters are more colorful and eye-catching and can speak to an illiterate audience, they may tell us less about overall advertising campaigns in terms of longevity, typicality, and target audience. It is also probable that their dissemination was more restricted to the city, while newspapers made their way to rural villages, where they would be read aloud and pored over even among the illiterate.[40]

Since this project represents the first systematic cultural study of the content of imperial Russian advertising, an exhaustive analysis of all advertising within the mass-circulation press was beyond its reach. Therefore, I focused on four of Russia's most popular mass-circulation newspapers, using two methodologies to combine maximum chronological span with in-depth analysis of content. For chronological breadth, I sampled two newspapers with the greatest longevity, one from each capital city. For a more comprehensive study I examined all available issues of the two papers with the widest circulation in Moscow and St. Petersburg respectively. The two newspapers sampled for longevity were *Peterburgskaia gazeta* (*Petersburg Gazette*), which ran from 1867 to 1917, and *Moskovskii listok* (*Moscow Sheet*), which ran from 1881 to 1918. In each case I surveyed two weeks' worth of issues (one week in May and one in November) every five years.[41] Appendix A shows a quantitative breakdown of advertising in *Peterburgskaia gazeta* throughout most of its run, highlighting the growth in various kinds of advertisements over the decades.

The second approach aimed at a more consistent examination, scanning entire runs (except for a few gaps in the available holdings) of the two most popular daily newspapers in prerevolutionary Russia: Moscow's *Russkoe slovo* (*Russian Word*), which ran from 1895 to 1917, and St. Petersburg's *Gazeta-kopeika* (*Penny Gazette*), which ran from 1908 to 1918.[42] In addition I looked randomly at another well-established newspaper, *Russkie vedomosti* (*Russian Record*), the so-called "professors' paper," in order to take into account socioeconomic diversity of audience. As with any first study, many future opportunities for research remain, such as a comparative study of advertising in the daily press and popular journals, a more comprehensive study of commercial posters, and a close examination of classified advertisements, all of which fell beyond the scope of the present work.

The majority of advertisements examined here appeared in the twentieth century, particularly in the period from 1905 to 1914. Newspaper advertising before the 1890s tended to be unimaginative, merely citing inventories and the name of the business. Rarely were illustrations used until the turn of the century, either in Russia or the West. Improvements in lithography and, in particular, the introduction of half-tone engraving in the 1880s and early '90s allowed newspapers themselves to use illustrations, an advance that naturally influenced advertising as well.[43] In conjunction with illustrations, the 1890s saw the advent of slogans and verse in advertisements, forming part of the shift in emphasis from information to persuasion that is one of the defining characteristics of modern advertising.[44]

In addition to international advances in printing and publishing, the economy played a role in Russia's advertising development. The upswing in the nation's economic performance from 1908 until the outbreak of war in 1914 allowed businesses to pay more attention to creative advertising.[45] The last six or seven years of peace thus constituted advertising's heyday in prerevolutionary Russia, and this fact is reflected in the predominance of examples from that period.

While advertisements are available in abundance as primary sources for this topic, the same, unfortunately, cannot be said for archival sources on prerevolutionary Russian advertising. The Soviet regime had little room for so bourgeois a topic as commercial advertising, and most of what has survived has done so because it was part of other records or collections that were deemed to hold greater value. Print advertisements themselves survived largely due to the fact that they were an integral part of newspapers, which libraries preserved. Indicative of the Soviet attitude toward the business of advertising, the records of Russia's biggest advertising agency, L. and E. Metzl, were largely sacrificed to a paper shortage.[46] There are no "mother lodes" of archival resources for the advertising industry such as exist, for instance, for long-lived advertising agencies in the United States.[47]

Despite the paucity of archival primary sources on the Russian advertising industry, enough does survive in scattered holdings to piece together advertising's growing role in late tsarist Russia. The few extant manufacturing company records relating to advertising together comprise an outline of its increasing importance in consumer industries; newspaper records present a fuller picture of advertising's importance to and relationship with the popular press; the archives of the imperial court reveal a great deal about the importance of state awards granted at national exhibitions to the advertising of manufacturers and traders; governmental investigations into businesses' trustworthiness during the First World War are a researcher's boon in preserving most of what we know about Russian advertising agencies; and censorship records have much to tell us about the administration's difficulties in overseeing the rising tide of advertising. These sources, along with printed leaflets and advertising booklets, trade journals, how-to manuals, and law codes comprise the foundation for the first part of the book, which seeks to reconstruct the history of advertising as an industry and an aspect of modernization in imperial Russia.

Chapter 1 dips back into the eighteenth century to trace the growth of modern advertising in Russia from its precursor, the street sign, to the flourishing of print media by the turn of the twentieth century. This chapter also looks at the institutions and people behind advertising, as well as the varied responses to it from the business community. Chapter 2 examines the relationship between state and advertising, both in terms of regulation and reward. Censorship of advertising remained a thorny issue for advertisers and authorities alike, not to mention the press. Yet traders and manufacturers continued to vie for governmental endorsements awarded at trade and industry exhibitions, greatly desiring the advertising value of an official state seal or medal.

The second part of the book analyzes some of the major themes apparent in the advertisements themselves: visions of progress through consumption; the gendered messages of commerce; and consumer culture's appropriation of Russian culture. Chapter 3 explores the emphasis of Russian advertisers on consumption as a modernizing, civilizing influence, especially for the rapidly increasing lower classes that were tripling the size of Russia's main cities from the mid-nineteenth to early twentieth centuries. This chapter looks at ways in which manufacturers promoted consumption as a new form of community transcending class at the same time that they often demonstrated paternalistic attitudes toward lower class consumers. In one of the paradoxes of Russian consumer culture, those promoting the vision of modernity in commerce were sometimes simultaneously trying to stem the pace of change.

Chapter 4 challenges the assumption, both of the time and in much subsequent scholarship, that early consumer culture was overwhelmingly directed at and adopted by women. Shifting away from the more common focus on Western societies in consumer culture studies to the particularities of late imperial Russia, and looking through the lens of the daily press rather than fashion or ladies' journals, reveals that men emerge as full participants with women in consumption, despite the prevalent perceptions that this was a female activity. Advertisers trod a fine line, appealing to gendered norms while seeking to draw men into the supposedly feminine arena of consumption.

Finally, chapter 5 explores ways in which advertisers both honored Russian cultural themes and simultaneously undermined them through commodification and humor. Although advertising touted the new, many of its appeals were clothed in the guise of traditional culture. Whether it be through images of Mother Russia, the Fatherland, invented traditions of historical jubilees, or appropriation of the intelligentsia's classical canon, advertisers linked their commodities to a shared heritage that suggested continuity in a world of rapid transformations.

The analysis found in the second half focuses on the intentions of advertising's producers rather than on audience reception, not because I deny consumer agency (even with the benefit of modern marketing research, advertisers cannot fully control how consumers will reinterpret, appropriate, mock, ignore, or simply enjoy their work),[48] but rather because there are so few sources through which to ascertain audience response to particular advertisements. Advertising is the business community's deliberate communication with the public. Its intentionality renders it readable in terms of the tactics that advertisers thought would work. Advertisements, of course, are not transparent reflections of their creators' minds. They are purposefully manipulative, seeking to encourage new and greater needs and to mold consumer behaviors. Yet this very manipulation can be telling of cultural and social perspective. Embedded as these advertisers were in the same time and place as their audience, they could not help but project contemporary perspectives about what they believed would resonate culturally. As media scholar Jib Fowles points out, when advertising strays too far afield from the symbols of its own culture, it produces no meaning and therefore no impact.[49]

Central to the modern experience as consumption has been, the role of advertisers in producing a culture of consumption is significant. In his early work on consumer society, Jean Baudrillard noted that marketing helps create the system of coded values in which goods stand for things beyond their function.[50] In late imperial Russia the symbolic system of consumer culture was in its formative stages, unsophisticated by our own standards, and yet foreshadowing to a remarkable extent the approaches of later consumerism. Reading advertising as a visual and textual strand in the evolving discourses on modernity in tsarist Russia not only sheds light on the tactics of creating consumer culture, but also retrieves some of the business community's collective voice as it negotiated the challenges and promise of what still seemed the path to a prosperous future.

PART

ONE

THE DEVELOPMENT OF
MODERN ADVERTISING IN RUSSIA

To "advertise" literally means to "turn toward" or "call attention to."[1] In this broadest sense of drawing public attention toward objects of trade, advertising goes back to ancient times. The local blacksmith or shopkeeper advertised simply by establishing a business with the purpose of attracting customers; a traveling street vendor advertised his or her trade in the act of displaying merchandise. In Russia, at least as far back as Muscovite times, tradesmen hung samples of their wares outside their shops to draw in customers.[2] But they also developed more active tactics to sell their merchandise. Hawking, in the literal sense of calling out in the street, was a means common to many societies for dispensing news and goods; the Latin word for this practice, *reclamare* (to shout out loud), is the root of the word for advertising in several European languages, including the Russian *reklama*.[3] As in other cultures hawking goods in Russia became an aggressive practice of pressuring passersby to stop and make purchases—described in Russian by the verb *zazyvat'*, which means "insistently to invite or induce someone to approach." The "invitation" was then followed by haggling over price.

Traditional trade practices such as these continued well into the twentieth century in Russia, but industrialization, urbanization, growing literacy, improved printing technologies, and rising consumerism put increasing pressure on the commercial marketplace to modernize. Zazyvat' was a central aspect of merchant traditions that business modernizers from the late nineteenth century onward wished to eradicate in favor of more "enlightened" practices, such as print advertising and fixed prices.[4]

Modern advertising followed mass production as the clarion call of mass consumption. The public voice of the consumerism sweeping much of European society, advertising's modernity lay essentially in encouraging a universal culture of consumption, rather than just the acquisition of luxuries by the well-to-do.[5] To accomplish this, advertising had to combine both persuasiveness and pervasiveness. While examples of commercial rhetorical flourish and print advertisements can be found before the era of modern advertising, only the onset of affordable, varied periodicals that the public could and would buy facilitated the spread of advertising on a national, socially inclusive scale. Before the 1860s in Russia, advertising remained a sporadic phenomenon with a reach dependent upon its viewers' class and location. With the development of the mass-circulation press and the rise of consumer industries, it became a national phenomenon.

The shift in tone from "announcement" to "advertisement" encapsulates the character of modern advertising. An announcement (*ob"iavlenie* in Russian) simply informs; an advertisement seeks to attract attention and to actively persuade someone to buy. In Russia, although the terms ob"iavlenie and reklama were often used interchangeably, it was reklama that concerned both proponents and critics of modern marketing. Straightforward announcements of events or statements of a shop's inventory continued to exist alongside the developing rhetoric of advertising, but the latter defined the modern trend, as well as critics' negative responses to its intrusiveness.

The "shouting out" of modern advertising was part of the rising volubility of unofficial voices making themselves heard in late tsarist Russia; it was not overtly political, but it was still potentially destabilizing for traditional monarchical control, as well as unsettling to the sense of cultural leadership among the nation's elites. This chapter examines the context for the emergence of reklama—the phenomenon of modern advertising—in the imperial period. It traces advertising's preindustrial exemplar, the shop sign, as a recurring flashpoint for Russians' frequently negative responses to images of trade from the eighteenth century. It addresses advertising's diversification and symbiotic role in the rise of the mass-circulation press from the late nineteenth century, a period that also saw the rise of advertising agencies. These agencies were mediators between businesses and the press, although they were not the creators of the advertisements themselves. The chapter infers as much as possible about that most elusive aspect of Russian advertising history, the creative process. And finally, it explores the increasing adoption of modern advertising by Russian commerce, as the business community itself expanded, diversified, and modernized.

SHOP SIGNS AS PRECURSORS OF MODERN ADVERTISING

Shop signs foreshadowed modern advertising both in creativity and in the polarity of responses evoked. Designed initially for illiterate or semiliterate populations, shop signs were as much visual as textual communications for trade. It is this convergence of art and commerce that triggered discomfort in many who saw the two fields as diametrically opposed. Commerce carried a connotation of unseemliness in much of Russian cultural history, but the long-term failure to suppress shop signs indicates the irrepressibility of tradespeople's need for advertising, as well as the regime's often grudging acceptance of its economic necessity.

Ranging from simple painted names to elaborate representations of goods, shop signs were more than literal signs; in the eyes of rulers and commentators from the eighteenth century into the twentieth, their character and proliferation carried semiotic weight, signifying economic health, aesthetic values (both negative and positive), and even moral impropriety, depending upon the predominant interests of the observer. In St. Petersburg especially, from the days of Peter the Great and his successors, the desire among rulers and intellectuals to promote an Enlightenment sensibility of architectural regularity (*reguliarnost'*) for the Western-style capital created an ongoing tension with the often irregular and intentionally eye-catching accoutrements of trade. From the perspective of eighteenth-century reformers, shop signs, which sometimes included three-dimensional, oversized models of goods suspended into the street, embodied the vulgarity and disorder of old-world trade. In the twentieth century's bifurcated gaze, shop signs were still seen by some as emblems of a bygone era (although now one subject to both nostalgia and disdain), but in their ubiquity and diversity the signs were also taken as indicators of the rising tide of modern commerce. Outdated or modern, distasteful or charming—the judgment depended on the viewer's notions of what "modern" should mean. Recurring targets of both disapproval and admiration, shop signs served as lightning rods for opinion about the aesthetics of urban space throughout the imperial era, particularly in the capital city.

Shop signs first spread from western Europe to Russia in the late seventeenth century. With the increase in international trade and the influx of Western customs under Peter I, Russian and foreign traders and guilds adopted European trade symbols, such as the depiction of a lion holding a pretzel to denote the German bakeries in St. Petersburg.[6] Although few of the earliest signs survived, there is ample evidence to suggest their prevalence in the eighteenth century, at least in the capital city.[7]

Embedded throughout Russian society, and especially among its upper echelons, lay a deep-seated vein of negativity toward trade. The basic dishonesty of the tradesman was assumed, as evidenced by the oft-cited business saying, "If you don't deceive, you won't sell." Petty merchants were seen as narrow-minded, despotic tricksters, while the rising industrialists of the late nineteenth century, despite their better educations and surface polish, were largely seen to be self-centered profit mongers, unreformed at core.[8] Shop signs, then, could be visible reminders of a "dirty" occupation.

Empress Elizabeth (ruled 1740–1762) expressed just such displeasure at being forced to see the trappings of common trade on her regular routes through the city. In 1742 she ordered that eating houses and their signs be removed from major streets. Not content with this measure, in 1752 she decreed that no shop signs of any kind remain on main streets, "as today there are a multitude of them for various trades, visible right opposite Her Majesty's very courtyard."[9] The offensive signs were consequently relegated to backstreets and inner courtyards, as were the merchants themselves the following year. Catherine II (ruled 1762–1796) was able to see beyond the vulgarity of the commonplace and recognize the hindrance to convenient trade that such a consignment to the alleyways imposed. In 1770 she revoked her predecessor's decree, allowing merchants and their signs to return to the capital's major thoroughfares. She did so with the stipulation, however, that the signs meet the standards of "decency" (*pristoinost'*). Specifically forbidden, for example, were depictions of men's undergarments or funeral paraphernalia, both of which forced to mind subjects best left out of polite conversation.[10]

Throughout the nineteenth century shop signs became an increasingly ubiquitous part of the urban landscape. They were not only painted on panels above and beside doorways but in windows and the glass of nearby lampposts. As in other European capitals, the oversized models of merchandise suspended over merchants' doors might include a giant glove, for example, or a massive leg of ham. In the absence of an outright ban, shopkeepers imaginatively appropriated both two- and three-dimensional spaces, extending commercial signs into the supposedly noncommercial areas beyond their thresholds.[11] In the process, they began to make advertising an inescapable aspect of the urban experience.

Not everyone saw the signs in a negative light. With the proliferation of street advertising, a visitor to St. Petersburg in the 1840s called the city's main artery of commerce, Nevskii Prospekt, "a kind of picture gallery."[12] The prevalence of signs was not limited to the wealthy center of shopping. An anonymous commentator in 1848 noted the more primitive versions of shop signs that decorated the poorer streets; although he found them amusingly inferior, he still recognized them as a form of art and an expression of the merchants' taste. This sympathetic assessment was ahead of its time, as demonstrated by the fact that the author felt the need to justify his choice of such a humble theme for educated readers, declaring that "in a well-organized state there is no subject unworthy of observation by a curious person."[13]

While Nevskii Prospekt may have maintained the status of a gallery in this art of commerce, the shop signs of the smaller streets and outer regions, such as the Vyborg side of the Neva, developed along the lines of folk art. Unable to afford the services of more expensive artists, the majority of small business owners turned to modest local talent. In these areas the influence of European style was less evident. The absurd proportions of a rooster standing a head taller than a bull,[14] or the common grammatical mistakes in lettering may have elicited smirks from more literate passersby, but such signs provided a valuable commercial outlet for native Russian art that would be "discovered" by the avant-garde in the early twentieth century.[15]

During the nineteenth century the early tendency of shop signs to indicate the activity of the business, sometimes including a depiction of the owner at his work, gave way more commonly by mid-century to pictorial inventories of goods.[16] These included as many items as possible, so that a customer would be well informed as to the increasing diversity of goods that the shops offered. In a largely illiterate or semiliterate society pictures were more important than text. And in an overwhelmingly Orthodox society, iconography struck a familiar chord, even though in the service of commerce rather than God.

The predominance of the painted image over the word was less noticeable on the major thoroughfares, where customers could read not only Russian but quite likely French and German as well. The merchants left nothing to chance in engaging passersby, however, as the visiting novelist Théophile Gautier noted of Nevskii Prospekt in 1858:

Golden letters trace their full and slender lines on fields of blue, on black or red panels; they are stamped out and applied to glass façades, repeated at every door; profiting from the angles of the street, they round curves, extend the length of ledges, use projecting awnings, descend down basement stairways and seek every means of compelling the eye of the passerby. But perhaps you don't know Russian, and the form of the characters means nothing more for you than an ornamental design or a piece of embroidery? Here to the side is the French or German translation. You still haven't understood? The obliging sign pardons you for not recognizing any of these three languages; it even assumes that you might be completely illiterate, and presents a lifelike depiction of the goods for sale in the shop it is advertising. Sculpted or painted bunches of golden grapes indicate a wine merchant; further along glazed hams, sausages, tongues, tins of caviar designate a food shop; high boots, ankle boots, naïvely presented galoshes, say to feet that don't know how to read: "Enter here and you will be shod;" crossed gloves speak an idiom intelligible to all.[17]

This passage illustrates not only the luxuriance of advertising on Nevskii Prospekt (equaled, according to the author, only by the Swiss city of Bern), but also its abundance long before the economic growth of the late nineteenth century. On the eve of the Great Reforms, the center of Russia's capital was already an example of cosmopolitan commerce colorful enough to surprise a Parisian.

The interests of business had clearly displaced Catherine II's standards of "decency" in shop signs by the middle of the nineteenth century. A mid-century author lamented the windows and signs of funeral merchants that displayed small grave markers "standing . . . like a silent *memento mori*."[18] One such undertaker explained that his sign was in French as well as Russian partly for "tone," but also so that any French people dying in St. Petersburg would know that they could get good draft- and leakproof coffins at his shop.[19]

Hardly more decorous were the butchers, who had huge sides of beef painted on their signs—in one case the letters themselves composed of various cuts of meat.[20] Barbers often portrayed their auxiliary service of bloodletting, a seemingly macabre occupational linkage today, but one that was common in the West as well as in Russia at the time. Such literal and increasingly colorful depictions on shop signs persisted throughout the nineteenth and into the twentieth century, retaining their usefulness in the growing commercial sphere. The exotic was also popular, especially with tobacco vendors, who would often decorate their doorways with paintings of hookah-smoking Turks or American Indians replete with headdress and cigar.[21] Such stereotypical images (with all the exaggerations and errors that stereotypes entail) became the hallmarks of various industries.

Although some trade signs might follow formulaic patterns, the painter was responsible for the conception of the design, taking into consideration the specifications of the shop owner. Little information has survived about the artistic side of sign production, but in the nineteenth century this work was often combined with the business of icon painting (reinforcing the iconographic nature of shop signs). A typical studio would have one master painter and ten to fifteen apprentices.[22] Toward the twentieth century, shop sign painters either tended to establish independent specialized businesses or constituted the artistic departments of house-painting companies.[23]

In the early twentieth century, the aesthetic value of shop signs came under contentious debate, both as a matter of urban visual blight, echoing eighteenth-century concerns over architectural regularity, and as a division of artistic opinion among the avant-garde. The preservationist movement of the 1900s and 1910s sought to preserve and revive the classical Empire style of architecture favored in the era of Alexander I (ruled 1801–1825).[24] In contrast to the revival of the pre-Petrine Russian national style favored by the last two tsars (Alexander III, ruled 1881–1894; Nicholas II, ruled 1894–1917), the preservationists favored the clean lines and simple elegance of the Napoleonic era. The debate over styles implied definitions of national identity (European versus Muscovite Russian) and thus carried the passion of patriotic and political as well as artistic meaning. Concerned as the preservationists were with the harmonious façades of buildings, the increasing size and prevalence of shop signs in the early twentieth century perturbed them. Traders needed to attract a more anonymous public as the urban population soared with worker immigrants who were unfamiliar with word-of-mouth reputations. That meant bigger and more eye-catching signs.

The inevitable conflict between the interests of architectural purity and trade reached its peak in 1913, just as the preservationist movement was at its height. At their Fourth Congress, the Permanent Committee of All-Russian Architects concluded that, unlike early nineteenth-century shop signs, which by virtue of their moderate size had been appropriate to the "architectural magnificence of Catherinian and Alexandrine buildings," the "extraordinary largeness" of contemporary signs "disfigured not only individual buildings, but whole streets."[25] The paintings' lack of artistic merit was spoiling the look of the city. The architects forwarded their conclusions to the St. Petersburg city governor, who shared their sensibilities and, in January 1914, ordered that shop signs henceforth contain only the name of the firm, without additional text or paintings. He too felt that the depictions of meat, sausages, animals, vegetables, and laundresses were "tastelessly painted" and only appropriate to the illiteracy of earlier times. In 1914 the signs were "extremely unfavorable" to maintaining the smooth running of the capital as well as covering the "often artistic and stylish" façades of buildings.[26] More than 170 years after Empress Elizabeth's decree against trade publicity, it seemed at first that the capital's authorities had decided the matter in favor of the architectural purists.

However, the governor's order elicited protests and appeals from merchants and trade organizations, which banded together to protest the governor's decision to remove their signs. They contested the governor's positive assessment of the literacy level in the country, asserting that "our cultural development is still not at the necessary height" to do away with pictorial signs (a claim substantiated by the writers' own grammatical errors). The petitioners went on to say that not only servants "but also very many educated gentlemen seek this or that establishment by its sign and not by its lettering but by the type of product" depicted. The governor would serve the city better, the merchants added, by addressing the dirt in the streets and markets rather than inoffensive shop signs.[27] Despite his own sympathies, the governor was eventually forced to back down and recall his order when the Department of Trade sided with the merchants. In this age of industry and trade, the central government's priorities, it turned out, placed the interests of commerce over those of refined taste.

Against this backdrop of contention between architecture and trade, certain artists of the Russian avant-garde who were seeking national roots for creative inspiration turned to folk art forms such as the popular print (*lubok*) and shop signs. The work of artists such as Mikhail Larionov and Natalia Goncharova, for example, reflect the influence of shop signs in both content and style.[28] In the medium of shop signs, we find an unusual case of the mercantile sphere, so often derided by the intelligentsia, influencing art in ways other than through patronage from wealthy merchant art lovers.

It was through the artists' lively interest in the commercial art form of shop signs that the primitivist Niko Piromanashvili was discovered by members of Larionov's circle in Tiflis, Georgia. In 1912 he was earning his living painting signs, mainly for taverns. Examples of his work were brought to Moscow to form part of the "Target" exhibition arranged by Larionov in 1913, the first exhibition to display shop signs alongside works of recognized artists.[29]

Given the commonly elitist attitudes of the art world toward popular arts and commerce, the avant-garde concern with shop signs provoked predictable derision from critics, and many fellow artists even among the avant-garde found the new interest absurd. For Alexander Benois, a leader of the World of Art movement, art was a vehicle for the highest truth and beauty, with the artist serving almost as priest in this religion of beauty.[30] He denounced the "clowns" who were "shouting about signs, about going back to primitive ways and outrageous stuff like that." Another critic even proclaimed the equation of shop signs with art as "blasphemous."[31]

The popular press responded to the intelligentsia's contradictory attitudes toward shop signs with amusement. With the artistic debate ongoing, it was easy to satirize the possible fate of the signs that the preservationists wanted removed. A 1914 cartoon in the journal *Novyi satirikon* (*New Satirist*), entitled "On the Destruction of Painted Signs," showed an out-of-work sign painter mourning the imminent removal of his creations outside each of his former clients' shops: a butcher, a tobacconist, a grocer, and a clothier. Addressing the characters in his signs, he cries, "Farewell, fine young man, dressed in the latest fashion, admirably shaved and coiffed—farewell to you as well, fine lady, beautified at the salon; I didn't begrudge you the most expensive colors—farewell lady, with whom passing schoolboys fell in love, farewell, farewell!" In the last frame, the unemployed sign painter happens upon his "old acquaintances" at an art exhibition. "But they didn't recognize their creator, since now they cost thousands and called themselves 'works of the futurists.'"[32]

In a final irony, many of the signs survived on the streets long after the shops they advertised had been closed. Despite the "phobia of the commercial"[33] that carried over from the prerevolutionary intelligentsia to the new Bolshevik leaders, even the new Communist regime did not immediately remove the shop signs. For at least three years after the October Revolution, these "street emblems of the former capitalist system"[34] remained over businesses that no longer existed, advertising goods that were not available. The visual representations of trade had outlived two centuries of fluctuating opinion over their existence and worth because they served the populace effectively as signposts for meeting material needs and comforts in Russia's major centers of commerce.

It is in shop signs that we see the first dovetailing of art and trade, which is in large part why in Russia the signs seemed an affront to some and charming to others. Historically, shop signs have constituted the initial step in claiming urban space for not just the practice, but also the iconography of trade. In that sense, they were indeed precursors to modern advertising.

ADVERTISING'S DIVERSIFICATION IN THE
NINETEENTH CENTURY—FROM STREET TO HOME

In the nineteenth century, advertising broke beyond its in situ moorings outside the shop to colonize a growing diversity of urban space, both public and private. From posters to packaging, newspapers to public transport, advertisers utilized a multiplicity of surfaces to turn urban dwellers' attention toward consumer goods.

During the second half of the century, streets across Europe witnessed the flowering of an increasingly popular combination of art and commerce in the form of the poster. Facilitated by advances in printing technology, posters had the advantages of low cost, variability, and multiplicity. A merchant or manufacturer could order hundreds of copies of his advertisement at no extra effort for himself and little extra cost. He could then place them throughout the city, instead of just in front of his shop. Walls, fences, station platforms, the sides of public transport—all became viable locations for advertisements. During the 1870s entrepreneurs introduced poster columns into Russia, new urban landmarks devoted solely to advertising.[35] Placards were also posted on specially designed boards and in kiosks. Even in Russia's smaller provincial cities such advertising locations became a common sight. A Poltava printer who had acquired the rights to rent out advertising spaces claimed in 1904 that his town boasted 574 boards and 12 kiosks for posters.[36]

Educated Russians were readier to accept posters than shop signs as a potential art form. This was largely due to French influence, with artists such as Henri Toulouse-Lautrec lending legitimacy to the medium. There was even encouragement in the official art world for accomplished artists to turn their attention toward improving the quality of Russian poster design. In the 1880s the Academy of Artists put out the first art posters by Russian artists as advertisements for their annual ball.[37] And commercial posters were included in the 1897 International Exhibition of Art Posters, staged in St. Petersburg, with over seven hundred entries from thirteen countries. The Russian selections, however, were predominantly for publications and entertainment events.[38] This exhibition did much to encourage a subsequent union between art and commerce in Russian poster production. Now, without the former fear of stigma, Russian artists could openly supplement their incomes through commercial design. Such was the case with Ivan Bilibin, who created posters for the steamship company Kavkaz i Merkurii and the beer factory Bavariia.[39]

As advertising diversified, the street increasingly became commercial terrain. The boundary between shop and sidewalk blurred with modernized versions of *zazyvat'*; the merchants' pressure tactics now took printed form as salesmen inundated passing pedestrians with free advertising flyers, booklets, and price lists, distributed in large quantities. Once drawn inside the shop by these media, a customer might be given a complimentary calendar (containing advertisements as well as dates) or a free trinket, such as a pencil or comb with the company's named inscribed on it. By the end of the century, some firms were also giving out coupons to tempt people to sample free or discounted merchandise.[40]

Advertisers found other public venues to promote their businesses. The sides of public transport commonly sported mobile advertising, then as now. And the worlds of commerce and art overlapped on the stage, with owners of private theaters in St. Petersburg supplementing their incomes by renting out space on the stage curtains for advertising, forcing theater-goers to look at "all possible kinds of addresses" during the intermission.[41] Despite the common conception that ubiquitous advertising belongs to the twentieth century and beyond, clearly the urban residents of the nineteenth century, even in "backward" Russia, would have found it difficult to ignore the advertisements that filled their streets and public places.

Advertising reached further than just public locales, however. Even before radio and television brought endless advertisements into individual homes, commercial publicity found ways to reach into the privacy of the domestic hearth. There were three main ways in which businesses achieved this blurring of public and private space: on packaging, in newspapers and magazines, and by delivering advertisements to private homes.

In the nineteenth century, delivery of advertising notices to homes was hardly the tidal wave of catalogs and mailings we experience today. Yet, as in the West, by the 1880s catalogs connected provincial homes with urban consumption networks, and trade cards announced new merchandise to residents through the mail.[42] Although Russian businesses probably did not send out trade cards in the millions that their counterparts did in the United States from the 1870s, the practice of informing fashionable ladies and gentlemen of the arrival of the latest styles goes back at least to the 1840s in Russia.[43] Some businesses sent lengthy and elegant epistles describing their merchandise or announcing the opening of a new shop for elite clientele, while others merely delivered a visiting card with their advertisement on the back. The fact that many examples of such mailings are preserved in the personal archives of distinguished families clearly shows that recipients of this type of advertising did not yet consider it "junk mail."[44]

While home-delivered trade cards and letters were probably reserved for the elite, even the poorest urban residents took advertising home in the form of brand names, trademarks, and commercial designs on product packaging. In Britain branding appeared in the eighteenth century for some luxury goods, but the period in which brand packaging flourished throughout the industrializing world was the mid- and late nineteenth century, when the increase in ready-made consumer goods created the need for product differentiation. In earlier days, most dry goods were sold in bulk, and packaging existed purely for the functional purposes of transportation. But when rival companies saw the need to appeal directly to consumers by visually distinguishing their products from their competitors, they began to invest in attractive and distinctive labels and wrappings.[45] While other forms of advertising served to introduce and promote products, brand packaging existed primarily to facilitate consumer loyalty through name recognition.

By the late nineteenth century, there can scarcely have been a home in Russia's major cities without brand names on its shelves. It was not just the expensive perfume bottle that was decorated with an alluring label, but also the common household items from soap to cigarettes that trumpeted their contents' worth with as much imagination as the merchants could muster. In the course from shop to home, brand packaging was perhaps the most pervasive form of advertising, although few consumers probably thought of it as such.

The medium that contemporaries would have identified as the most prolific disseminator of advertising was the mass-circulation press. By the late nineteenth century, most of the Russian popular dailies dedicated about a third of their page space to advertisements, rising to half of page space in many cases during the early twentieth century.[46] This most lucrative—and eventually most common—form of advertising had to await the developments of the 1860s, however. Before that, while official government notices, classifieds, and some private trade advertisements were printed in independent periodicals, the use of this channel for commercial purposes was heavily restricted, both by the small circulations of newspapers and journals and by governmental controls. The Russian government maintained a near monopoly on advertising before the reform era, reserving the right to take in paid advertising for its own state-sponsored periodicals. By not allowing this right to independent newspapers, it deprived them of an important source of income. Even an 1838 law permitting individuals to place classified advertisements in private publications was of limited impact, since authorities retained arbitrary control to decide which publications would be granted the privilege.[47]

Independent periodicals would have to wait until the reform era (specifically 1862) for the eradication of restrictions on taking in advertising.

The new potential to form a financial base through paid advertising re-moved one of the main obstacles to the development of a commercial press in Russia.[48] But one other major hurdle was still to be negotiated before publishers could easily issue newspapers daily: that of mandatory prepub-lication censorship. Censorship regulations were revised in 1865, allowing publishers in the larger cities to request exemption from preliminary cen-sorship if they deposited five thousand rubles with the state to cover fines for potential publishing offenses.[49] The state also retained the power to bar an offending periodical from accepting advertisements; evidently this source of income was seen as a privilege rather than a right (as indeed was publishing an independent newspaper altogether). The favored punitive measure in case of infractions, however, was the temporary prohibition of street sales, a source of revenue that played an increasingly important role in mass circulation.[50]

The newly favorable conditions for periodical publishing occasioned a sharp rise in the number of daily newspapers published in St. Petersburg throughout the reform years, with a greater than threefold increase, from five in 1860 to seventeen in 1891. Moscow's press responded more slowly, but also steadily increased from two to eleven over the same time span.[51] Although many papers failed after only short runs, those that survived reached increasingly large audiences due to their affordability and popular format. The first "boulevard" newspaper, *Peterburgskii listok* (*Petersburg Sheet*), went from a circulation of 9,000 in 1870 to 128,500 in 1916, an increase almost ten times the rate of population growth in the capital city during the same period.[52] And it was soon only one of several similarly widely read papers.[53] The reforms of the 1860s had indeed created a springboard for the successful takeoff of the Russian mass-circulation press.

Russia was not very far behind the West in this development. Only in the previous decade had Britain undergone the changes necessary for the birth of a commercial press. The repeal of a tax on advertisements (1853) and of the Stamp Act (1855), which had included taxing newspa-pers, removed the obstacles that had previously made mass-circulation newspapers cost-prohibitive. Lacking the restrictive regulations of Russia and Britain, both France and the United States produced their first com-mercial mass-circulation publications somewhat earlier, in the 1830s. The relative concurrence of these international developments was, of course, inextricably tied to broader trends. Without the technological advances of the industrial revolution and its secondary results of urbanization and the growth of literacy, there would have been neither sufficient means nor audience for publishing on such a broad scale.[54]

What part did advertising play in the new commercial press? In order to keep prices low, publishers could not rely on subscriptions alone. The income from street sales was initially low and never enough to supplement subscriptions entirely. To be successful on a mass scale without state sponsorship required a thriving income from three sources: subscriptions, advertising, and street sales, with the first two most important of all.

Aleksandr N. Bokhanov, one of the few Soviet historians to have seriously examined prerevolutionary advertising, claims that advertising income was insignificant in the commercial press up to the 1890s because the newspapers had low advertising rates and inadequate circulation to tempt businesspeople to invest in their column space.[55] This dismissive claim reflects Bokhanov's predominant interest in the advertising of large industrial and financial concerns. Unfortunately, there are no surviving records to check income figures for the earliest years of the Russian commercial press. Yet, if we include all types of advertisements—classifieds and small businesses as well as large—and look at the amount of space given to them, we see that advertising's role in the new press was substantial, even from the beginning in the 1860s. In 1864, *Peterburgskii listok* already devoted forty-five percent of its pages to advertising and *Birzhevye vedomosti* (*Stock Market News*), twenty-nine percent.[56] Bokhanov is correct in saying that newspaper advertising rates were low in the 1860s—from eight to ten kopeks a line for the most basic kind of advertisement (a script-only, one-time notice using the smallest print on the back page). It is also true that this basic rate rose; in 1895 *Russkoe slovo* (*Russian Word*) charged fifteen kopeks a line.[57] At the same time, however, the cost of producing a newspaper was also rising. As circulation increased, so did expenses for paper, production, and distribution.[58] Thus the absolute rise in rates does not necessarily mean that the relative weight of advertising income rose.

Although business records for newspapers are scarce for the earlier decades, data from the 1880s furnish a fuller picture of advertising's importance to periodical publishing.[59] Accounts for two successful newspapers, *Russkie vedomosti* (*Russian Record*) and *Russkoe slovo*, provide particularly rich information about the financial contribution of advertising. While the circulation of *Russkie vedomosti*, the so-called "professors' paper" directed at professionals, never reached the heights of *Russkoe slovo*, whose audience spanned all the middle and much of the lower strata of urban society (even achieving popularity among rural villagers), income data show their equal dependency on advertising (see appendix B, tables B.1 and B.2).[60] In addition, data for *Rech'* (*Speech*), a newspaper that consistently ran at a financial loss, suggest not coincidentally that failure to attain a high level of advertising income meant a paper would struggle to survive (table B.3).

Advertising was a significant source of income from the time of the earliest records of *Russkie vedomosti* in 1883, bringing in close to one-third of all revenues at that time. This relative importance grew to almost one-half of total income by the 1910s. Even when a spike in circulation during the revolutionary events of 1905 was followed by a decline to more normal sales income, advertising income remained high. This suggests that, no matter the fluctuations in readership caused by current events, *Russkie vedomosti* had earned a lasting reputation as a desirable vehicle for publicity.

Data for *Russkoe slovo* (table B.2) show advertising income as a percentage of total expenses, rather than income. This is useful for demonstrating the skyrocketing costs of a fast-growing newspaper, with the growth in expenses generally outpacing rising income from circulation sales. To achieve success it was not enough to sell ever more papers. Publishers always had to find more advertisers, something that *Rech'* failed to do quickly enough (table B.3). In addition, this struggling newspaper demonstrated a heavy reliance on street sales that may have discouraged advertisers who were interested in stable circulation figures from investing more.

It is difficult to know exactly how much was earned in each case from classified advertisements, since newspaper accounts record advertising income as one lump sum. This category of advertising, due to its occasional nature and simple format, can have been financially significant only in its quantity. *Russkoe slovo* could easily fill up to two pages in each issue with requests for employment or offers of rooms and personal goods in small print.[61] By 1912 *Peterburgskaia gazeta* averaged over 240 classifieds a day (see appendix A). Nevertheless, classified advertisements were not sufficient to make any major periodical financially viable.

From its inception in the 1860s, the mass-circulation press was thus forced to solicit commercial advertising from a merchantry that initially saw little need to spend profits on new forms of publicity. As we have seen, the merchants already filled the streets with their signs. Just as shopkeepers would have to rethink their advertising tactics under the pressures of the modern market, periodical editors had to adapt to a commercialized world of print media, in which simply presenting the news was insufficient for ensuring viability. Not only did the mass-circulation newspapers have to collect advertising, for the sake of their own survival they had to play a facilitating role in encouraging merchants to accept modern print advertising as a necessity.

To this end, newspapers would often have on their payrolls a person in charge of collecting and supervising advertising. In addition to a salary, this employee was paid a percentage commission on each advertisement obtained. As the paper grew, it might hire several in-house agents to specialize in separate areas, such as theater, banking, or commercial enterprises. It was up to these employees to approach merchants and persuade them to invest in publicity. This was often an uphill battle, requiring patience and perseverance. Initial failure, advised a publishing manual, "must not have the effect of weakening the energy of the publisher's representative," but he should go back to a potential client a second time or even repeatedly. Such energetic and "solid workers," the author complained, were unfortunately hard to find in Russia, where initiative was not always well rewarded.[62] The manager of *Rech'* realized that without "the element of personal interest" (i.e., a commission), it was unrealistic to expect significant results from employees pursuing commercial accounts. This newspaper paid its solicitants four to five percent commission, potentially doubling their small salaries.[63] During the 1910s the advertising department at *Rech'* counted up to nine people, including office workers who were responsible for receiving classifieds and supervising the accurate printing of advertisements.[64] Given that *Rech'* never rivaled more successful newspapers in advertising revenue, we can assume that papers such as *Russkoe slovo* would have employed significantly larger, or at least more diligent, advertising staffs.

ADVERTISING AGENCIES

The entrepreneurial spirit necessary to pursue accounts was far more evident in the advent of independent advertising agencies than in newspaper employees during the last quarter of the nineteenth century. With the rise of this new enterprise, newspapers found the tables turned, as they themselves were solicited to accept advertisements. Part of the general trend toward specialization and professionalization occurring in late imperial Russia, the new agencies signaled the transformation of print advertising from a secondary, if important, source of income for newspapers into an industry in and of itself.

It was an industry with modest beginnings throughout the Western world. The first advertising agencies developed in western Europe and the United States in the middle of the nineteenth century, a decade or two before they appeared in Russia. They functioned as independent intermediaries between the press and advertisers. Acting solely as placement services, they facilitated both the collection of valuable income for the publishers and the distribution of advertisements on a broad scale for merchants, who could now deposit their announcements in one place to be sent to as many publications as they wished. The agencies profited by buying newspaper space in bulk at as large a discount as they could negotiate and selling the space piecemeal to advertisers at a slight discount on the periodicals' published rates.

In its initial form, the advertising agency employed no copywriters or artists, let alone market researchers. Salesmanship and creativity were left to the merchant to worry about. As Stephen Fox writes of this "prehistoric" period in the development of advertising in America: "To work in advertising demanded no particular knowledge of copy or design or the product being celebrated. Instead it required an acquaintance with the periodicals in any given territory, some sense of the going advertising rates, and—in particular—a rare gift for haggling."[65]

Such was the status of the fledgling industry when the precursors of advertising agencies appeared in Russia during the 1860s. Although the firm of Ludwig Metzl, founded in 1878, is widely credited with being the first advertising agency in Russia, this claim is problematic. Other preexisting businesses that dealt only with classified advertisements sometimes evolved into broader agencies, taking on diverse functions, such as translation services, as well as commercial advertising. "Bureaus of announcements" date back at least to 1864, as shown by A.A. Stepanov in his overview of prerevolutionary newspaper advertising.[66] However, the Metzl agency was certainly a pioneer in size. Ludwig Metzl, a Czech-born Austrian who was twenty-four years old at the company's founding, built up an enterprise that maintained primacy in the Russian advertising industry until the First World War. The single-owner "office of announcements" (*kontora ob"iavlenii*), L. Metzl and Company, was established in Moscow, with branches soon opening in St. Petersburg and Warsaw. In 1891, Ludwig accepted his brother Ernest as a full partner, and with a financial boost of 30,000 rubles from a German investor, Julius (Iulii) Rosenfeld, the newly registered L. and E. Metzl and Company officially became a trading firm (*torgovyi dom*).[67] Branches in Vilnius and Lodz completed the company's network in the Russian Empire, but the Metzls also boasted international branches in Berlin, Paris, Boston, and Buffalo, New York.

The partnership between the brothers was never equal. Ludwig received fifty percent of the profits, while Ernest shared the remaining fifty percent with Rosenfeld. In 1900 Ernest died in debt, having sold his furniture in an attempt to pay expenses incurred by his own long illness and his son's education.[68] All rights to the business reverted to Ludwig, who in 1905 took on his St. Petersburg manager, hereditary honorary citizen Grigorii Mikhailovich Epshtein, as a junior invested partner.[69] An attempt to turn the business into a joint stock company (*aktsionernoe obshchestvo*) was approved by the government in 1907 but never came to fruition; illness caused Ludwig's prolonged absence from Russia, and sufficient investors could not be found. Nevertheless, the company enjoyed unparalleled success. In 1914 L. and E. Metzl and Company earned more than 3,500,000 rubles from operations in the Russian Empire, with profits of 328,125 rubles from its branches in the capital cities alone. It listed 330 employees on its Russian payroll, including 95 in St. Petersburg and 84 in Moscow.[70]

Though unrivalled, the Metzl company was far from unchallenged. Many others, Russians and foreign residents alike, jumped on this profitable bandwagon of the advertising business. Figures for the early proliferation of advertising agencies in St. Petersburg are difficult to assess since city directories remain the only source for many of the smaller firms. In the directory *Ves' Peterburg* (*All Petersburg*) advertising agencies were initially grouped together with information bureaus (*kontory spravochnye*), which might or might not offer advertising placement; only a few specified their services in such areas as housing or employment referrals. In Moscow, however, the city directory, *Vsia Moskva* (*All Moscow*), listed advertising agencies (*kontory ob"iavlenii*) separately. In 1896 there were already thirteen in existence there, and as many as seven in St. Petersburg. By 1914 the number of advertising agencies in Moscow had risen to thirty-one, and in St. Petersburg to thirty-six (by this time advertising agencies were differentiated from information bureaus in both cities). By the eve of World War I, the pioneer agency of 1878 had become only first among many, and although the size of the advertising industry was still small compared to that of the United States, it was firmly established in the Russian Empire.[71]

Who were the businesspeople who competed with L. and E. Metzl and Company in this new sphere? Detailed information to answer this question is regrettably scarce. Apart from sketchy archival records for a handful of companies, the major source of information is the agencies' own listings in the city directories. It is clear, however, that this new field of enterprise reflected the ethnic and social complexity of the late imperial Russian business community—a community that this chapter considers in more depth in its last section. Of the thirteen agencies listed in *Vsia Moskva* in 1896, seven were of Russian ownership, judging by their names.[72] Even if the other six were foreign citizens (which should not be assumed), the advertising industry in Russia obviously did not remain a foreign preserve.

Nor, interestingly, was it a male one. The city directories also attest that, of those same thirteen agencies, five were owned and run by women. This fact flies in the face of accepted notions of women's limited roles in the Russian merchantry at the turn of the century. The ability to hold one's own in negotiations with mostly male clients did not fall within the traditional perception of female strengths. Yet sources suggest that women constituted a substantial element within the industry. This was also the case during the 1890s in America, where historians have found that women were a significant presence in advertising, even though the profession was dominated by men.[73] The recent emergence of the field in both countries meant that its membership was less established than those of other businesses, and women were able to take advantage of this flexibility to find a new livelihood. The very fledgling nature of the industry gave women more chance to enter it, since there had not been enough time for traditional male networks and attitudes to develop. A circumstance that may have facilitated women's involvement in advertising in Russia was the fact that it was possible to run a registered advertising agency from a private apartment, as some women did. Thus a minimum of independent resources was required to begin such a business. The number of women in advertising suggests that accepted gender roles in business were changing by the twentieth century, especially in newer fields of enterprise.

The significant proportion of women in advertising was even larger than evidenced by the city directories. A company with a male name might actually be managed by a woman. Archival records for the advertising agency of Bruno Valentini, for example, reveal that it was in fact run by his sister-in-law, Luiza Ivanovna Valentini, after the founder's death in 1911.[74] In a form letter to clients informing them of the death of "our chief and companion," Luiza requested that they transfer their loyalties (and their accounts) to her. She went on to manage the firm under her brother-in-law's name until 1916, despite the subsequent sale of the business to a friendly competitor. The strong presence of women in advertising suggests a far more active (if often hidden) female role in late imperial Russian business than most historiography, with its emphasis on the mercantile elite, allows.[75]

The majority of Russian advertising agencies operated on a small scale. The Valentini agency, founded in 1900 in St. Petersburg, never came close to the turnover of Metzl and Company. Even in 1913, when Russian advertising had reached its prewar peak, Luiza Valentini's clientele was limited. The firm grossed 76,472 rubles, a mere two percent of Metzl's 1914 business volume.[76] In 1916 the Valentini office employed only two people besides the owner, both Russian women.

More successful, but still modest in comparison with Metzl, was the advertising agency of A.Z. Remizov and Sons in Moscow. Aleksandr Zakharovich Remizov opened his office in the 1880s and was thus one of the earlier Russian advertising agents. In 1906 his two sons, Aleksandr and Ivan, also entered the firm, and according to a background check submitted to the newspaper *Rech'*, the three prided themselves on a reputation for diligence and discretion in their business dealings. Despite their respectability and the firm's long duration, its annual revenues reached only about nine percent of Metzl's (300,000 rubles in 1912).[77]

As the competition in the capital cities grew, Ludwig Metzl maintained his overall predominance to a large extent by establishing strongholds in the provincial press. It was much harder for these periodicals to obtain all the advertising they needed to survive, and many chose to grant Metzl a partial or total monopoly on advertising collection in return for a guaranteed minimum income. With agents travelling the empire, even where they had no offices, L. and E. Metzl and Company could provide intermediary services between publishers and merchants on a vast scale.

In the case of an exclusive contract with a periodical, as with *Odesskie novosti* (*Odessa News*), for instance, a Metzl agent would be attached permanently to the paper to run the advertising department. In other cases publications might collect their own local advertisements but leave Metzl with exclusive rights on the rest—a partial monopoly. By 1915 the company had contracted partial or total rights to collect advertising for almost two hundred periodicals throughout the Russian Empire.[78] As a private company with a national network and no state sponsorship, Metzl represented a relatively new level of entrepreneurship for Russia, made possible by the belated construction of railways, the ongoing modernization of business, and the encouragement of foreign investment in terms of both funds and expertise.[79] Foreign-owned but largely Russian-managed, the Metzl company provided what John McKay has defined as the healthiest type of foreign entrepreneurship—one that manages to "educate, change attitudes, and infuse a missing dynamism," thereby encouraging new domestic initiative.[80] To a large extent Metzl played this role in the Russian advertising industry, an industry that was in itself part of the modernizing trend in turn-of-the-century Russia.

Ludwig Metzl's personal motives, however, were hardly altruistic, and nationalist critics made exaggerated complaints about the firm's near monopoly in the field. In March and April of 1914, right-wing Duma members, unwittingly foreshadowing later Bolshevik policy, went so far as to propose that advertising should become a state-run enterprise because Metzl held rights to almost all advertising collections for the Russian press (an exaggerated claim), and therefore profits on advertising were going to foreigners.[81] The fact that Metzl and Company did bring in huge profits was due to its size, which allowed it to offer better terms to advertisers. Since it brought in more advertisements, the newspapers gave it bigger discounts, which meant lower rates for business customers. All advertising agencies extended credit to their advertisers—this was one of their major appeals over dealing directly with the publishers—but thanks to its larger turnover, Metzl could offer more than most. Thus the scale of L. and E. Metzl and Company kept it consistently ahead of the competition.

In addition to the provincial periodicals, Metzl enjoyed some success in gaining contractual rights with publishers in the capital. A new and struggling newspaper might feel it had little choice other than to entrust the collection of a third or more of its potential income to the experience of an established advertising agency. The St. Petersburg newspaper *Rech'*, which began daily publication in 1906, acknowledged this inevitability when it negotiated a five-year contract with Metzl to begin in October 1906. The document was ten pages long and covered every eventuality of their future relations.[82] Metzl was granted exclusive rights in return for a guaranteed income to the paper of from four to five hundred rubles an issue. If this average was not delivered through advertisements, the difference would be made up in cash by Metzl. The newspaper's editors saw this arrangement as an unwelcome necessity while they gained experience and widened their clientele. They were not able to escape the relationship even when the contract expired, however, but merely modified it to a partial monopoly, with the right to collect certain types of advertisements themselves. In 1912 the advertising department at *Rech'* brought in 11,359 rubles to Metzl's 133,408.[83]

Despite the evident difficulty of competing with the likes of Metzl, advertising was a new field that was seen by quite a few enterprising individuals as potentially lucrative. One did not have to be an advertising agent to try one's luck. In addition to all the pamphlets and calendars put out by individual businesses, people in towns throughout Russia petitioned the censorship authorities in St. Petersburg for the right to publish periodical advertising sheets (*listki ob"iavlenii*) that would offer their pages to local merchants for a fee. Not all these would-be publishers were granted permission, especially before 1905, but over 130 requests to put out general advertising sheets found their way to the authorities between 1876 and 1917.[84] The relaxation of censorship in the post-1905 years encouraged attempts at this endeavor, with 47 requests over the five years from 1905 to 1911 compared to 12 for the preceding half-decade.

Other attempts to cash in on the advertising industry were not quite so aboveboard. In 1912 *Russkoe slovo* editor Blagov received a telegram from the editor of the *Russkaia Riv'era* (*Russian Riviera*) newspaper in Yalta, requesting confirmation of the activities of a student named Lissner, who claimed to be working for the Moscow paper. In the name of *Russkoe slovo*, Lissner had been collecting advertisements at "extremely low prices." Blagov lost no time in informing his colleague in Yalta that he had absolutely no knowledge of Lissner, who was obviously a fraud. The next day the feckless student was arrested, and he confessed to the forgery of *Russkoe slovo* stationery.[85]

A new field of industry that opened up channels for individual enterprise in a society traditionally lacking in such opportunities, advertising presented chances for national and international profit and greater gender diversity, as well as fraudulent opportunism. Without this new industry the mass-circulation press that formed a central element of the emerging public sphere in Russia would have remained unviable. Aggressively self-promoting and yet simultaneously behind the scenes, the advertising industry's infrastructure facilitated and reflected the growing flexibility of modern Russian commerce and society as a whole.

THE MESSAGE CREATORS

Advertising's infrastructure is skeletal without the substance of message. It was the creators of copy and image who promoted the values of modern consumption. And yet this side of the industry remains unfortunately elusive for imperial Russia, largely due to the subsequent regime's dismissal of prerevolutionary advertising as bourgeois ephemera. It is helpful, therefore, to examine general trends in advertising creation as they emerged in the West, since Russia's early advertising developed along similar lines.

Our contemporary conception of advertising's creators places them within the advertising agencies: Madison Avenue's army of talented specialists fervently imagining clever hooks with which to capture the public psychology on behalf of demanding but uninvolved clients, supported by extensive market research and plentiful budgets. This image could not be further from the circumstances of the late nineteenth and early twentieth centuries, regardless of the country. Advertising agencies did not start to offer copywriting and creative design until the 1890s, and then only rarely. In America, the shift toward advertising agents' thinking of themselves as more than business intermediaries began during the 1895–1905 decade.[86] There is no evidence that this transition occurred in Russia before the collapse of the tsarist regime.

Common wisdom in the West during the nineteenth century held that only a business owner or manager knew his company well enough to be able to write its advertising. As American historian Pamela Laird points out, many business owners continued to write their own advertisements even after agencies offered the service; to this day, many local owners still do. The determining factor was not modernity or wealth, in Laird's view, but whether or not the firm was still operated by its founder.[87] Thus, on one hand the creative shift toward professional advertising specialists was largely a twentieth-century phenomenon, but on the other hand an entrepreneur's sense of creative ownership might trump the general trend of professionalization, allowing both avenues of advertising formation—professional and in-house—to coexist.

In Russia, most existing evidence points to the continuation of merchant/manufacturer control of advertising content up to the First World War, whether through direct composition or the hiring of independent writers and artists. Agencies and printing companies could assist by showing the customer the selection of border designs and decorations at the printer's disposal, but the trade manuals of the time suggest that it was still largely the responsibility of the merchant to come up with his or her own message.

Tradesmen who wanted to do more than just list their goods and prices would often turn to the services of independent artists and writers. The city directories list a string of names under "artists," many of whom were no doubt glad to earn some income through commercial design. Most such designs were anonymous; after all, the advertisement was supposed to boost the firm's reputation, not the artist's. A contemporary commentator described the large numbers of artists eking out a living on advertising work in prerevolutionary Russia: "[They were the] masses of beginning, sometimes mediocre, sometimes hopeful and talented artists, sculptors, writers, poets—the artistic Bohemia, huddling in garrets, writing verses and tales on scraps of dirty paper, drawing on cigar box lids, eternally hungry, snubbed, living on hopes and in debt."[88]

This picture was doubtless exaggerated (the author demonstrated a taste for hyperbole), but even so, it confirms the creative source of much advertising. There is also fictive evidence that struggling authors sometimes turned their pens to advertisements. In his story "The Writer," Anton Chekhov describes the reduced circumstances of an old drunken writer who composes advertisements for a tea merchant. On presenting his crumpled piece of paper, the cringing scribbler apologizes to the merchant for any possible mistakes, explaining that he has been writing advertisements for three shops at once—a task "that would make Shakespeare's head spin."[89]

As Western experience shows, not only failed writers turned to composing advertisements. In western Europe and the United States advertising was often a source of income for writers who had not yet made a sufficient name for themselves to survive by writing solely for their own audience. Charles Dickens wrote advertising copy as a young man in the nineteenth century, and Sherwood Anderson, despite his loathing for the career, supported his family on advertising for over 20 years before being sure enough that he would succeed in his own right.[90]

Of course, as advertising grew into an industry, other people apart from failed or unconfident artists saw it as an occupational opportunity. Factories and larger businesses could usually afford to employ copywriters on a regular basis, and such writers might come from unexpected backgrounds. One of the most prolific composers of advertising in early twentieth-century Russia was Sergei Apollonovich Korotkii (born 1854), a nobleman and decorated veteran of the Russo-Turkish War of 1877–1878. Korotkii posed as Diadia (Uncle) Mikhei, whose tall tales and verses for the Shaposhnikov tobacco firm appeared frequently in the pages of several major daily newspapers in the 1910s. No Sherwood Anderson cringing at his own self-perception as a hack, Korotkii seems to have enjoyed his role as an enthusiastic and eccentric crusader for the tobacco industry and often featured his own picture in his advertisements (see fig. 4.17). In addition to writing advertising copy for cigarettes, he petitioned the government in 1905 to publish his own journal, entitled *Tobacco*, to cover every aspect of the beloved product from cultivation to marketing.[91] Both in his lengthy petition and in his advertising, Korotkii showed himself to be a man as obsessed with tobacco as he was with his medals and military rank (evoking a real-life Kovalev, Gogol's hero of "The Nose").

Korotkii not only gloried in including his own image and credentials in tobacco advertisements that appeared both in the press and in leaflets passed out free or sold for a kopek to the Russian public, but he often wrote himself in as a main character in his verse fantasies. As Uncle Mikhei, Korotkii experienced exotic adventures, travelled the world, placated devils (persuading them to take cigarettes instead of Russian souls back to hell) and even promoted his employer's excellent tobacco on Mars. In a wartime story, the German kaiser himself paid Uncle Mikhei a nighttime visit to discover the secret of the cigarettes that were letting Russia beat the Germans (this in 1915!). No comforter of the enemy, Mikhei lectured the emperor on his foul deeds and told him to go to hell, reinforcing his patriotism with a footnote about his own (Korotkii's) battle against other enemies in the Russo-Turkish War.[92]

As a writer of advertising, Korotkii's exuberant character certainly does not fit the image of an "artistic Bohemian" shivering in a garret, but neither does he represent the typical copywriter. Korotkii's idiosyncrasies aside, as advertising expanded and became more acceptable, its creators were more likely to include the enterprising and talented, who saw their occupation as a promising choice rather than a necessity born of failure. Whether advertising's authors were hired pens or business owners themselves, they became increasingly inventive as they sought to woo customers in an ever-more-competitive consumer goods market.

ADVERTISING AND THE RUSSIAN BUSINESS COMMUNITY

> Advertising in our age of free competition is not a luxury or superfluity, but a
> necessity.... To reject [it] is to reject railway travel and communication by tele-
> graph, or deliberately to close your eyes and say that it is now terribly dark.[93]

As it flourished in late imperial Russia, the advertising industry advertised itself to the Russian business community as an emblem of progress
without which no enterprise would survive the demands of contemporary
trade. In the modernizing city of that period, it was indeed no longer
enough to hang up a sign over one's door and establish relationships
with customers in the neighborhood in order to succeed in business. The
expanding population was increasingly anonymous, in part because recent
labor immigrants' continued ties to their villages hindered urban assimilation, but also because residential mobility within the capital was common
for all social groups. In addition, the rise in industrial growth and mass
production meant more and more companies were offering similar types
of goods.[94] Business owners were forced to think about the growing threat
of competition.

The advertising industry was quick to offer its help in meeting this
threat, proffering an arsenal of newspaper advertising, posters, leaflets,
packaging, promotional gift ideas, and coupons, all of which promised
to make companies stand out from their rivals. Did the merchants of the
Russian business community willingly embrace these new opportunities
for promoting their businesses, or did they resent and resist the pressure
to exceed the bounds of their traditional shop signs and street hawking?
Did merchants and manufacturers actively attempt to create a consumerist ethos, or did they simply react to the demands of modern commerce?
With western Europe and America often touted as the leading pioneers in
advertising, did members of the business community see the expansion of
this industry as a Western imposition alien to Russia or as an inevitable
and even desirable corollary of progress in the industrial age?

Inasmuch as the modernization of retailing in Russia was modeled
on Western practices, it contributed to tensions over Westernization
that had been ongoing since the reforms of Peter the Great in the early
eighteenth century. Even the very words for "shop" in Russian reflect an
East/West divide. *Magazin* (a borrowing from the French) is the term for
the more modern store that appeared in Russia in the nineteenth century
and was noted for its Western-style, glass display cases and fixed prices.
Lavka denotes the traditional Russian shop, which was usually smaller and
darker, with only one opening to the street; customers in a lavka at the
turn of the century would expect to haggle over prices.[95] From the 1880s

department stores, initially introduced by foreigners, were also changing the retail experience. In society at large and within merchant circles, some lauded and enjoyed these changes. Others saw them as one more step in the undermining of traditional Russian culture by Western influences.[96]

Modern advertising was also largely a Western influence at the outset and thus triggered similar ambivalence from conservatives about threats to Russian culture. And yet, those on the right who spoke out against it on nationalist grounds did so not in condemnation of advertising per se, but rather in an attempt to Russianize it. Just as the right wing Duma deputies mentioned earlier wanted a Russian state monopoly on what they saw as foreign domination over the business of advertising agencies, some publicists urged businesses to find Russia's unique path in advertising style and content. In 1898, for instance, the ultraconservative publisher of *Russkii trud* (*Russian Labor*) and onetime "hired pen" of the Moscow merchants, Sergei Sharapov, put out a booklet written by like-minded Aleksei Verigin, entitled *Russkaia reklama* (*Russian Advertising*).[97] Protesting the growing tide of what he saw as "slavish" imitations of Western advertising, Verigin proclaimed:

> Let [Americans and Europeans] write "Castoria" and "Pear's Soap" on their backs, bald spots, and walls, let them bake it into their bread, yell it out on the streets, sing it in church. That's their business, and if it's profitable, let them make a fortune. . . . With us nothing of the sort will work. It's a different social psychology. The Russian person is an enemy of any affectation, clamoring and impudence. We need business—serious, intelligent and, above all, *sincere* and likeable (*dushevnyi i simpatichnyi*). Only that kind of business will stir and find resonance with us.[98]

Verigin was not arguing here for no advertising at all, but rather (as the title of his booklet suggests) a specifically Russian style of advertising—more "sincere and likeable."

Regardless of the merits of Verigin's pronouncements about the natural pleasantness of Russian trade, we might expect his plea for a specifically Russian path in advertising to have found resonance with the business community, given the fact that the Russian merchantry had been intensely conservative and anti-Western throughout most of its history.[99] Yet interestingly, the sources suggest that while many merchants did resist modern, Western-style advertising, they did not do so primarily from nationalist sentiments. Rather, their resistance was much more prosaic, founded largely in inertia and an unwillingness to spend money.

This perhaps surprising level of indifference to the nationalist appeals reflects the fact that throughout the late imperial period fundamental changes had taken place in the character and composition of the Russian business community. Not only was the community no longer the sole preserve of the traditional merchantry, but the traditional merchantry was itself changing. I use the term "community" because it is helpful to denote the totality of those whose interests lay in commerce but recognize that the concept of community is tenuous at best in terms of self-definition for the late imperial business sphere.

By the end of the nineteenth century, the Russian merchantry was no longer a cohesive group, as Alfred Rieber has clearly shown. Once a legally protected and exclusive *soslovie* (social estate), the *kupechestvo* (merchantry) was becoming an increasingly porous and varied group whose members' only commonality was involvement in some kind of trade or manufacturing.[100] A decree of 1863 granted the right to engage in trade and industry to all, regardless of soslovie or nationality. Although the statute effectively rendered the kupechestvo obsolete as an estate, the term continued to be used as a nominally recognized status and a source of cultural identity until the revolutions of 1917. The kupechestvo suffered, however, from regional, social, ethnic, economic, generational, attitudinal, and official divisions that precluded united responses even in the face of its own demise. Nor can traders from the lowlier *meshchanstvo* (the petty bourgeoisie, which included small traders) be excluded from the commercial sphere. The boundary between the kupechestvo and meshchanstvo was not fixed; a *kupets* could easily become a *meshchanin* if at any point he could not pay his annual guild fee. In view of these circumstances, I use the phrase "business community" rather than the traditional term "merchantry" to include those who sold services as well as goods, those who manufactured as well as traded.[101]

In addition to its dilution as a social group, the traditional merchant community was also experiencing dynamic generational change. Many among the younger generation at the turn of the century were breaking free from the traditional restrictions and customs of their fathers, in social and educational exposure as well as in business practices. This was especially true in the capital and in centers of trade on the periphery of the empire, such as Odessa.[102] By the end of the nineteenth century, even in Moscow, which was considered the traditional heartland of the Russian merchantry, there existed between the more progressive entrepreneurs and the stubbornly traditional old merchants, "a wide variety of men in transition, who found themselves at various way stations along the kupechestvo's path of economic and cultural progress." The younger of these, "beneficiaries of secondary education, were likely to dress in what they imagined to be the latest Parisian styles, to immerse themselves in dime novels and in the comic operettas and light drama offered by Moscow theaters, and to copy their business methods from local German traders."[103]

Thus, on the one hand the traditional merchantry was changing from within as the older generations receded. On the other hand the boundaries were also being broached from without. As postreform legislation put trade and industry on an increasingly economic rather than social footing, the merchant soslovie expanded to include members of other social groups—especially the nobility and wealthier peasantry—and other nationalities.[104] Demonstrating this trend, as early as 1873 over fifty percent of the first merchant guild in Moscow had entered its ranks since 1861.[105]

The influx of non-Russian nationalities adds complexity to the definition of "Russian business community." Exactly how Russian was urban commerce in Russia? As industry and trade expanded across Europe in the nineteenth century, it inevitably crossed national boundaries and took on an increasingly international character. Russia was actively part of this process, inviting foreign participation in the fast-paced industrialization of the 1890s and laying railway lines to the West and the Far East.

On a more local level the picture was also heterogeneous. Even in Moscow, the full-blooded *kupets* inhabited the business community alongside a multifarious range of associates: the German businessman, married to a Russian woman and living all his adult life in his adopted country; the Jewish industrialist, claiming no other country besides Russia but still not fully accepted as a native; the foreign entrepreneur with factories thriving in Russia for decades. These examples are just a few of the myriad that could be given.

The imperial census of 1897 gives some insight into the national makeup of the Moscow and St. Petersburg business communities. In Moscow, twelve percent of those defining themselves as *kuptsy* claimed a non-Russian language as their mother tongue, as did six percent of *meshchane* (although not all members of that estate were in trade). In St. Petersburg, according to the same linguistic criterion, the rates of non-Russians were higher: twenty percent of kuptsy and eighteen percent of meshchane.[106] These figures represent only part of the picture, however, since people could easily engage in trade and industry without listing themselves in a mercantile estate. It is also impossible to account for those of foreign ancestry who already thought of Russian as their native language. Given the mixed constituency of the Russian business community, its boundary must be drawn geographically rather than ethnically.

This does not mean that national origins were not of perceived importance, especially from the viewpoint of native Russians. Segregation of foreign and Russian stores continued to exist throughout the imperial period, particularly in Moscow, with fashionable shopping districts still primarily identified with west European stores.[107] For the most part, however, the business community consisted of a complex and interacting mix of social and national elements, increasingly transcending traditional boundaries. The Russian business community incorporated all those engaged in commercial activities on Russian soil.

In the face of this diversity, it is small wonder that the nationalist appeal to pursue a uniquely Russian path in advertising found no practical resonance among members of the business community. Verigin and Sharapov's pleas for a specifically Russian style of advertising were ineffectual because they spoke to a past fast disappearing; they no longer reflected the composition of the Russian sphere of trade. With the simultaneous acculturation of Russian merchants to Western practices and of foreign business people to Russian society, there could be no such thing as pure Russian advertising. A feature of the international phenomenon of modern consumer society, advertising was as culturally mixed as trade itself.

This is not to suggest that advertisers did not incorporate Russian cultural motifs into their marketing approaches, a topic addressed in chapter 5. Nor does the disregard of Verigin's rhetoric mean that all merchants and manufacturers rushed to adopt broader advertising with open arms. In fact, turn-of-the-century journals devoted to Russian trade, as well as handbooks put out by the advertising industry, frequently lamented the obstinacy with which many small merchants resisted modern advertising.[108] These publications, which often cited Western techniques as models to spur on Russia's own progress in the advertising field, clearly did not consider foreignness the reason for the merchants' resistance, however. If they had, they would hardly have referred so often to the need to learn from abroad. Instead, they reproached merchants for repudiating something new, for being unwilling to accept the changing demands of business. The three characteristics repeatedly blamed for retail traders' obstinate rejection of modern advertising were inertia, fear of financial risk, and an ingrained disdain for extensive publicity.

The "old ways" of conducting trade carried with them a multitude of misconceptions and habits unsuited to the modern market, according to trade journalists. Their composite picture of an "old style" merchant was someone uneducated, who had learned on the job as a boy, lacked any sense of a calling, and trusted to the maxim "if you don't deceive, you won't sell." His major method of encouraging new custom would be to pressure passersby in off the street.[109] Stubbornness, laziness, and lack of imagination all contributed to what one writer called the "cowardly apathy" of Russian trade.[110]

Since advertising represented an investment without guarantee of return, many small traders were initially loath to put money into it. Not only did a merchant have to be willing to risk the cost of publishing his advertisement repeatedly in order to reach enough people, but he had to compose it himself or pay someone to do it for him. Either way, it challenged his skills and his pocket. Rather than deal with these demands, wrote one advertising proponent, it was easier for a businessman to complain with fellow tradesmen about slow sales and declare that "everything depends entirely on luck" anyway.[111]

A merchant could easily justify such a dismissal by adhering to the common belief that advertising was only necessary for shoddy goods and was used by swindlers (an ironic rationale if one is to believe contemporary critics' negative assessment of merchant ethical standards).[112] To advertise was to demean oneself. This notion was not unique to Russia in the dawn of the consumer age. The loudest and brashest pioneer of print advertising in much of the Western world was patent medicine, with its endless claims to cure everything from colds to cholera. Many a merchant of legitimate goods shrank back from such dubious company.[113] The phrase "advertised merchandise" came to sound "reproachful" and offensive to the ears.[114]

This reaction was slowly changing, however. As the Russian business community itself evolved, long-accepted notions broke down. The shift, not surprisingly, seems to have begun with the non-Russian merchants and manufacturers. In 1894 a St. Petersburg author, who wanted to encourage greater openness to publicity among Russian businessmen, lamented the fact that a "significant majority" of those advertising in the capital were "foreigners, Jews or Finns."[115] (Again, it should be noted that this comment was not a condemnation of foreign influence but a plea for Russians to jump onto the bandwagon.) As the twentieth century progressed, more and more references appeared in the trade literature to an increasing acceptance of advertising as an essential business practice throughout the community. In 1903 a Moscow trade journal declared this to be "the century of advertising."[116] "Advertising is acquiring wider significance" as each year of increasing competition goes by, wrote the editor of a new trade journal in 1907.[117] The old prejudices were waning, claimed an advertising specialist in 1908—"even the former inveterate enemies of advertising are running to its aid in one way or another."[118] "Scarcely any merchants now do not recognize the meaning of advertising,"[119] asserted a contributor to *Torgovyi mir* (*Trade World*) in 1910, and two years later: "Every year advertising is winning for itself a more and more honored place in our trade and industry."[120] The same journal, discussing the state of trade as the twentieth century's second decade began, editorialized, "The merchants are ready to reject the old ways of trade. They have become convinced of the uselessness (*neprigodnost'*) of them for the present times. They are ready to conduct their business on new principles, to strive towards this."[121]

The "present times" were defined in terms of sweeping socioeconomic change. With city populations burgeoning and consumer markets offering an increasing variety of goods as Russian industry multiplied, commentators turned to the metaphor of a maze to describe the new urban environment. The modern city, with its contemporary trade, was a "dark labyrinth" that confused seller and buyer alike.[122] Proponents claimed that advertising could guide the consumer through the maze, acting as mediator for the profusion of commercial novelties.[123] Thus advertising was to do more than just accompany rising commerce; it was to chart consumption for the bewildered participants of urbanization.

For the merchant the modern consumer was part of the problem. Urban shoppers, more mobile than their rural or provincial counterparts, switched merchants easily, yielding quickly to novelty.[124] Likened to a child spoilt by a ceaseless flow of new toys, the city customer was "with each day more capricious, more nervous, and demanding to be pleased."[125] In the same vein a socialist critic of advertising described modern Russian consumers with an intensity that ironically betrayed sympathy for the merchants' lot and aversion to the masses:

> Now the consumer appears before [the business owner] in the form of a silent, enigmatic mass, surrounding him on all sides and at the same time invisible: close enough to touch and always elusive; tirelessly demanding all kinds of goods possible and refusing them when they are offered; greedy for any novelty, which, however, is quickly declared out of date;—the masses, recklessly open-handed and at the same time haggling over a farthing, self-loving and always utterly indifferent to the part played by anyone who tries to satisfy their demands or guess their fantastic caprices.[126]

Through publicity, argued advertising's proponents both inside and outside the industry, a merchant could lure and tame the faceless, fickle crowd. Some early enthusiasts claimed a hypnotic power for advertising; publishing your name repeatedly would, "like the breaking of ocean waves," arouse the curiosity of the "public masses" and act "forcibly [*nasil'stvenno*] upon the will and feeling of the reader."[127] Most writers kept their assertions more grounded: advertise regularly, honestly (*dobrosovestno*), and with originality, and you would become a recognized name with a broad clientele.

In the bewildering tide of modernization, advertising's promoters employed both organic and mechanical metaphors to encourage merchant acceptance. The slogans "publicity is the soul of any enterprise"[128] and "advertising is to the merchant as fertilizer to the farmer"[129] comfortingly implied that this new practice was part of a natural and timeless world. Simultaneously, advertising as "the engine of trade"[130] and the "weapon of progress"[131] armed the merchant for the road into the future.

While the old prejudices against advertising did not entirely die, by the eve of World War I, the acceptance of the new practices among Russian merchant circles was enough to prompt one businessman to explain the proliferation of trade advertisements in the newspapers as "herd instinct."[132] The evidence of one popular daily newspaper, *Peterburgskaia gazeta* (*Petersburg Gazette*, see appendix A), shows that each issue in 1912 averaged eleven times as many retail traders advertising as in 1867 and almost twice as many as in 1897. The small traders of the Russian business community, if more grudgingly than willingly, were by and large adapting to advertising as a necessary tool of modern trade.

For all their hesitations, retail merchants were among the first to advertise regularly in the commercial press, adopting this medium from the 1860s, as opposed to the later appearance of brand-name goods manufacturers in the newspaper pages. From the 1880s, however, manufacturers as a whole showed a similar rate of increase in newspaper advertising (see appendix A). Although advertisements for brand-name products never equaled the quantity of ads for retail stores, numbers only tell part of the story. Manufacturers' advertisements tended to be bigger and more creative than those the small merchants could afford. Once they began to see the opportunities for publicity presented by the mass-circulation press, many manufacturers turned to this resource with enthusiasm, using it aggressively, prominently, and consistently. As in America producers of brand-name consumer goods soon outstripped retailers in innovation, if not in volume.[133] As Laird points out, it was manufacturers' success in marketing branded products that led to our contemporary association of modern advertising with brand-name goods.[134]

Thanks to both tsarist legislation requiring joint stock corporations to present annual reports to the government and the preservation of records from many prerevolutionary businesses, Russian archives contain sufficient data to give an overview of advertising policies for several major consumer goods industries.[135] Sources for manufacturing companies improve at the turn of the century, partly due to the increase in sheer number of business enterprises at that time[136] and also due to the growing trend of incorporation—transforming private firms into joint stock companies in order to increase capital.[137] Business archival records are not consistent as regards advertising. Many companies kept detailed lists of expenses, yet within a single firm accounting practices could change to include item-ized accounts one year but not the next. Nevertheless, an overall picture of budgeting policies does emerge.

Three consumer goods industries offer useful case studies to examine manufacturers' varied and evolving attitudes toward advertising. The toi-letries, tobacco, and tea enterprises all enjoyed broad market appeal across social and, to varying degrees, gender lines, and a relatively good source base has survived for each.[138] Although we might associate the toiletries industry with luxury goods such as perfume, these factories also manu-factured soaps and shampoos directed to a wide array of the population. The tea industry demonstrated a markedly different advertising approach from toiletries and tobacco; while the latter two advertised actively in the daily press, tea merchants generally ignored this medium, relying more on posters and packaging. In each case, however, individual, brand-name packaging was essential, since the growing consumer market forced these industries to reach purchasers individually, rather than through whole-salers buying in bulk. All three depended on brand-name reputation to compete with rivals producing essentially similar goods. The very con-sumer-oriented nature of the tobacco, toiletries, and tea industries thus made them a formative part of Russia's emerging national market. As such, it is hardly surprising that their owners would see the potential of advertis-ing, not only to fight competition but also to evoke consumer aspirations. Whereas the shopkeepers were simply trading the goods with which they were supplied, the manufacturers were designing and packaging products to create new demands. Innovation was thus essential to their survival.

The manufacturing sector was as much a patchwork of varied ethnic and social origins as the retail sector. The toiletries industry was dominat-ed, though not monopolized, by French owners, with Russians employed among the directors and managers. Although the largest tobacco company, La Ferme (Laferm), was founded by an Austrian, this field was predomi-nantly occupied by ethnic Russian and Russian Karaite (a Jewish sect[139]) entrepreneurs. Of the three the tea industry had the strongest connections to the traditional Russian merchantry, with two of the most eminent Mos-cow merchant families, the Botkins and the Abrikosovs, acquiring much of their wealth from the beverage.

It is probable that foreign ownership provided much of the early impetus for an active advertising policy in Russia's manufacturing sphere, though the paucity of data for the nineteenth century makes this state-ment largely conjectural. The evidence suggests, however, that once one manufacturer began to advertise in the daily press, competitors within the same industry were likely to do the same; thus the approach to advertising had more to do with intra-industrial practice than with the nationality of owners. As newspapers swelled with advertising at the turn of the century, and especially after 1905, many Russian firms invested in the media pages as much as their foreign competitors. Each in its own way, the consumer goods industries tackled the challenges of creating and fulfilling demand for their brand-name products.

The Toiletries Industry

The toiletries industry was one of the first to advertise its goods regularly in the daily press, going back at least as far as the 1870s.[140] The oldest and among the largest of the toiletries firms, Rallet and Company, exemplifies the industry's active engagement in advertising. Founded in 1843 in Moscow by Frenchman Alphonse Rallet, the factory subsequently passed through several owners, all of whom were French.[141] With established ties in western Europe, Rallet and Company initially obtained much of its advertising from abroad. Throughout the early twentieth century, however, the proportion of Russian-produced advertising increased. Whereas in 1904 forty percent of Rallet's advertising was imported,[142] by 1913 the percentage had fallen to about twenty-five.[143] The growth in domestically produced advertisements reflects the rapid accommodation by Russian printers and craftsmen to the needs of an expanding consumer industry.

The place that advertising occupied in Rallet's management concerns is demonstrated in the uniquely detailed minutes from the firm's weekly board meetings in 1898.[144] Advertising was the subject of discussion twenty-five times in conferences between February 7 and May 22, at which the chairman and two directors, among various other members of the board, considered issues of company policy, from hiring and firing to new product lines.[145] These discussions reveal both an extremely diverse and dynamic use of advertising and a cautious spending policy. While the company was willing to experiment with different marketing approaches, it did so with expenditures very much in mind.

Both the board meetings and the firm's accounts demonstrate the wide array of Rallet's advertising ventures. Newspapers constituted only one outlet; billboards on park fences, walls, and station platforms, posters and signs on public transport and theater curtains, advertisements in calendars, almanacs, and restaurant menus, gift pencils and surprise cards inside packages—all were employed after being individually discussed and approved or rejected by the directors of the company. Many of these outlets were proposed by representatives from the advertising agencies that were growing into thriving businesses themselves at this time in Russia. Rallet did not limit itself to one agency, but accepted ideas from five or six at any given time. If the price attached was considered too high, the representative was told to go away and rework his proposal. Competition among the agencies, each of course knowing that it had no monopoly on Rallet's custom, usually meant that a lower figure was arrived at forthwith.

Publishing companies also solicited Rallet with offers to include advertisements in their publications, such as calendars and books. These proposals were accepted or rejected on the basis of the projected readership, even more than on price. If a publication was not popular or sufficiently well known, the offer of advertising in it would either be turned down or given a small trial run before any large investment was made. The character of readership was also taken into consideration. The management decided to place an advertisement in the well-known publisher Sytin's 1899 "All-Purpose" (*obshchepoleznii*) calendar, for example, in view of its distribution among the "intelligentsia sections of the population."[146] If the board members particularly liked an idea, they would make the most of it. On discussing one publisher's proposal for a "summer companion" (*letnii sputnik*) to include train timetables and sports schedules, the directors decided not only to print a single advertisement on the inside cover, but to advertise on the outside cover and throughout the booklet as well. Such saturation advertising, they felt, would give the idea that the publication was their own. To complete this impression, they ordered an extra thousand copies to keep or distribute from the company premises.[147]

Rallet published advertisements in many central and provincial periodicals. Great care was taken that these regular publications should have the desired effect. At one board meeting directors discussed the failure of a particular advertisement, though unfortunately they did not specify the reasons. Nevertheless, a new drawing presented by the chairman was accepted to take the place of the failed advertisement, along with a list of periodicals in which it should be published.[148]

Rallet dealt with many newspapers and journals directly, while with others it worked through various advertising agents. This varied approach suggests that convenience was not the main issue for the company, but rather obtaining the best deal was the goal, whether that be through an agency in one case or directly from a publisher in another. Overall, Rallet's closely supervised yet flexible publicity strategies indicate the high level of direct involvement on the part of the firm's middle and upper management in advertising policies and activities.[149]

Evidence from another major toiletries firm, Brocard, confirms that such practices were not confined to Rallet. Founded in 1864 by another

Frenchman, Henri Brocard, this company soon became Rallet's largest competitor in Russia. At least as early as 1893, Brocard employed a
full-time advertising manager, one Anton Rochette, to execute the firm's
detailed publicity agenda. As a middle manager Rochette received a salary
of 1,600 rubles a year in 1906, in addition to monthly commissions. This
was, of course, far less than the 9,000 rubles that the directors received
as salaries but still a respectable wage compared to the 500 rubles a year
of a regular office employee.[150] A photograph of the advertising office at
Brocard and Company in the firm's golden jubilee publication shows that
Rochette did not work alone but managed an entire department.[151] The
Brocard company diversified its advertising as much as Rallet, both in
methods and media.

In many ways, manufacturing companies like Rallet and Brocard fit
Alfred Chandler's definition of the modern business enterprise, which in
turn helps explain their wholehearted adoption of modern advertising.[152]
The diversification of functions within the same firm, the inclusion of
separate departments run by salaried managers, the management of their
own marketing rather than relying on wholesale distribution—all placed
these manufacturers squarely in the realm of modern business, with its
direct links to the consumer and consequent emphasis on public image
and salesmanship.

The multiple advertising needs of such companies further illustrate the
variety of employment created by advertising in the urban economy. Even
in advertising agencies there were special areas of expertise, some dealing
mainly in billboards and posters on trains and railways, for example. In
addition to keeping professional agents busy, companies like Brocard and
Rallet would simultaneously contract advertising work with several printers, some of whose engravers spent much of their time on commercial
posters and labels.[153] Manufacturers of pencils, combs, and fans could also
find their way into the advertising accounts of Rallet and Brocard, supplying the thousands of free trinkets that these companies used to woo
customers. Bottle factories manufactured flasks and jars custom designed
for each product. Other contractors specialized in doing nothing but dis-
tributing advertising—pasting posters on walls and handing out leaflets.
Others still made a living painting signs or supplemented their incomes
writing commercial verses. From the early 1890s Brocard's advertising
accounts mention payments for the composition of verses (*stikhi*).[154]
As the consumer gained importance in the late nineteenth century, the
increasingly complex advertising industry became a field in which sundry
craftsmen, workers, and employees found a livelihood and in which many
manufacturers took an active interest.

Rallet and Brocard's level of commitment to advertising was far from unique for the toiletries industry, nor was it simply the result of foreign ownership. The Moscow firms of A.M. Ostroumov and S.I. Chepelevetskii and Sons, two smaller but active competitors of the French-owned companies, also made regular appearances in the advertising pages of the daily press by the late nineteenth century.[155] Chepelevetskii and Sons was founded before the 1880s and owned by a large Russian Jewish family of Moscow merchants.[156] Aleksandr Mitrofanovich Ostroumov founded his company in 1892.[157] The investments in advertising of these two Russian firms, judging not only by the evidence of advertisements themselves but also by surviving company records, were equal to or even greater than that of the French firms in proportion to their size.

The records of Ostroumov, Brocard, and Chepelevetskii show that these companies were willing to spend the equivalent of anywhere from forty to almost one hundred percent of net profits on advertising (see appendix C). Their advertising budgets did not remain static but generally grew along with sales. The industry as a whole typically spent between 2.5 and 4.5 percent of sales income on advertising before the onset of World War I.[158]

Whether the firms' advertising increased sales or vice versa is a problematic question. In his analysis of American advertising, Michael Schudson finds that the rational textbook method of assessing an advertising budget based on the revenue increase it creates is in fact impossible to verify due to lack of all the relevant data. In order to determine their advertising budgets, most companies, even today, simply come up with a set percentage of either sales or profits from the last year or of estimates for the next. A study quoted by Schudson found that past sales were more likely to influence advertising decisions than was advertising likely to increase future sales. In other words, sales tend to create advertising at least as much as the other way around.[159]

Until the immediate prewar period there is little to tell us how Russian firms determined the level of their advertising budgets. Nevertheless, in examining the figures from Moscow's toiletries industries, it appears that these turn-of-the-century businesses may already have estimated their advertising budgets based on sales. In the case of Ostroumov in 1901–1902, however, advertising continued to grow even when sales temporarily fell, suggesting an already institutionalized faith in advertising as essential to the company's vitality. Advertising was not considered a dispensable item on the company's list of expenses but rather an integral part of creating and maintaining a consumer market for its goods.

It is also important to note that, while the advertising expenditures listed in company accounts include newspaper advertisements, posters, price lists, and giveaway trinkets such as pencils, they do not include packaging or labels, even though these were an important part of the public image of a company's products. If labels and packaging were added, advertising expenditures would be greatly increased—in some cases tripled—for most manufacturers of brand-name products.[160]

The Tobacco Industry

While the toiletries manufacturers' embrace of active advertising came early in the Russian context (by the 1880s), other industries followed suit as the competition for brand loyalty intensified in the twentieth century. By the 1900s brand-name cigarette (*papirosy*) advertisements were prominent and regular features on the front pages of several popular mass-circulation newspapers. Since advertisements on the front page generally cost twice as much as those on the back, location in itself is an indication of a business's emphasis on advertising. Even though the tobacco manufacturers were slower to adopt this kind of print advertising, they became enthusiastic users of the medium during the last decade of the tsarist era.

Tobacco had been processed in Russian factories beginning in the 1850s. By 1908, there were 241 factories in the Russian Empire producing over 58,000,000 rubles worth of snuff, cigarettes, cigars, and pipe and chewing tobacco a year.[161] Of the 241 factories, nine companies dominated much of the advertising in the national market; all but one of these were founded and run by ethnic Russians or Russian Jews.[162]

To a great extent the tobacco companies' advertising followed an industry-wide pattern similar to that of the toiletries firms, but on a smaller scale. In general, their advertising represented from one-third to one-and-a-half percent of sales in the prewar period. It is unlikely that the difference in expenditure lay in newspaper advertising, given the consistent presence of tobacco (especially cigarette) advertisements in the mass-circulation press after the turn of the century. The tobacco firms also engaged in poster and billboard advertising but were less involved in other marketing approaches, such as giveaway trinkets and elaborate packaging.

The tobacco manufacturers' early neglect of publicity is evident in their poorly differentiated accounting for this expense before 1900. In 1898 the La Ferme company's accounts defined its advertising as simply "publications and signs" (*vyveski*).[163] The Gabai company's lack of emphasis on advertising in that same year is clear from the fact that advertising was lumped together with a list of miscellaneous expenses that included lawyers' fees and painting the fence![164] By the 1910s, however, Gabai's marketing was greatly diversified, encompassing not just newspaper advertisements, but posters on fences, in parks, and on theater curtains. The firm also dispersed over three thousand rubles' worth of "advertising matches" in 1911.[165]

The leading companies almost all paid attention to advertising by the 1910s, and those firms that did not were slow to appeal to a broad market. Rostov-on-Don's Asmolov and Company, for example, neglected advertising because it concentrated on a more elite market, selling mostly cigars, pipe tobacco, and expensive cigarettes. This firm's lack of advertising reflects the assumption prevalent in the early days of most consumer societies (and as we have already seen, definitely widespread in Russia) that a quality product is its own advertisement and does not need other promotion. The attitude is confirmed in this case by an article promoting Asmolov and Company in 1910, that ends: "To talk of the quality of the cigarettes and tobacco put out by the factory is completely superfluous (*izlishne*), since their great distribution speaks for itself."[166] In 1913 Asmolov's directors finally agreed that their neglect of the mass market should be rectified, but rather than change their own factory's production, they bought out a smaller, struggling firm that was already equipped to produce cheaper cigarettes.[167]

In 1912 the firms of La Ferme, Bogdanov, and Dukat formed a syndicate in order to control competition and consolidate the increased capital that higher excise taxes and the pressure to automate production had made necessary.[168] Budgeting and accounting procedures subsequently became more standardized among these firms; by the eve of the First World War, both La Ferme and Dukat had stated policies of allocating one percent of turnover to advertising.[169] In the case of La Ferme, this policy represented a doubling of the firm's advertising budget in comparison with the late nineteenth century.

Despite the syndication the tobacco companies' advertising remained independent. It is almost certain that, like the toiletries manufacturers, they created internal departments to deal with advertising management as their marketing activities grew more complex. There is proof that this occurred in the case of Shapshal, which employed a full-time advertising manager with a salary of 2,400 rubles a year in 1914.[170] Nearly all the major firms also employed copywriters like Sergei Korotkii (who wrote initially for La Ferme and after 1905 for Shaposhnikov) to provide the endless verses and stories that characterized so many cigarette advertisements on the front pages of papers like *Gazeta-kopeika* and *Russkoe slovo* in the prewar period.[171] This use of verse and fiction was an approach much less used by the toiletries companies—another indication that a business's advertising methods tended to be determined by patterns within its own industry.

The Tea Industry

An examination of the tea industry's advertising policies shows yet again that companies responded more to the tactics of their direct competitors and to changes within the industry than to any generalized trend in advertising. The tea companies differed entirely in their marketing approach from those of either the toiletries or tobacco companies.

Tea first appeared in Russia in 1638, when a Mongol khan sent some as a present to Tsar Mikhail Romanov. Its popularity spread slowly throughout the subsequent centuries (the Russian samovar is a product of the eighteenth century), accelerating greatly in the late 1870s, when the Russian navy established ties in Chinese and Indian ports, shipping tea back in bulk to Odessa, to be processed in Russian factories.[172] Tea plantations within the Russian Empire began to prosper in the 1880s, but most of the unprocessed leaves still came from abroad.

Initially, the large tea factories in Russia seem to have dealt for the most part with wholesale buyers. Advertising thus occurred more at the retail level, with individual shopkeepers including tea in their list of goods for sale. In a report to shareholders in 1903, the large firm of K. & S. Popov Brothers, founded in 1842, talked of the sweeping changes that had altered their business since the early 1880s.[173] On the buying end, the opening up of the East to Russian trade meant that the companies now needed representatives in China and India, as well as Central Asia and London. Selling had also changed. Whereas they had previously only dealt with a few large-scale customers, each buying in the hundreds of thousands of rubles, now the majority of their custom went to small consumers with accounts in the tens as well as the hundreds of rubles.[174] To deal with this business, the Popov company had seven branches throughout the Russian Empire and some abroad. In addition, they ran their own retail shops in Moscow, St. Petersburg, and the Caucasus.[175] The trading house of Wogau & Co., a wholesale concern dealing in many materials and foodstuffs including tea, described the late nineteenth-century trend to incorporate retail selling in the tea industry, necessitating "widespread advertising."[176] In 1893 it formed a new company, Karavan, to deal with both the retail and wholesale tea markets. Karavan maintained its own retail shop in Moscow.

There is little archival information on the tea firm of one of Moscow's leading merchant families, the Botkins. While accounts for 1913–1914 include a long list of trade expenses, advertising appears nowhere among them. This absence suggests that the company continued exclusively in the wholesale market, unlike its competitors. The firm was not thriving in the early twentieth century, suffering a loss of over 140,000 rubles in the 1907–1908 fiscal year.[177] It is worth speculating that this decline may have been precisely due to a failure to change with the times in terms of marketing.

"Widespread advertising" was essential to the retail market in an industry where companies' products differed very little beyond the label. For the individual consumer there was no bulk discount to ensure the loyalty of a customer. Unlike the toiletries manufacturers, who often developed products in their own laboratories, the manufacturers of both tea and tobacco broached the national mass market using similar resources and processes, differentiating their goods largely through packaging and advertising claims.

The tea industry, coming to retail sales as it did only at the end of the nineteenth century, developed a somewhat different approach to advertising than we have seen so far. In addition to product packaging, which was a large expense and an important part of the public appeal for all three industries, the tea companies placed a heavier emphasis on posters and in some cases almost entirely ignored advertising in periodicals.[178] The Vysotskii tea company, for example, showed a marked predilection for poster advertising. The accounts of this firm lack total expenditures for advertising, but a wealth of detail reveals an extensive advertising policy. Vysotskii & Co., probably the largest tea firm in Russia, simultaneously engaged the services of at least eleven printing companies to fill its continual orders for posters, labels, decorated boxes, and calendars. Just one of these printers could run up an account with Vysotskii worth ninety thousand rubles in a single year.[179] As an example, one printer's modest account for one month includes up to 24,000 copies of one poster, with the order being repeated in various quantities throughout the year.[180] Ten thousand copies cost Vysotskii one thousand rubles. Clearly this company placed great stock in its poster advertising. There is no evidence at all in its accounts for any advertising in periodicals.

As the leading companies entered the retail market, they experimented to discover which approaches would work best in attracting individual consumers. Three years' worth of future estimates for advertising in the Popov firm between 1902 and 1906 (table 1) reveal a great deal about the management's thinking, even though the expenses allocated in theory were not fully spent in practice. Judging by its absence in 1903–1904, the expenditure on calendars in 1902–1903 was an experiment deemed unsuccessful, or too expensive, for this firm. Instead, a far larger amount of twenty thousand rubles was contemplated for special advertising boxes, a category not discarded but greatly reduced two years later. Estimates for publications were tentatively increased the second year but more than halved by 1905, and this at a time when many other manufacturers were placing advertisements more and more regularly in the press. Meanwhile, a temporary decrease in projected poster expenses in 1904–1905 was more than made up for by an almost two-fold jump in 1905–1906. All of these variations demonstrate the experimental character of advertising in the tea industry, barely out of its first decade in retail sales (see table 1).

TABLE 1 ——K. & S. Popov Brothers projected advertising expenditures

1902-3		1903-4		1905-6	
Publications	10,000	Publications	11,000	Publications	5,000
Calendars	10,000	Advertising boxes	20,000	Advertising boxes	7,000
Posters	16,000	Posters	14,000	Posters	25,000
Price lists	8,000	Price lists	4,000	Price lists & supplements	6,000

Source: TsGIA g. Moskvy, f. 766, op. 1, dd. 1, 2.

Accounts for the Popov tea firm point to another difference in advertising practice from the tobacco and toiletries companies, although whether this was industry-wide is impossible to tell without further evidence. Rather than base their advertising budget on sales, by 1912 this firm stated its projected spending at about thirty thousand rubles a year "independent of turnover."[181] Whether or not this was a shared practice, obviously the Popov company had developed a steady advertising strategy by the 1910s.

The main determining factor in marketing strategies appears to have been intra-industrial practice and the need to compete with the methods of immediate rivals in the same business. Nevertheless, since the 1870s the toiletries, tobacco, and tea industries had, each in its own way, incorporated advertising into their budgets to the point that it had become an integral part of their business policies. The manufacturers, whose job it was to stimulate public interest in new products as well as selling existing goods, were not simply responding to changes in the world of commerce as had many small merchants but were actively engaged in creating a consumer market.

CONCLUSION

The plethora of advertising in postreform Russia was perceived as something qualitatively as well as quantitatively different because it reflected changes demanded by the modern market. By the 1910s the Russian business community as a whole had largely accepted that advertising was now an intrinsic aspect of trade. Manufacturers of consumer goods saw the value of advertising somewhat later than small retailers, but they soon emerged as among the most creative advertisers in the daily press. If the small merchants' acceptance of modern advertising was initially more grudging than enterprising, they nevertheless ultimately acknowledged the necessity to adapt, and those who opposed advertising did so more out of inertia than a nationalistic resistance to Western influences. Even Verigin, a public adversary of Western imitations, conceded that advertising (in its ideal "Russian" form, of course) could be a "weapon of civilization" and "a significant spur to technological progress and enlightenment."[182] In the final analysis, both he and the merchants accepted that progress required change. Traders and manufacturers were pragmatic; what concerned them was the ability to survive and overcome the competition, much more than ideological debates over Westernization.

Advertising, manufacturing, and trade each fed the others' progress, further boosting economic growth and consumer activity. Similarly, advertising and the mass-circulation press emerged in symbiosis. Newspapers sought advertising, income from which made possible the very existence of a nongovernmental press. Without advertising the published forum for Russia's nascent public sphere would probably have remained limited to predominantly intelligentsia circles. In turn, without newspapers the primary messengers of consumption would have remained shop signs and posters on city streets; the voices of consumer culture would have permeated urban and rural homes much more slowly.

In Russia as well as in the West, advertising was both a consequence of and a formative influence in the process of modernization that opened new opportunities in business and creative endeavor for men and women alike. While the size of the Russian advertising industry was small in relation to that in Western cities such as London or New York, its growth was vigorous, and its potential social and cultural impact was perhaps more radical in a country that had so long resisted the dramatic changes inherent in industrialization and social mobility.

What did this growth in advertising mean for the tsarist regime, which desired the economic benefits of modernization but preferably without the experience of modernity? The next chapter looks at the relationship between advertising and the state, exploring tensions created when a regime is happy to grant (and even sponsor) commercial publicity for its trade and manufacturing but seeks to do so within the constraints of monarchical sanction and authoritarian control.

TWO

SEALS OF APPROVAL AND

STAMPS OF CENSORSHIP

Governmental Approbation and Regulation in Advertising

As the business community communicated daily with the population through its advertising, one might assume that the tsarist regime, which saw any public forum as potentially dangerous, would regard this commercial publicity with suspicion. To some extent this was the case, and all merchants had to consider the constraints of censorship and trade regulations when they advertised. Yet the Russian government also played a significant part in boosting the commercial reputation of select merchants and manufacturers, granting what amounted to imperial endorsements through exhibition awards and royal warrants, both of which bestowed the right to display the imperial insignia of the double-headed eagle on signs and advertisements.[1] To merchants trading in a competitive environment, such official seals of approval were sought after and jealously guarded once attained.

The Russian government thus played a dual role of support and supervision in the field of commercial publicity. Both sides of the coin constituted traditional autocratic functions of control, here through favor, there through regulation. But as Russian society increasingly challenged the legitimacy of autocracy in the early twentieth century, how desirable did state favor remain as a means of maintaining public reputation? And to what extent was the government able to maintain control over the burgeoning field of advertising? The first part of this chapter addresses the various means through which the government granted its approval and shows the business community's ongoing hunger to receive it despite the changing political climate. However, while the tsarist regime saw itself as the benevolent bestower of awards, evidence shows that traders sought these favors primarily for their marketing value rather than as tokens of subject loyalty.

The second part of the chapter examines the government's increasingly ineffective role as the regulator of advertising. The character of the Russian autocratic regime—specifically its continued reliance on censorship rather than legislation—rendered it particularly ill-suited to control the consumer marketplace, and authorities proved unable (or perhaps disinclined) to manage the growing tide of advertisements, especially in the years between 1905 and 1914. The preference for censorship over national legislation, no matter how futile the former proved to be, reflected the state's greater affinity for personalized controls than for impersonal rule of law. It stands in contrast to Western countries' increasing legislative responses to advertising abuses, ad hoc and inadequate as even those may have been.

IMPERIAL HONORS

The most sought-after endorsements among manufacturers and merchants from the reign of Nicholas I (1825–1855) through that of Nicholas II (1894–1917) were those imperial honors that awarded the right to display the state seal, emblazoned with the double-headed eagle, on store signs and advertising. A select few came by these awards in one of two ways: by winning prizes at trade and industry exhibitions, or by gaining the title "Purveyor to the Court of His Imperial Majesty." Of the two methods, the prizes awarded at trade and industry exhibitions were easier to attain and among the most widely incorporated into company advertising (see examples in figs. 4.2, 4.9, and 5.17).

Trade and manufacturing exhibitions were similar to annual trade fairs in that both of them displayed and sold goods brought together for a limited time, but while the principal purpose of exhibitions was to compete for prestige, that of trade fairs was to sell. Trade fairs (*iarmarki*), such as the largest held in Nizhnii Novgorod, had played a crucial role in the Russian market for centuries and continued to do so long after their Western counterparts languished. Only in the second half of the nineteenth century did the development of modern transportation and the proliferation of permanent urban trade centers undercut the fairs' economic significance.[2] While trade fairs fuelled the nation's trade and industry through commerce, manufacturing exhibitions sought to do so through celebration. These shows were held to inform and impress the public and to encourage excellence in industry by presenting and rewarding the best that the country or region could offer.

The practice of publicly displaying manufactured goods began in England in the mid-eighteenth century as a result of emerging industrialization. France and Germany soon followed suit from the 1760s onward. These early exhibitions were regional or at most national in character until London's Crystal Palace Exhibition in 1851, an event that is seen as a watershed in the public estimation of industrial progress.[3] The Crystal Palace Exhibition initiated an era of international expositions in which Russia began to participate from the last quarter of the century.[4]

Domestically, however, Russia began its own expositional tradition in the field of trade and industry with a manufacturing exhibition in St. Petersburg in 1829.[5] The initiative was state-sponsored but undertaken with the support of merchant representatives. Before rebellion in Poland and the poor harvests of the early 1830s set the Nicholaevan regime decisively in favor of preserving the economic status quo, the late 1820s had seen some active moves to foster industrial development. Under finance minister Egor Kankrin a manufacturing council made up of merchants, manufacturers, gentry, and scientists was formed in 1828 in order to advise the government and improve communications between industry and the bureaucracy.[6] One of the founding provisions of the council stated that it would be "compliant" with the goals of the new body to introduce an exhibition of "native" (otechestvennye) factory goods to be judged and awarded prizes. In October 1828 this provision introduced the statute decreeing the first exhibition in St. Petersburg, which was opened the next spring by the tsar himself in the St. Petersburg bourse.[7]

The official goal of the exhibition was "not only to acquaint the local population and foreign visitors with the achievements of Russian industry, but also to give the manufacturers the public respect they deserved."[8] In what historian Walter Pintner has called "the most spectacular of the measures taken by the state in the twenties to encourage development,"[9] the exhibition was thus intended to elevate the status of the manufacturing sphere in a society that customarily disdained the occupations of industry and trade. The public display was also implicitly an official impetus to bring Russian manufactured goods up to the quality of Western products. A journalist for the governmental publication *Journal of Man-*

ufacturing and Trade (*Zhurnal manufaktur i torgovli*) wrote effusively, and apparently without irony, that "even foreigners found items that were worth purchasing."[10]

From the beginning, the government envisaged that these events would be regular affairs, and the guidelines in the original exhibition statute remained the basic foundation for future shows. This and later statutes, incorporated into the law code of the Russian Empire, constitute among the best records of the evolving processes of granting trade and manufacturing awards throughout the nineteenth century. An examination of these laws elucidates the government's multiple purposes in sponsoring exhibitions. Representing the height of tsarist progressiveness in the era before major industrialization and reform, they were seen as promoting social well-being as well as regional and national economic pride.

As laid out by the 1828 statute, St. Petersburg would stage an exhibition every three or four years, and Moscow would host them in some of the intervening years. The exhibitors were charged no fee other than transportation, and their goods were not subject to guild or city taxes while on display. All types of factory and craft products were welcomed, barring only those too bulky to manage. Entry to the exhibition was likewise open to all visitors, except those of "improper" (*neprilichnyi*) appearance.[11]

The exhibition was the direct responsibility of the manufacturing council, which chose a committee from its members for the day-to-day supervision of the event. From this committee, the minister of finance appointed his own choice of chairman. The job of selecting the best examples of industry to receive honors was taken seriously. Throughout the exhibition the committee drew up a list of what it considered the most outstanding products. A week before the closing date, it presented this list to the whole manufacturing council, which inspected the items, heard the advice of "invited specialists" (*znatki*), and ensured that no item of superior excellence had been neglected.[12] Prizes of the first, second, and third order were then voted by ballot. First prizes consisted of silver and gold medals, forged specially for the occasion; second prizes took the form of public commendation (*pokhvala*) and inclusion in the subsequent account of the exhibition; third prizes consisted of monetary awards for domestic and artisanal crafts. The decisions of the judges were then submitted to the minister of finance, who sent them on with his comments for the opinion of the tsar. He in turn could award particularly worthy manufacturers with medals to wear around the neck or other special rewards. The honors granted to particular manufacturers were thus sanctioned by the monarch himself, creating a symbolic link between the throne and industries large and small.

Testimony to the importance that the government attached to these events lay in the fact that it staged them frequently and at state expense. There were exhibitions in Moscow in 1831, 1835, and 1843, and in St. Petersburg in 1833 and 1839.[13] The authorities genuinely believed that the exhibitions promoted industrial expansion. According to Pintner it was Kankrin's fear of overproduction that led to the reduced frequency of the exhibitions; a new policy stated in 1836 that the events were to be held every fifth year, alternately in the two capitals.[14] Nevertheless, that same year the tsar confirmed the right of provincial towns to stage their own industrial exhibitions, as Smolensk had already done. These events, acknowledged the tsar, "could not only satisfy curiosity, but could also be useful for competition towards the improvement of goods."[15] In other words, the government saw a direct response on the part of manufacturers to the stimulus of state honors.

In the 1840s Warsaw began to host exhibitions (1841, 1845), and as the capital of the kingdom of Poland, annexed to the Russian Empire in the late eighteenth century, this city was incorporated into the relay of official exhibition sites in 1848. By then the proliferation of industrial exhibitions was such that the original 1828 guidelines were deemed inadequate. These regulations were revised and expanded in a decree of January 21, 1848.[16] The new rules required heightened official control—indicative of the general increase in bureaucratization under the Nicholaevan regime—but also granted greater and more differentiated awards for manufacturers, a sign that this competition was still perceived as producing positive results.

The most important changes concerned both the extent of information required from manufacturers for official entry in the competition and the judging process itself, which was delineated in far more detail. To even submit goods at an exhibition under the 1848 regulations became a multi-leveled process involving reports from governors and manufacturers alike. Whereas the original regulations called only for each exhibitor to put up a sign with the owner's name and factory and compile a list of all the displayed goods and their prices, the new rules demanded an exhaustive list of data that covered every aspect of a factory's existence. This included the founding date, number of machines, recent improvements in mechanization, number of workers, and usefulness of the factory to its surrounding district. All had to be accounted for in a report on each establishment from the civil governor. Without this report goods were not eligible for awards, although they could be shown. In addition, manufacturers were to submit annual production and sales figures, indicate raw materials used, and list the number of workers employed outside the factory. With all this data the authorities acquired a sense of regional industrial development in addition to the information needed to record awards.

The governors were also required to name the enterprises in their respective provinces that, in their opinion, most excelled in production methods and factory maintenance, especially regarding worker safety and welfare. This last information was initially sent to the governmental official with ultimate responsibility for the exhibition in each city. For St. Petersburg this was the minister of finance; in Moscow it was the military governor-general, and in Warsaw the Governmental Commission on Internal and Spiritual Affairs. Only later were these recommendations sent to the primary judges.

Each city appointed its own committee for the direct supervision of its exhibitions. In the capital this was chosen from the manufacturing council, as before. In Moscow members were selected from the customs branch of the manufacturing council, and in Warsaw the committee was made up of both official servitors and well-known industrialists, with a chairman selected by the vicegerent. In each case the utmost care was to be taken to keep procedures within the strictures of officialdom.

Significant changes also appeared in the composition of the judging commissions under the 1848 decree. Rather than relying on the superficial observations of the exhibition committee officials (albeit with the "advice" of a few specialists), there was now a judging commission for each branch of industry, composed almost entirely of specialists in that field. More specifically, these were manufacturers, tradesmen, and others with technical backgrounds. They were to be chosen in part for their "impartiality" (*bespristrastie*), but even though a manufacturer was not allowed to judge his own goods, one wonders how well his rivals' products fared under his vote.[17] Nevertheless, this attempt at more informed judging, along with the expanded information base with which to appraise all aspects of productions, attests to a more thorough and considered attitude on the part of the authorities to the awarding of industrial honors. Clearly, these awards were not granted lightly.

The regulations of 1848 instructed judges to first keep in mind three basic factors: quality of goods, moderation of production costs and sale prices, and the state of the factory. While assessing quality, the judges were to consider not just the finished form but also the appropriateness of the raw materials and their processing. Low prices in themselves were not enough to act in the company's favor unless they were the result of scale of production or manufacturing improvements reducing costs. The use of cheaper materials was acceptable only if it did not affect the end quality of the product. In regard to factory conditions, the judges were to pay attention to the usefulness of the factory to its locality, technical innovations adopted, the importance and utility of the goods produced, and the adaptability of the manufacturing process for various markets.

Other factors were also taken into consideration. It was important to note whether the factory used native or foreign materials and to what extent its products decreased the need to import foreign goods. Unusually high levels of production and the introduction of entirely new fields of industry in a given region might also be cause for commendation. Both the extent to which the needs of the local inhabitants were satisfied by the factory's goods and the number of workers who were sustained by its employment should enter into the judges' discussions. And finally, concern for the welfare of the workers should be manifested not just in terms of sustenance and safety but also in insurance against poverty and helplessness in cases of sickness or "loss of strength."[18]

This lengthy list of stipulations reveals the government's increasingly studied purposes in establishing industrial exhibitions and granting awards. Its goals were to encourage domestic production that would be accessible to the broad population (with affordability not sacrificed to quality), to reward technical innovation, and to reduce Russia's dependence on imported goods and expertise. The role of industry in keeping the country abreast of Western developments and in a strong position as an independent power was thus implicitly acknowledged. If these goals seem surprisingly progressive for the prereform era, it should be remembered that the exhibitions represented the height of state activism in promoting industrialization and technical progress during the reign of Nicholas I. They also demonstrated a paternalistic awareness of industry's social, as well as economic, significance. By stipulating workers' welfare as a judgment criterion, the government hoped to instill in the manufacturers a sense of their importance in creating and maintaining social harmony through contribution to their local communities and the care of their workers. The tsar himself had stated at an earlier exhibition that, without the "energetic and paternal supervision of their morals," the workers would become "a *soslovie* (estate) as miserable as they are dangerous for their masters."[19]

With the imparting of such responsibilities to industry, the decree of 1848 also offered a more extensive range of awards. In addition to the earlier prizes, manufacturers could now win monetary rewards, and the gold and silver medals were each subdivided into large and small categories. Artisans and exceptional workers (recommended by their factories) were also eligible for commendations and small silver medals. The most significant addition as far as manufacturers and tradespeople were concerned, however, was the right to display the state seal on their signs and goods, and it is to their perspectives that we now turn.

This privilege of displaying the state seal quickly became one of the most sought-after official endorsements that a Russian merchant or manufacturer could acquire. Recognized merchants proudly placed the state seal on labels, shop signs, company stationery, and advertisements. The double-headed eagle signified quality sanctioned at the highest level; it was tantamount to a royal guarantee.

Only officially recognized exhibitions, however, could grant legitimate medals and the right to display the state seal. While small provincial exhibitions proliferated in Russia throughout the late nineteenth and early twentieth centuries, relatively few received the necessary approval from the Ministry of Finance (or the Ministry of Trade and Industry after 1905) to make them official. Russian manufacturers increasingly sent their goods to foreign exhibitions in Europe and the United States, but in order to be legitimate in the eyes of the authorities, these had to include official Russian participation or be announced in the government press.[20]

Placing an advertisement for a foreign exhibition in the *Government Herald* (*Pravitel'stvennyi vestnik*) was not a straightforward matter of submitting text and payment, even if these came through official channels. When the Dutch embassy in St. Petersburg requested announcement of a 1908 exhibition in The Hague, for instance, a Russian government agent in Paris was assigned the task of investigating the worthiness of the planned event. In spite of months of telegrams to and from Paris and memoranda between the ministries of Finance, Foreign Affairs, and Trade and Industry, the exhibition was almost over by the time the authorities reported back that it was not deserving of recognition.[21] Other foreign exhibitions suffered a similar fate at the hands of the Russian government.[22]

Unfortunately, many Russian manufacturers were not aware of these restrictions and took part in provincial and foreign exhibitions only to find their awards useless for publicity purposes.[23] One can imagine the disappointment of many merchants who were told that they could not broadcast their successes to the public. A semiliterate leather goods manufacturer in Tver province, respectfully requesting permission to wear the honorary cross and gold medal he had won in Brussels in 1910 and to depict them on his goods and bills, was brusquely informed that the exhibition had been a private undertaking and he was therefore not legally allowed to display his awards.[24] A Poltava sewing shop owner (the daughter of peasants), rewarded with a gold medal for participation in an exhibition in Rotterdam in 1909, was informed two years later that the event had not been recognized by the Russian government and she must therefore not use her medal.[25] Such examples are numerous.

Larger and more established businesses tended to be more aware of the regulations and were quick to cite them if they discovered a rival firm including illegitimate honors in its advertising. Iurii Nechaev-Mal'tsov, owner of a well-known glassware factory that had won the right to display the state seal at six separate exhibitions since 1849, complained to the Ministry of Trade and Industry in 1911 that a Vitebsk company, Galerkin and Sons, was manufacturing lamp glass with the state seal on it. According to Nechaev-Mal'tsov, his factory was the only one in its field to win this award at all the major Russian exhibitions. The Galerkin firm was therefore "committing forgery," Nechaev-Mal'tsov charged, by imitating the "so very deserved reputation" of his products and thus "misleading the public and causing [himself] substantial loss." To clinch his case, Nechaev-Mal'tsov meticulously cited an article of law forbidding the use of misleading labeling and the depiction of awards without the date on which they were won. In fact, the Galerkin factory had won the state seal at an exhibition in the Don region in 1909, which, unbeknownst to them, could not confer official awards. The Department of Industry promptly ordered the Vitebsk governor to tell Galerkin and Sons to refrain from using the seal or face the consequences in court.[26]

In a similar case of the same year, the Moscow Society of Perfume Manufacturers complained to the authorities about a small nonmember toiletries factory that was displaying an award won in an unauthorized provincial exhibition. This company was also ordered to stop.[27] Clearly, the incorporation of government endorsements into a company's public image was seen by owners as a distinction to be preserved and guarded.

Contesting these rights was also a way for small companies to challenge a larger competitor. In 1911 a second-guild St. Petersburg vodka merchant, Ivan Bauman, wrote to the Ministry of Trade and Industry concerning the predominant vodka firm, P.A. Smirnov. Along with several Moscow and Riga liquor manufacturers whom he was representing, Bauman questioned the validity of the varying awards (sometimes as many as eight state seals) that Smirnov publications depicted as company honors. The firm's agents, "traveling all over Russia with the goal of attracting large numbers of customers, to the detriment of the interests of myself and other vodka manufacturers," were holding up these awards to "uninformed tradesmen" (*nesvedushchie torgovtsy*) as legitimate proof of their products' superior quality. Convinced that no company could (or should?) have so many governmental honors, Bauman requested confirmation of each of them so that he could expose Smirnov's "unfair propaganda" to the authorities. Unfortunately for Bauman, Smirnov's claims were all genuine, won at officially recognized exhibitions in Russia and the United States. To top it off, the firm had been supplying the royal family for over a decade. After two years of unanswered appeals, Bauman was snubbed in a terse note from the Department of Industry telling him to mind his own business.[28] Goliath is not always leveled, but that does not alter the fact that this Russian David believed that aiming at the giant's state seal was the shot that might make the difference.

The importance attached to government endorsements by Russian merchants is evident not only from their competitive battles over these honors but also from the lengths that many went to in order to obtain them as they became harder to win in the usual way. From the 1870s the previously regular all-Russian industrial exhibitions became rarer, partly due to the country's official participation in international events. In 1876 the government decided to postpone the next exhibition, which was due to take place in Moscow, in favor of the international Parisian exposition of 1878.[29] Moscow did not finally host its exhibition until 1882.[30] This decline in domestic exhibitions deprived many manufacturers of their major means of winning the highest industrial honors. Some who appealed directly to the emperor for awards were successful, but in 1900 Minister of Finance Sergei Witte ordered that exceptions should no longer be made; medals and the right to display the state seal could only be awarded at recognized exhibitions.[31]

Still some merchants continued to petition the authorities, whether out of ignorance or determination. To mark the centenary of his family's watch-making business in St. Petersburg in 1912, Friedrich Ditmar penned a detailed account of three generations of "continuous activity in the field of native (*otechestvennyi*) trade and industry," which he hoped would earn his firm the privilege of the state seal. He was probably unaware of Witte's decree of twelve years earlier and no doubt disappointed by the blunt refusal sent by the Department of Industry.[32]

Others simply stretched the rules. Lodz linen manufacturer Borukh Gliksman, when caught displaying an unauthorized state seal in 1911, pleaded in justification that he had only used the emblem "on little labels" for his goods, not on the signs outside his business.[33] In an even more blatant case, a merchant in the Polish town of Suvalki put the state seal under the sign of his small shop (*lavka*) on the grounds that he was a salesman for the yeast manufacturers who had won it.[34]

Such machinations were increasing by the 1910s, as reports from the Ministry of Trade and Industry to the St. Petersburg city governor noted in March and April of 1911.[35] The governor was told to require those found improperly using the state seal to sign an affidavit not to do so in the future and to make them answerable to the law if they did persist.[36] It was important to protect the status of the award:

The depiction of the State Seal is the highest exhibition award, which has a special value not only in the eyes of manufacturers and traders, but also in the eyes of the vast masses of consumers—in their ignorance (*neosvedomlennost'*) judging the qualities of goods not by their inherent worthiness, but by outer signs of excellence on shop signs, labels, and so forth.[37]

The importance that the government attached to its awards is evidenced by the various stages of investigation required for confirmation of each prize. At the international exhibition held in Kazan in 1909, for instance, the council of experts recommended a total of 1,733 awards (the full array of medals and commendations was awarded in each of the many fields of enterprise), with reasons for their decisions included for every individual nominee.[38] The entire list was then vetted in detail by the Department of Industry, and any questions or objections were sent back to a representative of the Ministry of Trade and Industry for clarification. In all, there were queries on 330 of the 1,733.[39] Final confirmation could then take anything from a few months to two years. Of the fifty-six large gold medals originally proposed, thirty-six were confirmed in March 1910, four were rejected, and ratification of the other six took until the end of 1911, more than two years after the exhibition ended.

Little wonder then that some small manufacturers responded favorably when a new and seemingly easy way of obtaining medals presented itself. In the decade before the First World War, certain groups of enterprising and often unscrupulous profit seekers began making a business out of merchants' desires for exhibition awards. Traveling agents approached provincial manufacturers and offered to represent them at various exhibitions, taking a fee only if their goods won a prize. While there was nothing blatantly illegal about this practice, the agents did not explain to the merchants (who wanted the prizes entirely for their publicity value) that awards from most of these exhibitions would be officially worthless.

The governor of Ufa brought this matter to the attention of the Ministry of Internal Affairs in 1910. He reported that several manufacturers in Ufa were displaying on their labels, shop signs, and stationery, "for the purpose of advertising," the medals of various agricultural societies.[40] Not only were these medals therefore inappropriate for industrial products, but, he alleged, they had been bought from traveling salesmen rather than won at exhibitions where the merchants had clearly never been. In fact, the governor's knowledge of the law was lacking in both these regards. Manufacturers had never been required to accompany their goods to shows, since this would have imposed too heavy a burden on the running of their businesses, and an 1849 amendment to the law on industrial exhibitions allowed agricultural shows to include manufactured goods as long as they were of local production.[41]

Nevertheless, the governor's complaint, accompanied by police depositions taken from involved merchants and copies of the contracts drawn up by the salesmen, highlights both the shady nature of this enterprise and the reasons behind the merchants' willingness to cooperate. On the face of it, the deal offered by the agents was quite favorable to the manufacturer. The agents usually took on themselves all costs of transportation, display, storage, customs duties, and insurance and demanded no fee unless the merchant won a medal. All the owner had to do initially was to provide the goods. Fees ranged from seventy-five to three hundred rubles, depending on the agent and the type of medal won. Some merchants were evidently satisfied enough with the arrangement at first to engage the same agents repeatedly. The fact that they won medals every time apparently only belatedly struck them as suspicious. In one case it was only when the salesman demanded a higher fee after the fact that the deal turned sour. In all cases the merchants never saw their goods again and received only paper diplomas testifying to their awards. To receive the actual medals would cost more. Most did not see the point in paying for a piece of metal, even if it did carry the imprimatur of the tsar; the value for them lay in the reproduction of the award on goods and signs. In effect, from the merchants' viewpoint the whole purpose was advertising. Unfortunately, therein lay the agents' major deceit.

While exhibitions (official and otherwise) continued throughout the empire, it is ironic that the last great all-Russian industrial exhibition of the imperial period was held at the peak of Russia's industrialization drive—1896 in Nizhnii-Novgorod. Ordered by Alexander III shortly before his death and conceived by Witte to demonstrate "the results of protectionist politics," the exhibition was lauded by the French consul as reflecting, "in a clear vision, the work of fifteen years of transformation, I would say of economic revolution."[42] Almost ten thousand exhibitors took part, according to this witness, at a cost to the government of about ten million rubles. Unfortunately, the event was not the great popular success that the organizers had wished. This "most complete and most beautiful"[43] of Russian exhibitions was greeted for the most part with public indifference and had fewer visitors than that of 1882 in Moscow, despite the fact that the later exhibition was three times bigger.[44] A contemporary account blamed low attendance on "the most naïve, petty manifestation of still-not-obsolete Russian negligence"—the authorities' failure to advertise the event properly, with posters, flyers and newspaper announcements through the empire."[45] If the government was inept at vaunting its own achievements, it was nevertheless effective in giving the manufacturers their awards, and the endorsements of 1896 remained abundantly and proudly displayed in advertising throughout the early twentieth century.

A merchant did not have to win exhibition awards, however, in order to convey a suggestion of official approval in the firm's public image. Part of Sergei Witte's program of promoting Russian industry was to pass a law in 1896 protecting trademarks.[46] Upon request and for a small fee, the Department of Trade and Manufacturing in the Ministry of Finance (and after 1905, the Department of Industry in the Ministry of Trade and Industry) would give governmental confirmation of a trademark for a renewable period of from one to ten years. Any manufacturer could incorporate into his or her advertising this official ratification, if not of the product, at least of the label or factory emblem. Though this did not signify governmental approval, an impression of such was often given by including the words "confirmed by the government" or "registered in the Ministry of Trade and Industry" under the trademark or company name. Indeed, advertising manuals encouraged this practice to bolster a company's reputation in the public eye.[47]

Nevertheless, the attachment of solid official honors to the firm's name was naturally more desirable. With the decline in frequency of industrial exhibitions, there was only one other way for merchants to acquire the right to use the state seal, and this was open to very few. From the second quarter of the nineteenth century, tsars had been granting the privileged title of "Purveyor to the Court of His Imperial Majesty" to favored suppliers of goods and services, a title that came to include the right to display the state seal. This custom of honoring merchants had already been in practice since the Middle Ages in Britain, where it was called the Royal Warrant. The warrant was initially just a title, but William IV began granting use of the royal coat of arms along with it in the 1830s, and his successor, Queen Victoria, formalized the procedure.[48] By the end of Victoria's reign, 1,080 firms were entitled to use the royal seal on their products.[49]

The antecedents of the Russian tradition can probably be traced back to Peter I, who originally founded a court office (*pridvornaia kontora*) to deal with the economic needs of the court, including the procurement of goods and supplies. Since Russian industry was not yet developed enough to satisfy the tastes of the eighteenth-century Europeanized court, the position of court supervisor (*faktor*) was created in 1742 for the purpose of ordering goods from abroad. For the rest of the century, this post was filled by foreign merchants, who were allowed to maintain their own trade businesses in addition to their court duties. In the nineteenth century, with the expansion and improvement in Russian manufacturing, Russian merchants gradually obtained access to the imperial court. Alexander I granted the first-class (*pervostateinyi*) merchantry the right of entry in 1807, and in 1824 he extended the right to all first-guild merchants.[50] It is unclear exactly when the title "Purveyor to the Court" was first granted in Russia, but the honor was already valued among manufacturers by the 1840s. In August 1826 Nicholas I had created the Ministry of the Imperial Court, initially to deal with all matters concerning the ruling household.[51] Through this ministry the emperor conferred the special title upon select merchants.

It was incumbent upon merchants or companies to request the honor, which was not given automatically. The Office of the Ministry of the Imperial Court investigated the petitions, which were often addressed directly to the tsar. The investigation consisted of confirming with the particular branch of the court that the merchant had indeed delivered goods consistently and satisfactorily. By the 1890s the ministry had a preprinted questionnaire to use in each case, asking not only about the quality of goods and the trustworthiness of the purveyor, but also whether his or her prices were reasonable. If the merchant or company received favorable answers on all points, the ministry then forwarded the request for the approval of the tsar. Even with a good report, however, petitioners were usually turned down if there was already a titled supplier of the particular merchandise to the family member in question.[52] Only a change in the emperor's tastes or the accession of a new tsar could make way for another title of purveyor to his court once that privilege had been bestowed for a given product.[53]

Merchants who supplied members of the tsar's family other than the royal couple were allowed to use the title with slight modifications, such as "Purveyor to the Court of the Grand Princess," or "His Highness the Tsarevich." These titles usually came with the automatic right to use the state seal, until February 1856 when, in what was no doubt an attempt to maintain the special value of the seal, Alexander II ordered that henceforth this privilege be confined to those who supplied the emperor and empress alone.[54] Suppliers to the rest of the royal family could instead depict on their shop signs the monogram of the personage in question with a special shield as background.[55]

Until 1900 there was no difference between the state seal granted at exhibitions and to purveyors to the court. In order to prevent confusion, however, and strictly enforce the rule that the seal could only be won at official exhibitions, Witte announced on July 28 the tsar's command that a distinction henceforth be made. Purveyors to the imperial court were given a year to change the depictions on their signs from a large to a small state seal with a smaller eagle than that displayed by exhibition prizewinners.[56] It is an indication of the government's emphasis on competitive industry at the turn of the century (especially under Witte's influence) that the expositional award should take precedence over that conferred on the monarch's favorite traders.

There were no restrictions as to the social status of the court title's recipients. Foreign and Russian entrepreneurs, large and small manufacturers, traders and artisans could receive the honor if their goods and services happened to please royalty. In 1859 a state peasant was even granted both seal and title for his dairy products and vegetables.[57] Regulations required, however, that the deliveries be continuous and of many years' standing (in 1861 this was defined as at least eight years).[58] These requirements were reiterated in the rejection of many appeals for recognition from hopeful merchants who had offered royalty a onetime or occasional service. A Smolensk tradesman who once gave Tsarevich Alexander Alexandrovich a box of candy and subsequently envisioned the royal child's monogram emblazoned on his shop signs was typical of this fervor to incorporate imperial symbols into a business's public image.[59]

Exceptions were made to the regulations if a member of royalty made a special request on behalf of a favored provider, even though this could lead to rancor among members of the trading community. An example of such a case from 1861 shows what failure to receive imperial recognition for services rendered could mean to a business. In preparation for a royal visit to Livadia, a pair of Odessa grocers were invited by palace officials to transport part of their shop to Yalta in order to supply the Crimean court. Not only did the palace stipulate that these goods be delivered in accordance with the firm's Odessa price list, but the owners, "in order to justify fully the trust placed in us," ordered special goods from abroad on their own account and "spared neither means nor—so dear for a merchant— time." They deemed these efforts worthwhile, in the hopes that they would both "earn the attention of the authorities" and the right to be consistent purveyors to the court whenever Their Imperial Majesties were in the Novorossiiskii region. "We anticipated this right even more so because, without it, society has the basis to prove that we did not justify the trust placed in us, which cannot but have influence on our trade." What was at stake here, as in all similar cases, was not so much imperial favor as public reputation. What galled these particular tradesmen most was that a fellow Odessa merchant, who had prepared clothing for the empress, was granted the title of purveyor to the court and now exhibited the state seal above her shop—"a circumstance that all the more forces the Odessa public to speak of our operations in Yalta badly, to the detriment of our turnover." The grocers never received satisfaction because the seamstress had acquired her title at the special request of the empress, and the Minister of the Imperial

Court was not willing to disturb the tsar with exceptional requests under any lesser authority.[60] These tradesmen's complaints nevertheless show that merchants primarily esteemed imperial honors for their advertising value rather than for any innate satisfaction in pleasing the tsar. In the merchants' opinions, the public paid attention to such marks of royal favor.

Despite growing disillusionment with the tsarist regime among diverse sectors of society, being named a purveyor to the court remained a matter of some import to the firms concerned right up until World War I. Those companies granted the title during the tercentenary celebration of the Romanov dynasty in 1913 were especially eager to announce their distinction in ceremonious fashion. Some took out large announcements in the paper to declare that they had won the title for this great occasion; their notices advertised no products, but rather, with the solemnity of an official decree, displayed the title and state seal—the best advertisement of all.[61] As long as the tsarist state was the center of authority, merchants and manufacturers were keen to appropriate the prestige of that authority and consolidate their reputations through the various imperial endorsements available to them.

THE LIMITS OF CENSORSHIP

Merchants and manufacturers may have valued legitimization from tsarist authority as a boost to their public reputations, but the expansion of their advertising strained the fetters of governmental censorship regulations in the late imperial period. On one hand the tsars were unwilling to revoke censorship control over advertising, even though it proved ineffective in the face of a booming commercial press. On the other hand they were remarkably resistant to passing national legislation to combat advertising abuses.

Initially, the paucity of laws regulating advertising was not unique to Russia. At the turn of the twentieth century, advertising was still a young and rapidly evolving industry in the West. Few countries by this time had enacted any thorough legislation to prevent abuses; responses tended to be ad hoc, dealing with individual problems as they arose. In Britain, for instance, the 1853 London Hackney Carriage Act prevented advertisements from being placed in such a way as to block ventilation and light in public transport. The 1889 Indecent Advertisements Act banned description of the lurid details of venereal diseases in patent medicine advertising, and the 1907 Advertisement Regulation Act enabled local authorities to stop large outdoor advertising from disfiguring public places such as parks.[62] In Germany also some of the first regulations, beginning in 1902, concerned the preservation of landscapes in the face of encroaching billboards.[63] In the United States, patent medicine advertisements were not regulated until the passage of the Pure Food and Drug Act in 1906, and the push for truth in advertising had to depend on a movement for professional standards from within the advertising industry itself at the beginning of the twentieth century.[64] Often, legislation was slow to address abuses; for decades writers and artists in western Europe as well as Russia were powerless to prevent their works from becoming part of commercial endorsements.[65] As Western countries addressed problems piecemeal through legislation, Russia resisted passing laws to tackle advertising problems even on an ad hoc basis. Instead, the regime continued in its preference for censorship well after the liberties resulting from the 1905 revolution rendered this system purely nominal.

The obduracy of retaining an unworkable system of control over commercial publicity is partly rooted in the fact that the last tsars were modernizers without being modern. They wanted an entrepreneurial economy under authoritarian power. All three of the last Russian tsars promoted progress in their own ways, despite the significant differences in their political outlooks. The Great Reforms shepherded through under Alexander II (ruled 1855–1881) included liberalization of censorship, allowing for the emergence of the mass-circulation press and its concomitant expansion of a major advertising medium. The state-sponsored industrialization drive begun by Alexander III (ruled 1881–1894) greatly increased the production of goods for sale to a growing population. And Nicholas II (ruled 1894–1917) had his grip on autocracy pried free enough by the Revolution of 1905 to allow limited civil liberties. Yet, as much as these rulers promoted modernization (willingly or not), they still saw their regimes as the traditional protectors of a gullible public. In an era before the notion of truth in advertising was supported with much legal framework anywhere in the world, perhaps this paternalism is understandable. It may go some way toward explaining the stubborn retention of censorship for advertising when other types of print media were given greater freedoms.

In broad terms, the censorship statutes of 1828 and 1865 forbade offending the church and Christianity, autocracy and government, the morality of the people, and the personal honor of individuals.[66] None of these strictures placed serious obstacles in the way of commerce. Nevertheless, all commercial advertising was subject to censorship, and this imposed logistical problems at the very least. The censorship reform of 1865, which allowed for publication of periodicals without preliminary (prepublication) censoring, facilitated prompt daily circulation of newspapers, but significantly, it did not exempt advertisements from preliminary review.[67] Such an exclusion obviously meant delays for the advertisers, but with sufficient forethought they could still inform the public of sales and new products in a timely fashion, given the cooperation of the authorities. However, an overzealous or vindictive bureaucracy could easily throw the whole procedure into disarray, as we shall see later.

From 1828 onward, the law required all types of posters and small (*melkie*) print advertisements to be submitted to the local police authorities for examination.[68] Unfortunately, the law did not define the word *melkie*, which led to recurring bureaucratic confusion. In 1873 the Chief Administration of Press Affairs put out a circular stating that only bibliographic and sheet music advertisements should go through the general censorship; presumably, all others were included in the category of those supervised by the police authorities. Yet others suggested that *melkie* meant "only announcements in the narrow sense, specifically small advertisements about buying and selling things, and offering services, etc."[69] Even this definition could apply to trade or classified advertisements, or both. The tendency became simply to include all types of advertisements not specified in the regulations under the catch-all label *melkie*.[70]

In addition to troubles over definitions, the application of the statute in relation to censoring advertising seemed to depend more on the decisions of regional authorities than on the letter of the law. Until the end of the century, the St. Petersburg city governor had all the melkie advertisements that were printed in the capital, both trade and classified, directed through his office for scrutiny. This situation lasted until 1898, when city governor Nikolai Vasilevich Kleigels finally assigned the duty to the local police for the "greater convenience" of the capital's populace.[71] He had in mind private citizens putting classified advertisements in the local papers, giving the example of a grieving widow who would no longer have to drag herself from her home on the outskirts to the governor's office in the city center just to have an obituary approved. Why this was ever necessary is unclear since, according to the 1865 censorship statute, it was the duty of the printer to submit publications to the relevant authorities for censorship.[72] In fact, it was the printer or, in the case of periodicals, the publisher who bore any punishment for infractions.[73] The advertiser suffered only by the cancellation or modification of his or her advertisement.

Whoever the intended beneficiaries might have been, Kleigels's order automatically applied to commercial advertisers as well as private citizens because the official regulations had still not differentiated between the two. According to *New Time (Novoe vremia)* publisher Aleksei S. Suvorin, the previous system of going through the city governor's office had been preferable because it allowed for "a certain uniformity."[74]

Such uniformity need not have been lacking from the new system if the city governor had stuck to the letter of the law and assigned censorship duties only to the office of the chief of police (*politseiskoe nachal'stvo*), but Kleigels determined that censorship should take place in the police station (*uchastok*) of the district where the printing shop of each advertisement was located. Suvorin complained that in St. Petersburg alone this meant that over forty district police officers were, no doubt grudgingly, spending much of their time reading advertisements. And naturally the resulting decisions were unpredictable.

Perhaps it was the officers' lack of enthusiasm for this tedious new task that allowed some questionable advertisements to appear in print. In their inspection of advertising, the main instructions were to prevent "fraud and the exploitation of trust" and to block any advertisements that helped spread depravity (*razvrat*).[75] In 1899, however, Kleigels accused Suvorin's paper, among others, of printing such notices as a woman proposing her "youth" to any takers or an offer of government posts in return for money.[76] In response, Kleigels ordered "the most attentive consideration of such advertisements and the unconditional banning of them."[77] As for potentially fraudulent trade advertisements (which in his mind included them all), the local police stations would be better equipped to check out questionable claims.

By 1900 this directive from above was causing chaos for newspaper publishers and advertisers alike in the capital. In April Suvorin wrote a long letter to the head of the Chief Administration of Press Affairs, Nikolai Vladimirovich Shakhovskoi, pleading with him to intervene since appeals to the city governor had only resulted in the latter's affirmation of all police decisions.[78] There had been no trouble abiding by the system for twenty-five years, Suvorin wrote, until suddenly in March the police officer at the second district Liteinii station began refusing advertisements for no apparent reason or simply because he himself did not know and therefore could not vouch for the advertiser. At Suvorin's protestations the officer directed him to send these advertisements for verification to the police stations located in each advertiser's district, a task those policemen refused as none of their business.

The situation reached ridiculous limits. A hosier's claim that "stockings the like of those from my workshop you won't find in any shop" was banned on the ground that it was unverifiable. A footman seeking work was not allowed to call himself "completely honest" because "to advertise oneself thus is uncomfortable (*neudobno*) from the moral standpoint."[79] A dog groomer (*sobachii parikmakher*) was banned from advertising simply because the policeman found the whole concept "unseemly" (*neprilichnii*). The officer's sensitivities notwithstanding, Suvorin commented sardonically, "such groomers do actually exist and they don't find their occupation indecorous."[80]

Suvorin felt that the whole attack on advertising in his newspaper was prompted by police vindictiveness over his recent publication of an article criticizing the police and fire departments. He buttressed this opinion by showing that an advertisement forcibly retracted from his paper had been printed in exactly the same form in the *Bulletin of the St. Petersburg City Governorship* (*Vedomosti Sankt-Peterburgskogo gradonachal'stva*).[81] Despite Suvorin's misgivings, evidence suggests that the crackdown on advertising was more a result of local overreaction to orders from above than any personal vendetta against *Novoe vremia*. The police may have combed this paper with special scrutiny because Kleigels had cited it as a major offender, but other publishers were suffering from equally arbitrary treatment of their advertising at the same time.

A few weeks after Suvorin's complaint, the editor of *Russia* (*Rossiia*), Georgii Sazonov, wrote to Shakhovskoi at the Chief Administration of Press Affairs claiming that he was losing the trust of his advertisers. Mistrust under these circumstances took on a "frankly offensive character, since the responsible editor of a non-censored publication is surrendering to the censorship of a police officer." It would be a good thing for the press, Sazonov added, if preliminary censorship for advertising—this "sad relic of the ancient past"—were relegated to the archives and advertisements were printed on the editor's responsibility.[82] Such a concession was not to occur.

The Chief Administration of Press Affairs and the Ministry of Internal Affairs did agree with Suvorin and Sazonov, however, that the city governor should not encourage such obstructionist intervention in advertising censorship since this was causing unnecessary problems in publishing and trade. An advertisement should not be blocked unless it contained within its own text clearly criminal or immoral tendencies. The police should understand that it was not feasible to check every potential exaggeration or falsehood, and they should also not forget that victims of advertising fraud had recourse to the courts in cases of abuse.[83] The latter point bespeaks the tenuous nature of Russian legal awareness at the dawn of the twentieth century, when even the police had to be reminded of the court's existence.[84]

In August 1900 the jurisconsult of the Ministry of Internal Affairs found that the local police officers had "in many cases demonstrated a completely wrong and arbitrary understanding of the new duties laid upon them," as well as "an insufficient understanding of the limits of authority." In the interests of protecting the population they had only succeeded in infringing upon the "rights and profits of the vast majority of honest advertisers." The jurisconsult found fault with the very notion of assigning censorship duties to the lowest branches of the police force because this was not the intent of the law: "The censorship of advertisements, not having, of course, such a serious significance as the censorship of other published works, is nevertheless given to the police authorities (*nachal'stva*)." Moreover, the consideration of advertising content from the social, political, and religious points of view demanded "more maturity (*razvitie*) and tact than can be assumed from the secondary representatives of the police."[85]

All these opinions were forwarded to city governor Kleigels, but he did little to correct the situation beyond directing the police to let through some of the advertisements specifically discussed by his superiors. In his view the inconveniences to the publishers and advertisers were (perhaps) regrettable but not as important as protecting the reading public, "often approaching any kind of advertisement with gullibility (*legkoverie*)."[86] Former Warsaw chief of police and a military man through and through, Kleigels epitomized the sternly paternalistic (and patronizing) official, unsympathetic to the needs of a modernizing economy and press.

Ultimately, it took a minor international incident to rein in Kleigels's customized system of advertisement censorship in the capital. In September 1900 the British chargé d'affaires in St. Petersburg turned to the Ministry of Foreign Affairs with a complaint from the manufacturers of Lea and Perrins Worcestershire sauce, whose advertisement had been running in several major Russian newspapers for over a year.[87] Now, the local police had refused to allow *Novoe vremia* to print this same advertisement without major changes to the text. The British complaint was passed on to then Assistant Minister of Internal Affairs Petr Nikolaevich Durnovo and to the Chief Administration of Press Affairs. Ordered by the latter to provide reasons for the refusal, Kleigels explained that the advertisement had contained the phrase "steer clear of any other so-called Worcestershire sauces." According to the police officer at the Liteinii precinct, "by affecting the interests of other traders, these words took on a polemical character."[88] It was clearly business as usual for the secondary representatives of the police!

On receipt of this explanation, however, Durnovo took the matter into his own hands and wrote to Kleigels demanding to know why the local police were still censoring advertisements and ordering the officer in question to release the original Lea and Perrins advertisement "forthwith (*nemedlenno*)."[89] After this incident, references to police arbitrariness in censorship disappear from the records, so we may assume that fierce reprimand by an assistant minister carried some weight.

Five years later, with the promulgation of the October Manifesto after the 1905 revolution, the printers of periodical publications freed themselves from the preliminary censorship of advertising by simply ignoring the regulations they had complied with for so long. When the government issued a decree on October 19 to the effect that publishers should abide by censorship rules until a new statute appeared, the St. Petersburg Soviet ordered the Printers' Union to refuse to print any publications submitted to censors.[90] The new statute of November 24, 1905, abolished preliminary censorship for all periodicals (the 1865 statute had allowed for exemptions upon request), but nothing was specified about advertising. Most publishers, it is clear, assumed that advertising was included and stopped submitting it for review. The St. Petersburg city governor appealed to the Ministry of Internal Affairs on this account in November 1905 and June 1906 and received confirmation that the censorship law as applied to advertising was still in existence and violators should be taken to court.[91] In the face of universal violation, however, the authorities were effectively powerless to stop uncensored advertisements from being printed. The most they could do was use the court system to punish offenders after the fact. Thus began the paradoxical situation that was to last until the imposition of military censorship in World War I: the government repeatedly insisted that preliminary censorship of advertising existed, whereas publishers and printers consistently acted as if it did not. The censorship apparatus had become little more than a paper tiger.

As is evident in the content of advertising after 1905, ineffective censorship made way for a pervasive stretching of the rules. In a few cases advertisements stepped on political or religious toes. In 1910 the Holy Synod raised objections to advertisements incorporating a cross[92] and in 1913 to the use of Gay's painting of Christ at Golgotha in conjunction with an advertisement for cigarette papers.[93] In 1911 the Moscow circuit court confiscated and destroyed 234,000 chocolate box wrappers carrying a portrait of Leo Tolstoy, not because this was seen as defaming a great author but because the picture was accompanied by the following words of the writer: "Land is like the air and the sun, it is the property of all and cannot be subject to ownership. In order for the land to become the property of everyone, people must recognize the sin of ownership."[94] It is indicative of the weakened state of censorship enforcement by this time in Russia that any manufacturer would dare to associate his goods publicly with such sentiments. Nevertheless, advertisements with dubious religious and political content were easily suppressed because they were exceptional.

Such was not the case with those that stretched the limits of moral propriety. After 1905 scarcely veiled advertisements for pornography, both books and pictures, abounded. Laura Engelstein has shown how such ads were part of a growing focus on eroticism that crossed genres, from the boulevard press to avant-garde literature, titillating many and provoking deep concern among others in Russian society during this period.[95] In an attempt to curb advertisements whose "coarse cynicism" was "clearly offensive to social morality," the Chief Administration of Press Affairs put out a circular in June 1910 that bemoaned the abundance of these ads and urged closer attention to preventing them.[96] In order to draw the boundaries of permissibility more clearly, this circular listed four types of advertisements that should never pass a censor:

1—Those for books that describe "the perversion of sexual feelings, prostitution, unnatural tendencies"; books that are statedly intended for adults only and therefore are read "with seductive interest."

2—Those concerning methods for preventing pregnancy.

3—Those for treatment of sexual impotency.

4—Those proposing "illegal liaisons."

Advertisements for birth clinics, treatment of female disorders, and venereal diseases (these three categories were significantly grouped together) could be allowed only if they were worded briefly and without listing the symptoms of diseases. Birth clinics could not specify that they were confidential—a common practice. Propositions for legal marriages and modeling services were permissible only if they did not include physical descriptions. All these clarifications, however, were entirely ineffective because from 1905 on advertisers and publishers ignored preliminary censorship.

In the 1910s the official struggle against advertising illicit material received a rare boost from the top of the tsarist government in an attempt to combat pornography. Russia's laws had included a ban on "corrupting images" since 1845, and censors throughout the nineteenth century had been instructed to block immoral material.[97] The renewed momentum to act against pornography in 1910 was part of a broader international campaign being conducted against the trade in sexually explicit publications. In May of that year, representatives of fourteen countries, including Russia, met in Paris to sign a cooperative agreement on the suppression of pornography. Ratified by Tsar Nicholas in October 1911, the agreement took effect in Russia on June 2 (15), 1912. The countries involved agreed to set up an international institution to share information that would help discover and suppress criminal pornographic activity.[98] Internally, each country was to deal with abuses according to its own laws. Thus, despite the heightened focus on the issue, no new laws were put into effect. As before, the charge of "corrupting morals" in Russia carried a five-hundred-ruble fine or a period of arrest from seven days to three months.[99] Not only was there no updated legislation, the existing law was rarely enforced.

Another category of advertising that became a major violator of censorship rules after the 1905 revolution was that of patent medicines. These advertisements had always been censored by local medical authorities, with the idea that they could discern harmful or misleading products in this field better than the police. Before 1905 the medical authorities had occasionally overstepped the limits of their authority in controlling the advertising relegated to them, although not to such extremes as the St. Petersburg police. Although there were no limitations as to appearance or form in medical and hygienic advertisements, the German makers of the mouthwash Odol—predominant in its field—complained in 1902 that they were being forced to limit their advertisements to the name and purpose of the product, place of sale, and price. The vague reason given was that "the virtues of this preparation do not correspond to the publications distributed about it." The company argued that, if their advertisements had an aggressively eye-catching appearance (*brosaiushchiisia v glaza vid*), this was necessary considering the character of the press itself, since only showy advertisements stood a chance of being noticed. They pointed out the contribution the firm had made to the "many hundreds of thousands in the population who had learned to value rational care for their teeth, the understanding of which doubtless favorably influences the people's health and is useful for the whole life of separate individuals."[100] The Odol manufacturers' pleas were to no avail, however; as long as advertisements were submitted for preliminary censorship, they were vulnerable to the officials who interpreted the censorship statute by their own idiosyncratic standards.

After 1905 the subjective judgments of censorship officials were no longer an issue, even in curbing advertisements for products with far more questionable claims than preventing bad breath. Patent medicine ads promised cures for every conceivable ailment, with sexual dysfunctions central among them (a topic explored further in chapter 4). The explicit ban on advertising medicines designed to affect sexual functions made no impact at all.

After the printers' boycott of censorship procedures began in 1905, the St. Petersburg medical authorities found themselves unable to stem the tide of violations and turned to the Chief Administration of Press Affairs for help. The result was yet another ineffectual circular reminding officials that the censorship laws were still in effect.[101] Another followed in 1911, denouncing those advertisements whose single goal was "profit for the inventors of various so-called medical treatments and systems, which by their pseudo-scientific content mislead trusting readers, for the most part those from the uneducated (*malorazvitye*) classes of the population."[102] These bureaucratic memos never produced the desired effect. Once the lid was opened on the Pandora's box of "creative" claims and titillating content in advertising, it proved very hard to close.

Postpublication censorship continued, but the system was overburdened, inefficient, and did little to curb abuses. On June 20, 1912, the head of the Chief Administration of Press Affairs, Count Sergei Sergeevich Tatishchev, sent forty-five sheets of newspaper advertisements to city governor Daniil Vasilevich Drachevskii, asking how any of them had passed police censors.[103] These clippings, taken from only one week's worth of newspaper issues, included advertisements for items such as the Ekzuber bust enlarger ("in just a few days you won't recognize your bust") and books with titles like "The World of Sexual Passions." For almost two months Tatishchev did not receive a reply, until he sent another missive wanting to know the reason why. What he was markedly unaware of was that from March 1911 the city governor's office had once again taken over all the duties of advertising censorship for purposes of uniformity, going back to the system that had existed in the capital up to 1898. Tatishchev's initial complaint had thus started an extensive search for the originals of all the advertisements, which had already been sent to the archives.

In his somewhat harried reply of August 14, Drachevskii brought out a litany of his own complaints about the censorship system. Every day his overworked staff had to deal with an influx of up to four thousand advertisements for examination. They would willingly do more, he avowed, but regulations did not require periodicals to send free copies of each issue to the censoring institution; therefore the governor's office had to buy subscriptions from the publishers they were overseeing. It was impossible to subscribe to them all, so they chose those that carried the most advertising.[104] Others could only be checked sporadically. This situation proves that censorship of periodical advertising was still occurring after publication, despite repeated official confirmation of the preliminary censorship rules. The governor's main weapon to combat offenses was thus the court system.

Since the first of the year (a period of seven-and-a-half months), Drachevskii's office had brought seventeen periodicals to court for advertising violations (see table 2 for frequency).

TABLE 2——Advertising censorship violations brought to court,
January 1–August 14, 1911

Periodical	Number of times charged in court
Gazeta-kopeika (Penny Gazette)	57
Novoe vremia (New Time)	36
Peterburgskaia gazeta (Petersburg Gazette)	23
Birzhevye vedomosti (Stock Market Record)	18
Vsemirnaia panorama (Worldwide Panorama)	14
Ogonek (Little Fire)	10
Sinii zhurnal (Blue Journal)	10
Rodina (Native Land)	9
Peterburgskii listok (Petersburg Sheet)	8
Rech' (Speech)	4
Vestnik zdorov'ia (Herald of Health)	4
Vechernee vremia (Evening Time)	3
Golos zemli (Voice of the Land)	2
Peterburgskii kinematograf (Petersburg Cinematographer)	1
Ves' mir (All the World)	1
Niva (Cornfield)	1
Vsemirnaia nov' (Worldwide Virgin Soil)	1
Total:	**202**

Source: RGIA, f. 776, op. 10, d. 387, l. 3.

Although the list found in table 2 includes both journals and newspapers, it is not surprising that the top three offenders are all dailies, as they had more frequent opportunity to overstep censorship regulations. Clearly, court action was meaningless. Most publishers, for purely commercial reasons, preferred to accept all the advertisers they could get and pay for any infractions later, because the fines were less than the advertising income involved. Even though the law allowed for substantial fines (100 rubles for avoiding censorship, up to 500 for immoral content, and in St. Petersburg up to 3,000 for violating rules about medical advertisements),[105] the penalties applied in practice were negligible. For all of *Birzhevye vedomosti*'s violations, the manager of the advertising department was made to pay forty rubles. A man charged with printing and posting uncensored posters was fined twenty kopeks. In November 1911 the publisher of *Gazeta-kopeika*, Mikhail Gorodetskii, had been let off altogether, even though (or perhaps as a consequence of which) in 1912 his paper was the worst offender.[106]

Thus, Drachevskii complained, he was fighting a losing battle. It could only be won if, firstly, all periodicals could be forced to send his office copies of their issues, and secondly, if the courts imposed higher fines. Neither of these requests was met. Tatishchev simply told Drachevskii to keep on taking offenders to court and informed him that the law strictly defined which institutions could require free copies of publications. The city governor's office was not one of them. Drachevskii even wrote back asking if he could then have the Chief Administration's old copies, since the statute of limitations allowed six months for prosecutions in these cases. The reply was negative: regulations required the Chief Administration of Press Affairs to keep its copies for two years.[107] The bureaucracy was literally stymied by devotion to its own rules. Censorship regulations, it appeared, had become more cumbersome and frustrating for the enforcers than for the press.

Why would the government prove so resistant to granting more substantive support to officials who were trying their best to fulfill the government's own regulations? In his study of post-1905 censorship, Caspar Ferenczi notes that the regime failed to increase spending for the censorship authorities for the entire period between 1882 and 1917, an era in which the number of Russian publications skyrocketed.[108] In other words, the censorship mechanisms were overstretched for all types of publishing. Ferenczi suggests that the ineffective censorship machinery was left as it was because the government never intended to use its full force except in cases that represented substantial threats, like the small revolutionary presses.[109] Interestingly, pornography was also seen as a political threat, as Paul Goldschmidt argues. The state viewed immorality as disobedience to God's law, and one who defied God was just as likely to defy the tsar.[110] Thus the law against immoral images, as well as the censorship regulations, provided the state with weapons ready to hand if it saw fit to use them against substantive dangers in print.

Perhaps, then, there was method in what appeared as bureaucratic madness to the likes of city governor Drachevskii. The government may have deliberately left the censorship authorities understaffed and underfunded, insisting that they fulfill impossible duties with limited resources, because it wanted the appearance of universal oversight while caring only about sustaining the power to stamp out what it saw as the dangerous offenders. In the meantime, meaningless court fines that served as no more than a tap (not even a slap) on the wrist helped keep up the façade of vigilance. This possible explanation still leaves unanswered the question as to why advertising did not benefit from the same liberalization in nominal regulation as other types of publications after 1905. I would suggest that the tsarist regime still clung to its self-image as protector of the gullible public, and in the absence of empire-wide legislation of advertising as a whole, censorship continued to allow it some oversight in the interests of the population.

The demand for national legislation on advertising in Russia came by and large from the business community itself. The first issue that prompted such a request was the increasing abuse of the word "sale" in advertisements. In November 1899 the *Trade-Industrial Gazette* (*Torgovo-promyshlennaia gazeta*) carried an article condemning the use of sales for unscrupulous competition and the dumping of poor quality goods.[111] Four months later, the Rostov-on-Don Committee of Trade and Manufacturing petitioned the local authorities to do something about the problem. Thus, in the interest of their own trade, the merchants themselves were urging legislation against the abuse of publicity. The result was a city statute forbidding the advertising of sales without prior permission from the head of police, to be given only in cases of legitimate sales, i.e., for the opening or liquidation of a business, or for biannual seasonal clearances.[112]

In 1901 the issue was referred to the Department of Trade, with the suggestion that steps should be taken on a wider basis than just Rostov-on-Don. The Ministry of Finance subsequently requested information from Russian consulates throughout Europe and beyond on any relevant legislation in force abroad.[113] Austria and Germany, it appeared, were the only countries to have a law, promulgated in 1896, controlling the use of sales in trade.

Meanwhile, similar complaints kept coming in from other cities as far afield as Vladivostok, and the issue was taken up by the popular press. Merchants claimed abuses were becoming worse as outsiders set up shop in town for a few months, published "screaming advertisements" and put up "importunate" (*zazyvaiushchiia*) signs, provoking a "special excitement" in the customer that caused him to "walk into the trap set by the crafty dealers," to the detriment of himself and the regular merchants.[114]

Despite such evocative and recurring pleas, the Russian government never acted on its survey of international law, preferring instead to rely on local legislation to deal with the problem. Each petitioner was referred to the solutions of other regions. Unfortunately, these local "solutions" were ineffective, partly because they did not carry the force of imperial law. On the eve of World War I, representatives of the business community and provincial officials were still periodically insisting on the need for national legislation to regulate unfair competition—to no avail.

Another questionable business practice that elicited a more active response from the government was the so-called "cooperative system" of selling general merchandise. Under this system, a merchant would sell a customer a sheet of coupons for a small sum, which the customer would then give out individually to acquaintances. On distribution of the whole sheet, the customer would receive cash or some "free" item, supposedly worth twenty-five times as much as the cost of the coupons. The merchant, for his part, would have roped in new customers, all of whom were potential coupon distributors themselves.[115] In theory, his business would grow exponentially, like a chain letter.

Advertising of the cooperative system had been banned by order of the ministries of the Interior and Finance in 1903, but the practice continued. In 1913 in cooperation with the above ministries, the Ministry of Justice and the Ministry of Trade and Industry decided to propose a law banning the system altogether. They found it to be unscrupulous in its perversion of the natural law of demand and exploitative in forcing the customers to do the merchants' "shameless advertising."[116] In addition, the very desire to receive twenty-five rubles' value for one was seen as immoral, "forcing the light-minded part of the population to attract as many other people as possible to buy the coupons and thus increase the number of unpaid agents advertising the firm, which receives profits quite out of line and, in its mercenary purpose, plays on such low elements of the human soul as reckless excitement (*azart*)." In fact, according to the Stavropol governor, some local peasants were so taken in by the promise of the cooperative system that they were selling their last property in order to buy up as many coupon sheets as possible! Despite the attention of four ministries, however, the cooperative system was still officially only "undesirable" rather than illegal when the outbreak of war in 1914 redirected governmental attention.[117]

In its attempted supervision of ethics in advertising, the Russian government proved both overreliant on a censorship system that no longer fit the realities of the modern press and popular tastes and unwilling to commit itself to broad legislation in response to evolving abuses on a national level. I would argue that this resistance is rooted in the long-term attitudes of tsarist power, that, since the days of Peter the Great, had paid lip service to the rule of law but remained wedded to autocratic sovereignty. Censorship represents a granting of permission from above, much as the regime granted trade and industry awards. Laws act independently of the ruler once established. Censorship is also potentially more flexible than legislation, allowing for changing standards based on personal interpretation of the guidelines. While this coincided with the whimsical character of personal rule, it also gave the state implicit leeway to be de facto more lenient than a de jure system might have allowed. Whether this leniency was intended or the result of stubbornness and incompetence remains an intriguing question.

CONCLUSION

The traditional self-image of the tsarist regime was one of benevolent control, granting favor to deserving subjects and using autocratic power for the good of the populace, including shielding them from corrupting influences. That this self-image persisted in the mind of the tsars right through the reign of Nicholas II is testament to its intractability in the face of contradictory realities. It also helps explain the anachronistic relationship between the tsarist regime and the business community, even as the Russian marketplace joined the Western world in welcoming consumer culture. In granting its seals of approval, the regime could stay true to its traditional role of bestowing awards on grateful subjects; this function continued unchallenged. However, in attempting, Canute-like, to control the incoming tide of advertising merely by repeating futile censorship orders, the government showed itself either unwilling or unable to adapt to market forces that flooded its institutional constraints.[118]

Merchants and manufacturers took double advantage of the government. On the one hand, they accepted and profited from tsarist honors when offered. The state seals and royal warrants that so soon would be ripped from shop doorways in revolutionary disgust retained powerful significance in advertising right up until the iconoclasm of 1917.[119] On the other hand, tradespeople and publishers ran more than a mile with the limited liberties conceded by the tsar in 1905. Yet merchants themselves pleaded for some legislation to stem unscrupulous practices in advertising in order to preserve fair competition and whatever public trust they enjoyed. To these pleas the government remained unresponsive.

The Russian case demonstrates that modern commerce could happily coexist with autocracy in some respects. Tsarist awards served the modernizing market, not despite their traditional form but precisely because of it. These symbols of traditional power accorded an aura of continuity and legitimacy to consumers unanchored by the pace of social and cultural change. Just as in Great Britain, monarchs did not mind some commodification of royalty, as it further popularized their public status. In contrast to awards, however, censorship did not serve the consumer market except through its complete failure to work.

That the content of advertisements provoked so much consternation among would-be censors illustrates the extent to which advertisers were testing cultural limits and promoting new individual and social possibilities as they reached out to potential customers. Part 2 turns to the advertising messages themselves and advertisers' attempts to create a consumer culture in the land of the tsars.

PART

II

THREE

CLASSROOM FOR CONSUMERS

Advertising Progress in the Urban Marketplace

Increasing urbanization makes the urban the primary level at
which individuals now experience, live out, and react to the totality of
social transformations and structures in the world around them.
—David Harvey, *Consciousness and the Urban Experience*

Advertising spoke a language of urbanity. To learn it, just as to
learn the language of another national culture, was to experience a
transformation—to acquire new perspectives, accept new assumptions, and undergo an initiation into new modes of thinking.
—Roland Marchand, *Advertising the American Dream*

Nowhere in Europe was urban life changing more rapidly than in Russia
at the turn of the twentieth century. Industrialization, belatedly begun but
forced ahead by the state at an intense pace during the 1890s, inevitably
increased social mobility. The Russian urban population almost tripled
from the 1850s to 1913; the growth was even more pronounced in the
two capitals, where the population size roughly quadrupled.[1] Largely due

to the influx of peasant laborers, early twentieth-century Moscow was, like New York, "a city of immigrants: almost three-fourths of the city's population had been born elsewhere."[2] St. Petersburg grew by an average of fifty thousand people a year between 1890 and 1914.[3] The result was a dramatically changing environment, not just for the newcomers availing themselves of urban opportunities in employment and consumption, but for all city residents.

The city served as consumer culture's classroom, presenting the latest commodities to an ever-broadening span of society. In that classroom the primer for Russia's emerging consumer culture was advertising, which used the multiple surfaces of the city as its media. Shop windows and signs, poster columns, walls, and trams were all pages in the text. The central medium, however, was the mass-circulation press, that phenomenon so emblematic of late tsarist Russia's blurring boundaries—between classes, "high" and "low" culture, public and private, liberal and conservative.[4] Mass-circulation newspapers represented the "democratizing of knowledge,"[5] and this applied to learning about consumer goods as well as events.

In contrast to advertising's text, its authors are not at first glance so easy to label as agents of change. It is common in the historiography of modern advertising to describe advertisers as proponents of progress— "apostles of modernity" in Roland Marchand's evocative phrase—but in the Russian context the conscious adoption of this role in the advertising of merchants and manufacturers had the added significance of suggesting a turnaround in their own public image.[6] Although expansion of trade and industry lay at the heart of the modernization process in urban Russia, the Russian merchantry is acknowledged by its historians as one of the most conservative segments of Russian society.[7] Thomas Owen points out that modernization theory, with its expectation that economic change will be accompanied by concurrent progress in political outlook, proved ill fitting for much of tsarist Russia.[8] Many merchants and manufacturers supported the conservative regime because they had long been dependent on state tutelage (*opeka*) to survive and thrive.[9] In the symbiosis between autocratic regime and industry, it is difficult to see the business community as a leading proponent of progress. To add to that incongruity, barring a few exceptions made for leading philanthropists, most Russians perceived merchants as resistant to change, selfish, petty, and corrupt.

Yet it fell upon the advertising merchants and manufacturers to promote trade and industry's visions of the progress and social benefit that modern commerce would bring. From their own need to expand markets and heighten demand for their goods, advertisers had to trumpet the individual and social necessity of their wares. To boost consumption they had to teach new needs to new customers. To keep up with the competition in growing consumer industries, ways had to be found to distinguish products, trigger shoppers' interest, and forge and maintain brand loyalty. As long as commerce was primarily associated in the public mind with the selfish motives of dishonest tradesmen, advertising would have limited impact.

And it was not just the perception of merchants themselves that had to be tackled in order to spread the messages of consumption. Traders and industrialists in Russia had to deal with the intellectual elite's "phobia of the commercial," an aversion that blamed commercialization for the degradation of "pure" culture.[10] This negative association was hardly unique to Russia, but the cause of the intelligentsia's disgust lay deeper than commercialization itself; it was rooted in an "ostracism of the everyday."[11] Russian radicals from the nineteenth century onward perceived a central opposition between *byt*, implying the "routine and stagnation" of daily existence, and *bytie* (spiritual being, not necessarily in a religious sense), which implied meaningful, "real" or "true" life.[12] Catriona Kelly points out that this opposition to the everyday did not apply across the elite political spectrum. Conservative Slavophiles valued the material and behavioral trappings of "appropriate *byt*" as a means of preserving the domestic traditions of Russian life, exemplified by the self-sufficient country estate or upright peasants and merchants.[13] Nevertheless, the Slavophiles, too, would disdain the brash commercialism of new brand-name goods.

One way or the other, consumer products belonged firmly to a much-berated sphere of *byt*, perceived either as a soulless entirety or in its modern (and therefore soul-corrupting) versions. Advertisers thus had to counteract hostility among the educated population to lauding the latest material comforts and at the same time turn around a widespread suspicion throughout society of their own motives and tactics in trade. In this sense the spread of consumer culture faced a strikingly different set of challenges in Russia than in Western countries. While advertisers in America and Great Britain certainly had to struggle to dissociate their goods from charges of "puffery" and the taint of patent medicine's wild claims, in the West entrepreneurship, industry, and trade were nevertheless inextricably linked with perceptions of the nation's progress. In America particularly the acquisition of material goods spelled success. In the eyes of the Russian intelligentsia, modern acquisitiveness spelled moral failure.

One way in which commercial rhetoric could soar above social prejudices against trade and materialism was by linking commodities to the greater good of individuals and society. Broadly speaking, advertisers developed two main ways to try to transcend the mundane perception of their business and spread the lessons of consumption. One, explored in chapter 5, was to associate their goods with quintessential aspects of Russian culture. To be a good Russian was to consume Russianness in all its commodified variations. The other major tactic, addressed in this chapter, was to jump on the bandwagon of progress and show the transformative potential of their goods to promote innovation, reward individual endeavor, and facilitate the civilizing influences of modern consumption—especially on the unkempt masses making the transition to urban life.

In linking consumption to civilization, advertisers could associate their agenda with the intelligentsia's mission to lift up the common people and thus promote an elevated cultural and social unity. The intelligentsia has been aptly defined as those Russians who were committed to "knowledge as a force for emancipating human beings from conditions and attitudes that were seen to deny their natural dignity and rights."[14] It was the self-proclaimed purview of this reform-minded amalgamation of educated individuals to usher in civilization to the common folk through the dissemination of high culture and progressive ideas, a process historian Stephen Frank calls cultural "colonization."[15] For the business community to suggest that their offerings of material goods would be part of the refining process of society thus demanded a radical shift in public perception of merchants and manufacturers. If consumption of commodities helped raise people up to modern standards of civilization, advertisers were implicitly aligning their commercial sphere with the civilizing mission of the cultural sphere. In so doing, they hoped not only to sell goods but also to project a corrective image of their own social worth.

Advertisers saw consumption as an integral component of modernity, but what exactly did that mean to them? This chapter examines specific examples of the multiple ways in which advertisers integrated their products into a modern agenda. The selected advertisements illustrate the claims that manufacturers commonly made for the civilizing, innovative, and problem-solving properties of their goods. These commodities were embedded in urban experience, promising lures, cures, and comforts for the conditions of city life, as well as an additional dash of magical excitement to spice up the potential satisfactions of material existence. They encouraged individual self-fulfillment, although within the constraints of the manufacturers' own class interests. The class-segmented audience for tobacco advertisements here provides a window into the ways in which that particular industry attempted to reconcile tensions between emerging class and consumer identities. Given the revolutionary era in which consumer culture developed in Russia, it is not surprising that manufacturers showed themselves to be more self-conscious and uncomfortable about encouraging material aspirations and consumerist ideals when advertising to members of the working class. Awareness of the working class was more apparent in early Russian advertising than in the usually standardized (and homogenously middle-class) advertising of the same period in the West.[16]

Even in Russia, however, class segmentation was generally less emphasized in advertising than the portrayal of a new kind of identification for the industrial age, one that would include all—the unifying community of consumers. By inviting everyone into a camaraderie based on shared appreciation of goods, consumer culture offered an alternative vision to that of a predominantly class-based society. And, just as consumption would unite the populace, it would tie Russia into the international community of consumers, allowing it to keep pace and compete in a modernizing global economy and culture. Altogether, through promises of belonging and individuation, comfort and adventure, innovation and civilization, consumer culture promised to usher the country into the modern age.

SOAP, CITY, AND SCIENCE— THE CIVILIZING PROMISE OF MODERNITY

As advertisers linked their messages to the civilizing mission of the intelligentsia, they joined the colonizing crusade to educate the rural population with the values of the city. These attitudes were not so dissimilar from those of European colonizers around the globe, given the cultural and social distance between the Russian peasantry and the educated urban classes. In his study of soap advertising in colonial Africa, Timothy Burke shows how Europeans saw their standards of hygiene as the "essence of civilization" in contrast to the perceived dirtiness of the natives.[17] From the perspectives of Russians, domestic colonizers were to their peasant neighbors as European colonizers were to African natives. Nineteenth- and early twentieth-century educated society in Russia looked on the manners and behavior of the lower classes as primitive and alien. The shock of activists, ethnographers, and health professionals at witnessing the ignorance of hygiene and the unrefined behavior among the urban and rural poor recurs throughout their writings.[18] Filth, the sharing of utensils, and superstitions that proved harmful to health were common sources of repugnance for the wealthier classes witnessing the lives of the poor.[19] By joining the movement to lift the common people out of their dirt and ignorance, manufacturers of hygiene products such as soap could sell their goods from the moral high ground of social benevolence.

That manufacturers liked to see their endeavors as socially worthy is evidenced by the elaborate publications some put out to celebrate their achievements. Pride in philanthropic as well as business purpose permeated the golden jubilee volume (1864–1914) of the Brocard toiletries company, for example.[20] The book lauded the altruistic spirit of the late founder, Henri Brocard, who was said to have been keenly interested in the "democratization of his goods," so that both hygienic and "elegant" (*iziashchnyi*) products could become accessible to even the poorer classes. With this goal in mind, he put out a brand called "People's Soap" (*Narodnoe mylo*), which sold for only one kopek a bar. Before this generous act, claimed the panegyric, soap had been virtually unknown in the villages, but thereafter the name of Brocard became "ubiquitous in the full sense of the word. Literally everyone began to wash themselves with "'People's soap.' . . . Thus, it is necessary to state as fact the undoubted influence of the cheaper production of hygienic toiletries on the tidiness and, consequently, on the health of the people."[21] Figure 3.1, which accompanied this text, shows

FIGURE 3.1 — "The appearance of soap among the people at the fair." Commemoration of Brocard's People's Soap. Source: *Zolotoi iubilei parfiumernago proizvodstva tovarishchestva Brokar i Ko. v Moskve, 1864–1914.* Moscow: 1915. *The golden jubilee of perfume production of the Brocard Company in Moscow, 1864–1914*

FIGURE 3.2—"Cleanliness is the enemy of microbes." Advertisement for soap from the firm of A.M. Zhukov. Source: *Russkoe slovo*, May 16, 1909.

peasant women smiling with delight as male vendors graciously offer them the sweet novelty of soap bars. The coyly flirtatious glance of the woman closest to the young salesman may reflect many peasant women's attraction to citified men, who were often seen as better marriage prospects. But the caption, "The appearance of soap among the people at the fair," adds greater significance to the encounter, suggesting the benevolent and almost mystical advent of something transformative and previously unattainable.[22]

Soap advertisers could just as profitably link their products with the benefits and concerns of science as with intangible powers. "Cleanliness is the enemy of microbes," declares the Zhukov company's slogan (fig. 3.2), in which microbial stick figures run in terror from the box of Zhukov soap.[23] This anthropomorphic image not only injects humor into the advertisement but also lends to its tone of didacticism. The selling point here is not sweetness, but fear of disease. In addition, for many in educated society, the mob-like microbes may also have suggested the "moral contagion" they associated with modernization's influences, particularly among the lower classes. The soap slogan thus projects a mission of educating as well as warding off the ignorant masses. With crowded, unsanitary housing conditions and regular cholera outbreaks in the major cities, this advertisement placed the Zhukov company in the ranks of those campaigning for public health through greater access to information and hygiene. It also echoed concerns about "social pathology and infection" that filled popular press stories on crime, as well as social scientists' worries over the spread of moral degeneracy in late imperial Russia.[24]

The Zhukov advertisement demonstrates the confluence of commerce and tsarist authority in its odd juxtaposition of symbols on the soap package. On one side of the box sits the trademark large beetle, which may at first glance seem to undermine the product's stated goal of cleanliness, but instead illustrates the company name (*zhuk* means "beetle"). On the adjacent side of the box, depicted in the same size as the insect, is the state seal, awarded to the Zhukov company at the 1896 industrial exhibition. The beetle's splayed-out pose mirrors that of the double-headed eagle in an almost comical symmetry, although mockery was certainly not the intent. Rather, this packaging illustrates the manufacturer's proud elevation of industrial production through tsarist endorsement; the humble beetle was found deserving by the imperial eagle. In terms of the civic mission of this advertisement overall, such an imprimatur could only add weight to the message that soap was a mighty foe of disease. And in the post-1905 era, if the microbes might also have the appearance of an unruly mob, the combined authority of tsar and soap appear also as an effective bulwark against chaos and disorder.

Individual commodities directly tied to hygiene could play an obvious part in the civilizing process, but the very fact that a product was manufactured in an urban factory enabled advertisers to tap into still-pervasive hopes that the city in itself might exert a progressive influence on backward, peasant immigrants. The lure of the city has a long, if ambivalent, history, especially in the modern era. In *Consciousness and the Urban Experience*, David Harvey eloquently summarizes the city as "the high point of human achievement, objectifying the most sophisticated knowledge in a physical landscape of extraordinary complexity, power, and splendor."[25] But it was also "the site of squalid human failure . . . full of agitations and ferments, of multiple liberties, opportunities, and alienations."[26] Russian villagers making the transition to the city, like their counterparts throughout the industrializing world, experienced the excitement as well as the bewilderment of the city's intensity. Semen Kanatchikov, in his personal memoirs of the transition from peasant to urban worker, remembered his first impression of the city's teeming trade:

What struck me most was the abundance of stores and shops: for every house, there was one store after another. "Who buys all these goods?" I asked my father. "Why, there are more stores here than there are people!" "Mother Moscow, she feeds all of Russia . . .," Father responded.[27]

On subsequently seeing the crowded apartment building in which he was to live as an apprentice, Kanatchikov's delight turned to "some kind of inexplicable terror before the grandiose appearance and cold indifference of my surroundings."[28] In historian Mark Steinberg's nuanced study of Russian working-class writers like Kanatchikov, the city forms a recurring motif as a symbol of progress and empowerment but also a cause of suffering, constriction, and cold disregard.[29]

The rhetoric of advertising naturally focused more on the positive aspects of urban modernity than the harsh realities of damp cellar rooms and squalor. But it did address the darker sides of city life—disease, alcoholism, stress, overwork, and overcrowding, for example—insofar as it sold products that claimed to assuage such ills. From advertisers' perspectives, the association of their goods with the fruits of the city constituted a plus, no matter whether those fruits were bitter or sweet. If the focus was on the opportunities of urban existence, then commodities could offer the promise of self-improvement through improved taste, innovation, and satisfaction. If the emphasis was on the travails of city life, then goods offered remedies for everything from typhus to suicidal tendencies.

The city represented the transformative present as well as the bright future, and in this light it was enough to place a given product in the urban context to suggest its quality and benefits. For example, a 1907 advertisement for Belousov tobacco tubes (*gil'zy*: empty cylinders made for filling with loose tobacco) depicts a peasant couple looking at a distant urban horizon. The man points his female companion's attention to large letters spelling out "XXth CENTURY" across the sky above the cityscape. The city and the new century beckon; no further text is necessary to make the association between city, progress, and product.[30]

The city was the arbiter of taste, as well as the nexus of progress. Another 1907 advertisement for a different cigarette tube factory, Viktorson, describes a newcomer from the provinces asking a policeman why the name Viktorson was so "glorified" in Moscow. After expounding the qualities of the tubes, the policeman concludes: "This isn't the countryside here, you know—it's the capital. They're good judges of everything, why not taste too?" The provincial, who accepts the superior status of city dwellers as a matter of course, promises to spread the news about Viktorson in the village when he returns.[31] These advertisements presented their products as part of a better, more informed world whose influence was reaching down from the enlightened heights of its urban centers to the less privileged rural population. Advertisers were not merely expressing their own prejudices in this attitude; they were taking advantage of the existing desire for city styles and commodities in the villages, especially among the young. Jeffrey Burds, in his study of peasant integration into the labor market, cites late nineteenth-century observations of workers who returned to their villages after years in the city expecting—and receiving—acceptance of their superior status among peers merely due to their urban polish.[32]

The city offered more than good taste and vague promises of a better future; it was also the locus of technological progress in pragmatic and exciting advances such as the development of electricity, the telegraph, and flight. As soap could control disease, electricity could dispel darkness (metaphorically and literally) with a power that appeared magical to the uneducated. Advertisements for Philips light bulbs depicted the practicality of electricity as demonstrated to overawed peasants and dumbstruck workers. One example shows an elderly peasant couple staring with delighted awe at a shining bulb as the ad copy touts the invention's economy and simplicity.[33] Figure 3.3, part of the same campaign, depicts a bespectacled professor pointing with one hand to a glowing bulb and with the other to the words "Philips light bulb—economical and simple" on a blackboard. In front of him sits a row of burly, open-mouthed men, a most uncomplimentary portrayal of workers seemingly struggling to get the new concept of electrical power through their Neanderthal-like skulls.[34]

Electricity, harnessed by modern man's genius, could now be explained and imparted in the form of the light bulb to the common folk for the improvement of their lives. In one simple image the modern benefits of education, technology, and commodities converge. The assumption evident in such advertisements, that the benefits of enlightenment were to be generously imparted by the educated to the ignorant, shows that the advertisers' attitudes were in keeping with the growing number of those among the cultural colonizers who wanted to improve the common lot. These advertisements also reflect the broader modern assumption that technology alone would improve humanity. As Georg Simmel observed of turn-of-the-century Germany, technical advances were heralded "as though the electric light raised man a stage nearer perfection, despite the fact that the objects more clearly seen by it are just as trivial, ugly, or unimportant as when looked at by the aid of petroleum."[35] That new commodities would elevate life to the significant and beautiful was one of the notions essential to the entrenchment of consumer culture.

FIGURE 3.3—"Philips light bulbs, economical and simple." Source: *Russkoe slovo*, October 2, 1911.

Steeped in the Enlightenment belief that man could conquer the elements, promoters of industrial products portrayed human ingenuity's ability to rival and even improve upon nature, as in another advertisement for light bulbs put out by the Russian distributors of Westinghouse products. The only rival of the Vertex light bulb, claims this ad, is the sun. In the accompanying image, a single, oversized bulb illuminates one side of the earth, as the sun weakly peers out from the other. The sun, reduced to a comical face smaller than the earth, is actually a poor rival to the planet-sized light bulb in this advertisement's version of the modern industrial universe.[36]

Products such as light bulbs were clearly offshoots of technological progress, but there did not have to be a direct link between product and technology for manufacturers to suggest one in their advertising. The Koeler company, for instance, illustrated its advertisement for eau de cologne with a dirigible floating above Moscow, accompanied by the slogan, "Higher than all eau de colognes in quality."[37] The Shaposhnikov tobacco company claimed that its brands were the cigarettes of choice for the intrepid aviators who became public heroes with their aerial daring during the 1910s and whose exploits were covered widely in the mass-circulation press.[38] "An aviator must know which kind of cigarette to take, sweeping up into the heights, remember only, Eva!!"[39] With no other connections than visual and textual juxtaposition or unsubstantiated endorsement, such ads attached their products to the coattails of the popular fascination with technological innovation.

In some cases, a commodity actually metamorphosed into an unrelated modern invention. A 1910 cigarette advertisement shows a "telegram from the Dukat factory in Moscow," carried along telegraph poles made of giant cigarettes, bringing the message, "Try new Bis cigarettes."[40] With the sense of importance and urgency that was associated with the telegram as a form of communication, the product is both message and messenger, announcing to the Moscow public its own momentous arrival by telegraph. Modernization itself became a commodity through which to bring news of other commodities.

There was, in fact, nothing noteworthy at all about the advent of yet another cigarette brand in that already crowded market—all the more reason, then, to suggest the opposite. The more inundated the consumer was with choices of goods, the more creative the advertisers had to become. As the population of the major cities expanded by the tens of thousands every year, increased demand for goods intensified competition among the consumer industries. Product diversification was one way of fighting for a slice of the market. New brand names, packaging, and sales pitches for essentially identical products (especially in industries such as tobacco and cosmetics) were attempts to woo consumers away from rival firms and keep customers loyal through apparent variety.[41] The naming of things is a means of creating attachment to them, as media scholar Jib Fowles points out. Names suggest intimacy, almost as if commodities were members of the household, like a pet.[42]

At the same time as brand names create familiarity, consumer culture demands constant reinvention and dynamic marketing. Thus, the ongoing introduction of new brands situated manufacturers as agents of change. Brand naming implicitly connected goods with notions of modernity, whose "aesthetics of transitoriness" and values of "change and novelty" have been noted by contemporary critics and subsequent scholars alike.[43] Consumer culture's emphasis on the "ever-new," to borrow Walter Benjamin's phrase, mirrored the scientific emphasis on technological innovation and allowed advertisers to bask in the progressive glow of modernity. In the unrelenting pace of change that characterized the late imperial Russian city, advertising rendered novelty a virtue. One of the most common slogans, "the very latest!!!" (*posledniaia novost'!!!*), made newness a selling point in and of itself. New meant better. Even when the innovation rested only in the invention of a new cigarette package, it was announced with the bold lettering and blaze of exclamation marks of a groundbreaking discovery. That no real change had occurred supports Benjamin's point that the "ever-new" was really a cover for the "ever-same" drumbeat of salesmanship that drew consumers into the endless promise of meaning beyond function in their constantly acquired goods.[44]

While the link between new brand names and progress was tenuous at best, manufacturers of consumer goods did play a substantive part in the nation's industrial progress as their production processes grew increasingly mechanized. In the industrial age factories were synonymous with the idea of progress. Manufacturers rarely shared the Romantics' horror at rural scenery disfigured by factory chimneys and smoke. On the contrary, industrialists both in Russia and the West proudly displayed smokestacks and industrial landscapes as dominant motifs in their advertising.[45] In her study of this phenomenon in American advertising, Pamela Walker Laird has found that the incorporation of the manufacturer's factory in his advertising was more about his pride of ownership and competition with other industrialists than a reflection of popular taste (in fact, she states, it was more likely an insult to public taste).[46] The factory was one of "the new instruments of power," and its depiction signified the owner's status and success.[47] Thus, smokestacks were not hidden but rather exalted as proof of progressiveness. Large manufacturers implied, or even stated explicitly, that a bigger factory meant a better product. The industrial skyline was a symbol of the modern, to be surveyed as one might admire a work of art.

Indeed, advertisers of this era, in Russia as well as the West, interlaced industrial and artistic motifs, placing them on an equal footing. Factory smoke became curling, art nouveau–style border designs for advertisements, or classically dressed young women framed factory scenes. The Moscow cosmetics firm S.I. Chepelevetskii and Sons decorated its company letterhead with a panorama of its extensive factory—chimneys, smoke plumes, and all—yet bordered the design with a beautiful woman picking roses (fig. 3.4).[48] Factory scenes like this were thus romanticized, conflated with symbols of the very purity the critics felt was being destroyed by industrialization. For a perfume company the accompaniment of roses was natural enough, but the point is that the inclusion of the factory was also seen as positive advertising and seemingly not contradictory. Smokestacks gushed sweet progress, not pollution.

Industrial production signified purity because it was seen as an advance on the dirty workshops and cottages of handcrafted goods. The Markov wine processing plant sold its "purified" wine with labels featuring its smoking factory (classically framed with decorative drapes[49]), and many manufacturers touted increased mechanization as a selling point for clean, desirable goods. Mechanization allowed manufacturers to keep pace with demand by producing more goods more quickly. Yet, in terms of advertising impact, such technical advances went beyond their functional benefits. Quality was purported to improve automatically as machine labor in production grew and human participation decreased. Central to this belief

FIGURE 3.4—Letterhead of the S.I. Chepelevetskii and Sons Perfume Factory in Moscow, 1916.

Source: Central State Historical Archive of the City of Moscow.

was both the pride in technological progress and the concern over hygiene. The educated population's perception of the working class and peasantry as the unwashed, uncivilized masses combined to associate mechanization with notions of cleanliness and quality.

The Russian tobacco industry proudly advertised the rapid automation it underwent in the late nineteenth and early twentieth centuries. In 1897, for instance, the Moscow company La Ferme promoted a new brand of cigarettes as one of the "wonders of technology . . . produced from beginning to end on *machines*, without the touch of *human hands*."[50] Similarly, the St. Petersburg company, Kolobov and Bobrov, advertised its Brio brand as "mechanical cigarettes," picturing a lone woman pulling the lever of a machine much larger than herself.[51] The starkest example of valuing machine over human production is Katyk's advertisement for tobacco tubes (fig. 3.5).[52]

The prominent slogan "WITHOUT HANDS" is literally depicted by a peasant woman with amputated arms, while the text emphasizes that "the marvelous tubes of Katyk are manufactured without the touch of hands; only with machines. That is why Katyk's tubes are the most hygienic. REMEMBER THIS." The (unsurprisingly) stone-faced and unkempt woman could no longer taint the product. This image taps into the misogynistic vein in Russian popular culture and also attempts to alter the perception of the manufacture of tobacco tubes, which had been the third largest women's domestic industry until mechanization of the process began in the late 1890s.[53] Katyk was thus graphically challenging the still-recent association of its goods with rural, and presum-

FIGURE 3.5—"Without hands." Advertisement for Katyk cigarette tubes. Source: *Russkoe slovo*, July 25, 1907.

ably unhygienic, domestic production. Though this grotesque image was probably an attempt at humor (which this company's advertising often employed), its message of machines besting human labor is clearly intended to be taken seriously.

There may also be another, unspoken subtext at play in the case of this advertisement. Russian Orthodox culture carries many tales of religious icons "not created by hands" (*nerukotvornaia*), inspired by a sixth-century legend that Christ himself created the first icon by miraculous means.[54] Strangely then, in order to suggest its product's superiority to a specifically Russian audience, the Katyk ad may well have been drawing on a widespread religious resonance, in addition to bruiting the very secular benefits of machine production. The advertisement's slogan "WITHOUT HANDS" (*bez ruk*) does not employ quite the same term as that used for an icon, thereby allowing the advertiser to avoid the offense of blasphemy while still including a tongue-in-cheek suggestion of his product's immaculate manufacture.

Paradoxically, the very people who would be undercut by increasingly mechanized techniques of production were among the consumers targeted by these advertisements touting machine labor. Industrial society's civilizing mission not only sought to uplift and cleanse the lowly peasant-workers, it also sought to control and minimize their importance in the workplace, keeping mass-produced goods free of the backward taint of those who made them. In the world of production, modernization was a double-edged sword, bringing both opportunity and constraint.

The world of consumption, in contrast, opened its arms to all. Consumer culture offered, in Stuart and Elizabeth Ewen's phrase, "the democracy of surfaces"—the appearance of equal access to desirable goods through cheap mass production of formerly luxury commodities.[55] The real luxuries remained, available only to the wealthy and advertised with images of exclusivity, but advertising's overarching message was that everyone could enjoy the privilege of consuming. The universality of consumer culture's appeal is a large part of what makes it modern from the second half of the nineteenth century. Manufacturers had to include the lower classes in their conception of the marketplace if they were to succeed in disseminating the modern, universal consumer ethic. This was especially relevant in selling inexpensive goods like cigarettes, affordable to workers, most of whom (among males) saw tobacco as a necessity, rather than a discretionary expense.

Unlike the more prolonged development of industry in the West, however, Russia's working class and its consumer culture were emerging at the same time at the end of the nineteenth century. This led to contrary impulses for manufacturers, who were concerned to mold workers and consumers simultaneously; how could they reconcile their desire to restrict the worker and free the consumer when they were one and the same person? Consumer culture's preferred version of the modern city was a "City of Mirrors," whose "glittering showcases . . . reflected the image of people as consumers rather than producers."[56] In the case of tobacco advertising, however, the reflections of consumer and worker often blurred into a double vision that proved difficult to resolve.

WHEN WORKER AND CONSUMER CONVERGE— TOBACCO ADVERTISING ADDRESSES CLASS

Tobacco consumption in Russia has been imbued with conflicting cultural meanings since its introduction in the seventeenth century. Banned for seventy years (far longer than in other countries), it was seen as a threatening foreign influence, potentially fomenting moral and social disorder.[57] Peter the Great overturned the ban in 1697, using tobacco in his bawdy court revelries (including as a parody of church incense in mock religious ceremonies)—and in the process strengthened the association in Russians' minds between tobacco and secularizing influences.

The popularity of various tobacco products changed over time, but they were mainly the preserve of the upper classes until the second half of the nineteenth century. Snuff, popular in the eighteenth century, came to be seen as "a quaint habit of older women" by the nineteenth.[58] Pipes gradually gave way to cigarettes (*papirosy*), while cigars remained a luxury product for the elite. Significantly, smoking was a predominantly urban practice in all its forms until the late nineteenth century. Only in the postemancipation decades did the habit spread among peasants. Konstantine Klioutchkine, in his analysis of tobacco's cultural meanings in nineteenth-century Russian literature, finds that smoking stood for liberation from social conventions, a manifestation of individual independence and progressive views. To smoke was to be modern.

With the growing accessibility and popularity of cheap packaged cigarettes in the second half of the century, smoking also came to be seen as "one of the more democratic habits" available to all urban males.[59] Tobacco's popularity rose during the period of the Crimean War (1853–1856), a conflict that precipitated Russia's path to modernizing reforms under Alexander II. Klioutchkine notes that this confluence of liberating politics and new habits of consumption further entrenched the linkage of tobacco and freedom in people's minds.[60] By the late nineteenth century, the humble cigarette carried weighty cultural resonance across all social classes.

Advertising cigarettes, therefore, was potentially rich symbolic terrain. As the industry increasingly mechanized production, tobacco manufacturers were doubly active in advancing the modern agenda, both technologically in the means of production and culturally in the promotion of a commodity that implicitly signified modernity. In light of this context and the growing demand for its products (annual output increased from 6 to 10.4 billion cigarettes between 1897 and 1908), tobacco advertising offers the best case study through which to examine how manufacturers perceived their audience in terms of class, precisely because the industry marketed multiple versions of essentially similar goods across the social spectrum.[61] Success demanded the targeting of brands to particular audiences. Products were often differently aimed at lower- and upper-class customers (as well as to men and women, a topic discussed in chapter 4). Although all classes bought cigarettes by the end of the nineteenth century, the brands came in varying quality and price. More expensive brands generally ranged from six to twelve kopeks for a packet of ten, whereas the cheaper brands sold for half that price or less, at five or six kopeks for a packet of twenty. Most cigarette brands of all factories fell within these two price ranges during the decade before World War I, making differentiation of target audience easier to discern. Even if some better-off smokers economized and bought cheap tobacco, the intended audience of consumers for the lower-end cigarettes was the lower classes, as the content of the advertisements quite often made clear.

As the market for their products stretched across the socioeconomic spectrum, the tobacco manufacturers found themselves in the rather uncomfortable position of expanding appeals to a working-class clientele made up of people who might simultaneously be their customers and employees. While they clearly wanted working-class customers, the tensions evident in many advertisements for cheaper brands of tobacco show how the manufacturers sought to encourage consumption while still controlling consumerist aspirations among the working class. Unfettered consumption without moral constraint was, after all, one of the main sources of complaint from educated society about the "degeneration" of the Russian peasantry experiencing the temptations of urban life.[62]

The tobacco manufacturers' appeals to working-class custom tended to fall into three main categories. The first echoed Russian liberals' attempts to draw in working-class political support by promoting universal, rather than class values, evoking the spirit of *nadklassnost'* (literally "above-class-ness" or "classlessness"). In this approach class distinctions disappeared, from the liberals' perspective in the world of politics and from the manufacturers' perspective in the world of cigarette sales. The second tactic, referred to here as "the vicarious elite," exemplified the modern consumer ethic, in which consumption of the right goods purportedly elevated the status of the consumer. According to this approach, the correct choice of cigarette rendered the smoker one of the elite. The third category represented a combination of the traditional paternalism of the factory owner and the assumptions of the educated reformers about the need to guard lower-class morals. In this paternalist/reformist mode, cigarettes would render the smoker an ideal worker, a boon to bosses and society alike, as well as a blessing to himself. Ironically, the ideal worker in this category was always portrayed as male, even though women made up the majority of the workforce in the tobacco industry. This is partly because the primary target for tobacco advertising was male, but it also reflects the normative assumption that proletarians were men.

Classlessness and the Brotherhood of Smokers

Russian liberals' notion of classlessness derived from their belief that a primary identification with class would undermine their emphasis on universal individual rights. Therefore, they preferred to avoid the word "class" when writing about workers' issues, seeking to transcend such distinctions in the spirit of classlessness.[63] In a sense the interests of industrialists (whatever their personal politics) demanded a commercial version of the liberals' agenda: universal individual rights of consumption. Perhaps it is not surprising, then, that some of their advertising echoed the liberal appeal to classlessness.

The possibilities of transcending class boundaries through consumption of a single type of cigarette were touted in a 1913 advertisement for a Bogdanov company brand, Smirna (the name of a city in Turkey).[64] To smoke Smirna was to become a member of the "brotherhood" of smokers, depicted by a line of identical smokers in fez hats. The image suggests the unity of a fraternity, a brotherhood, as the advertisement states, of "old and young, orthodox and non, rich and poor, knowledgeable and ignorant, family men and bachelors"—differences that would fade in the pleasure of smoking this cigarette. The play on words in the slogan, "Smirno (peacefully, or tranquilly) Smirna appeared!!" suggests that the tranquility of this good smoke would erase unimportant distinctions based on education and income level, age, family status, even religion. The emphasis on brotherhood would have a special resonance for workers recently transplanted from their villages. In his study of the transition undergone by peasant-workers in St. Petersburg, S.A. Smith notes that, in the absence of native family networks, brotherhood loyalty replaced the filial bonds that predominated in the villages.[65] Most of these workers lived and worked with fellows from their own home regions, forming a bond to mitigate the anonymity of the city and provide mutual support (as well as rivalry between regional groups). The term *zemliachestvo* refers to this community based on migrant workers' shared geographic roots (*zemlia* means "land"). In consumer culture, however, advertising took notions of displaced bonding several steps further, transcending both geography and class.

The scope of the brotherhood of smokers was carried one step further in a 1910 Bogdanov advertisement for Kapriz (Caprice) cigarettes (fig. 3.6).[66] With its humorous caricatures of right- and left-wing, upper- and lower-class types, this image portrays a leveling of politics as well as class. The promotion of non-partisanship (*nadpartiinost'*) as well as classlessness was another tactic of the liberal reformers. Adopted here for the purposes of consumption, political and socioeconomic differences fall away in these men's insistence on smoking only Kapriz.

The comic nature of such depictions demonstrates a conscious distancing from the advertisements' claims, suggesting that the advertisers knew, and knew that their audience knew, how imaginary the smoking fraternity remained. It was a transparent, if resonant, fiction but one that

FIGURE 3.6—"Right, left, upper, lower, smoke only our Kapriz. 20 for 6 kopeks." Advertisement for A.N. Bogdanov Tobacco Company. Source: *Gazeta-kopeika*, September 18, 1910.

in this case would include everyone in the shared humor. In contrasting the projection of classlessness for the cheaper brands with the images in advertisements for more expensive cigarettes, however, we might wonder if the advertisers' laughter did not contain a hint of nervousness. That the cross-class brotherhood of smokers was more palliative or joke than fact for the poorer consumers was underlined by the frequent association of more expensive brands with a quintessentially bourgeois lifestyle. A 1910 advertisement for the Shaposhnikov factory's expensive Krem cigarettes, for instance, depicts a portly, self-satisfied gentleman in a fine suit and monocle deriving "nothing but pleasure" from his tobacco, as well as his luxurious—and solitary—surroundings.[67] In the world of consumer culture, the notion of transcending class was most relevant for those who had more material cause to wish for it. For all the democratizing significance in the pleasure of tobacco, the reality was as transient as a whiff of smoke.

The Vicarious Elite

In the second category of tobacco's sales pitches for the cheaper brands of cigarettes, manufacturers sought to defuse working-class identity, not by erasing differences but by lifting the workers up out of their lowly poverty to a vicarious association with the elite. Most often this was done simply through selection of brand names. A number of cheap brands were given grand labels such as Roskosh (luxury) or Zolotyia (golden). The implication was that smoking these cigarettes would bring the sensa-

FIGURE 3.7—"Zolotyia cigarettes. 20 for 5 kopeks. The tobacco factory of A.N. Bogdanov Company, St. Petersburg." Source: Russian State Library poster collection.

tion of luxury or gold; no doubt some who did smoke them recognized with bitter irony that inhaling this richly named, cheap tobacco would be the closest they could hope to come to experiencing luxury and wealth. The unattainability of the reality behind the names was clearer still in the case of Tsarskiia (tsar-like) cigarettes, for who, even among the elite, could hope to live a tsar's existence? The further the reality, the more harmless the dream.[68]

Even beyond allusions to royalty, some manufacturers invoked an element of spiritual salvation in advertising their cheaper brands. The following is a verse for the Dukat Company's Tsarskiia cigarettes:

In life's difficult moments,
When I burn with anguish,
I smoke Dukat's Tsarskiia,
It's as if a burden rolls off my soul,
And grief is far away,
And things become cheerful,
And so, so easy.[69]

Words were not even necessary to convey the message in the poster advertising Bogdanov's Golden brand (fig. 3.7).[70] The packet of cigarettes, surrounded by shining light, is greeted by a peasant and a worker as if they are witnessing a revelation from the heavens or hailing the advent of a spiritual savior. The placement of the cigarettes on this poster would have been immediately significant to any Russian, as the icon corner of every peasant hut was found high in the corner to the left of the front door. In this advertisement Bogdanov's cigarettes are transfigured into a religious icon, and the worker and peasant are its worshippers. This is taking consumption to transformative heights, indeed.

Both of these first two advertising approaches that were common in tobacco advertising—the nicotine-induced approximations of material and spiritual salvation and the classless community of smokers—represent adaptations to the Russian context of more widespread methods of appealing to consumers since the advent of modern advertising in the late nineteenth century. The basic messages of belonging and of transformation of status through consumption are still overwhelmingly with us today, even if the historical particulars are very different. In these two categories the manufacturers were adapting to the modern marketplace by approaching their poorer customers as consumers, despite the persistent differentiation of class. The same cannot be said of the third category of advertising appeals, which was rooted in far more patronizing attitudes.

The Paternalist/Reformist Agenda

Didactic portrayals of ideal workers constituted the largest of the three categories that tobacco advertisers used to target working-class consumers. This suggests that the paternalist approach most closely reflected the manufacturers' own attitudes; it was certainly the tactic least likely to resonate with workers themselves, except perhaps those few members of the worker intelligentsia who were attempting to educate themselves and shared the upper-class disdain for perceived lower-class backwardness.[71] The messages in this group represent heavy-handed social, as well as commercial, propaganda. A 1913 Shapshal advertisement, for instance, featured this little verse (a typical example):

He who is resigned to his fate
He who is clever, dexterous in labor,
He who is not a mischief-maker,
That person always smokes our Kumir!!![72]

Kumir (idol) cigarettes created the ideal worker, although in this example, hardly an idol of the heroic variety. That such an overtly patronizing sales pitch could be printed in *Gazeta-kopeika* (*Penny Gazette*), a working-class newspaper, is testament to the persistence of paternalistic views among Russian industrialists on the eve of revolution. Apart from its folk ditty (*chastushka*) format, it is difficult to see this as an advertisement intended to attract working-class consumers. Indeed, its content is in direct opposition to the often bawdy subjects of popularly created chastushki.[73] The purpose seems rather to assuage the manufacturers' anxieties through attempting to control their own workers.

That the lower-end customers targeted by the manufacturers sometimes were their own workers was made explicit in a 1910 series of advertisements for the Shaposhnikov and La Ferme factories. Both of these companies used verse in their advertising, usually signed by "Uncle Kornei" for La Ferme or "Uncle Mikhei" for Shaposhnikov. This personalizing device may have been the brainchild of one man: Sergei Apollonovich Korotkii, a self-styled crusader for tobacco who wrote countless advertisements in newspapers and pamphlets and was certainly the writer behind Uncle Mikhei. A nobleman and decorated veteran of the Russo-Turkish War of 1877–878, Korotkii initially rented out his literary skills to the La Ferme Company, but began working for Shaposhnikov around 1905. He was thus the avuncular voice behind Shaposhnikov's 1910 attempt to advertise to its own workers.

One advertisement in this campaign purported to reproduce correspondence from the "hall porters, doormen and watchmen of the Shaposhnikov factory to Uncle Mikhei, expressing their appreciation for the company's Mashinka brand of cigarettes."[74] These workers supposedly wrote the following verse:

In our monotonous lives,
We are all drawn to fashionable Mashinka,
You pay a five-kopek piece for twenty,
And you enjoy yourself like anything!!
They aren't cigarettes—they are delight,
Merci, Mikhei! Regards! Compliments!![75]

A second advertisement carried Uncle Mikhei's gracious reply to the grateful workers, but the ruse of this "correspondence" was ludicrously exposed by a mix-up in printing dates: Uncle Mikhei's reply appeared the day before the initial "letter." The proletarian guise was thinly drawn to begin with, not least by putting French words into the mouths of porters and watchmen.

In good paternalist style the expectation of gratitude from workers for their bosses was a common thread throughout many of the advertisements in this third category. Another was the manufacturers' concern about working-class morality, especially in the areas of alcohol consumption and sexuality. In this regard the paternalist tactic joined with the reforming mission of the educated elite, whose perception of innocence among the common folk steadily gave way to anxiety over the corruptive influence of the masses during the postemancipation era. Anxiety turned to alarm after the peasant disturbances triggered by the 1905 revolution.[76] One of the main targets of reform was peasant drunkenness, and tobacco manufacturers could conveniently capitalize on the fact that their goods produced their desired effect without intoxication. They could side with the temperance movement by preaching the virtues of cigarettes over liquor for both health and happiness. The Dukat company, for example, depicted its happily sober workers in a poem entitled "Labor and Rest":

> The whistle has blown and the factory folk
> Are already going to rest after working all day . . .
> One hurries home, one drops into the tavern,
> Yes, and there'll be friends there to drink tea with,
> They remember the village, acquaintances, family,
> And dream of time off towards Ivan's Day.
> Fellow countrymen discuss sowing and mowing . . .
> "Young lad! Give us Tsarskiia cigarettes!!" . . .
> In the smoke of the cigarettes from the firm of Dukat,
> The hours while away—everyone is glad of the rest.
> Look: time is flying, it's already time to go home,
> Each having taken his Tsarskiia with him for tomorrow.
> In the morning the whistle calls everyone early,
> The factory worker goes to work once again,
> He begins to smoke, cheerful and glad,
> Invigorated by Tsarskiia, from the firm of Dukat.[77]

Here is the perfect worker, happy to snatch a few hours' rest with friends, drinking tea not vodka, rejuvenated by a cheap cigarette, and cheerfully reporting to work on time. He subsumes himself willingly, if wistfully, to the routines of modern factory life and is content with his lot. Simple lives require only simple pleasures. Such a worker would naturally never go on strike or make revolutionary demands on the owners. Such a worker was no threat—and such a worker probably did not exist. Compare Dukat's picture of contentment in the factory to actual workers' songs of the time, and the contrast is clear. From the late nineteenth century, so-called "factory songs" of the workers bemoaned their hard existence, as for example in "from morn to night we toil working in the factory, really like in hell (*chisto kak v adu*)."[78]

In the paternalist projection, however, not only were cigarette-smoking workers happy at work and with friends, they also kept their marriages intact, thanks to the correct choice of tobacco. An advertising verse for the Ottoman company was purportedly written by a worker who claimed his wife loved him better now that he smoked the firm's Berezka (birch tree) brand, a "wonderful creation," due to which he had stopped gambling and drinking and had received a raise.[79] Another advertisement for the same brand, with a verse explicitly entitled "A Proletarian Ditty" (*proletarskaia pesenka*), equates the pleasure derived from wife and cigarette:

> I married very young,
> Took a beautiful wife,
> And—from Ottoman's—I smoke
> Berezka, and that alone.
> Both are tasty, both are sweet—
> Both Berezka and my wife—
> And they give me strength
> To clamber upwards from my day.[80]

The sexual implications of this verse are quite explicit, yet within the legitimate bounds of marriage. In those advertisements that fall into the paternalist/reformist category, there are few hints of extramarital sexuality. Occasionally, other advertisements for the cheaper brands might appeal to lower-class consumers through out-of-reach sexual fantasies of orientalist goddesses, but when it came to suggestions of real life, the pleasures of the working class were to be kept strictly inside the realms of moral probity.

Such strictures did not apply further up the social scale. On the contrary, when sex was used to sell the more expensive brands of cigarettes, it was nearly always extramarital. Shaposhnikov's Uncle Mikhei cast an upper-class smoker, the "bon vivant Serge," directly in the "demimonde" of prostitution.[81] Serge is depicted equally enjoying his expensive cigarette and his elegant female companion. Similarly, a portly, monocled gentleman in a caricatured advertisement for Rua, one of Shapshal's higher-priced brands, seems to practically drool over his cigarette at the much younger beauty under his wing (fig. 3.8).[82]

If Foucault is right in asserting that sexuality as a social discourse was originally the creation of the bourgeoisie, then the fact that the working class was outside the bourgeois purview also adds an element of territoriality to the separation of moral categories evident in Russian tobacco advertising.[83] The manufacturers were part of a bourgeoisie that was still very much seeking its own definition in the last few years of the imperial regime, and this insecurity only fuelled the need to draw social parameters. Nevertheless, the moral division was a futile one, not only because it ignored social realities (such as the fact that prostitution existed among all classes), but also because cigarettes of both price ranges were advertised in the same newspapers. Tobacco manufacturers could hardly have supposed that working-class readers would not notice the allusions to illicit sexuality and bourgeois lifestyles in the other advertisements. Perhaps the fatuity of the attempted propaganda only emphasized the advertisers' own view of the workers as unsophisticated children, unschooled in the ways

FIGURE 3.8—"Rua cigarettes. 10 for 6 kopeks." Advertisement for the Shapshal Brothers Company. Source: *Gazeta-kopeika*, June 8, 1913.

of the world, potentially dangerous yet still susceptible to the influence of straightforward moral tutelage. Yet this conclusion does not credit the manufacturers with much sophistication either.

The likelihood that the tobacco manufacturers actually believed that their moralizing messages would work is slim, but their persistence in them ultimately says more about their own difficulty in moving beyond the stereotypical relations of paternalism than about their understanding of the workers. Stereotypes only remain as long as they trigger knee-jerk reactions. The manufacturers found it difficult to pry loose their own protective reflexes to be able to treat workers as fellow consumers in the modern marketplace. The obstacle surely lay as much in their failure to transcend their own self-perceptions as in their fear of workers' rebelliousness. As James von Geldern has pointed out, history has to allow the influence of absence of identity, as well as its presence.[84] The industrialists' fallback to the paternalist attitude reflects the lack of a full-fledged, modern identity to fit the changing society in which they now found themselves. The dilemma of the tobacco advertisers was not simply one of how to sell their products to a particular group of customers but of how best to reconcile their own conflicting positions as both old-style factory bosses and modern promoters of commerce. In addition, they had to reconcile their customers' dual identities as workers in need of control and as independent-minded, modern consumers. By attaching themselves to the moral crusade active in educated society, manufacturers could combine their paternalism with the reformist agenda, thus satisfying their traditionalist instincts in the guise of forward-thinking social regeneration.

TEACHING CONSUMPTION IN THE COMMUNITY OF CONSUMERS

Although tobacco manufacturers' attempts to mold working-class smokers into ideal consumers (and workers) were among the most heavy-handed tactics found in late imperial advertising, it was not uncommon for advertisers to act as tutors in consumption across the social spectrum. Advertising's task was, after all, to disseminate a new primary self-identification for all—that of consumer. Among a population in which social mobility was still a new idea for the vast majority, the promise of fulfilled aspirations on an individual and a community level was both radical and comforting in its implications. In the context of tsarist Russia, it was still radical to suggest that individuals did not have to accept their appointed lot but could make their own choices and forge their own paths. Advertising's promise of self-actualization through consumption implicitly encouraged consumers to reach for more. This resonated with an increasing emphasis on selfhood in late imperial Russia, in popular culture as well as among the intelligentsia and beyond.[85] Steinberg notes that the assumption of collectivity in Russian culture is an oversimplification even for the eighteenth century, but the late nineteenth century witnessed the development of "a wider civic discourse . . . in which we see heightened awareness of the personal self, obsessive introspection, and a growing sense of the moral and social implications of acknowledging the self."[86] Thus, the assertion of individual needs and aspirations in commercial advertising echoed broader undercurrents in Russia's changing social thought, even while these developments threatened the mindset of the traditional regime, with its reliance on the people's collective identities and responsibilities.

In contrast to its radical implications, advertising's promise of comfort manifested itself in two major ways: the couching of commodities as known anchors of material and cultural life in unsettling times and the offer of membership in the community of consumption. Both approaches suggested security and assured support, whether in the form of tangible goods or imagined camaraderie.

Advertising, then, had to speak simultaneously to individuals, separate social classes, and across the social spectrum. Its appeals to individuals were helped by the shift from traditional forms of consumption, in which goods were passed down from one generation to the next, to modern consumer culture in which the push is toward endless consumption of new goods for each individual.[87] (In this process advertisers played both benefactor and beneficiary, multiplying the very goods that would elicit new needs and increase their own profits.) Urbanization also facilitated the natural increase in individual demand. Fowles points out that urbanization promotes heightened individuation due to its dismantling or loosening of traditional community ties. For market purposes this increases consumption, as migrants to the city must replace the basic goods for which they would have formerly relied on their village household or community.[88]

While increased demand from individuals benefited trade and manufacturing, advertisers needed their appeals to speak to many, not just a disparate few. Consumers must be made to feel good about their individual choices, while being part of a larger consuming community of similarly wise, tasteful, and discerning persons. Like the imagined bonds of citizenship in Benedict Anderson's analysis of national community—imagined because members would never personally see all their compatriots[89]—advertising's lens projected the bonds of consumption as a bridge across the anonymity of strangers in the social mélange of city life.

Well before twentieth-century critics argued over whether consumer culture imposes conformity or expands choice, advertisers seem to have intuited that the promise of both might hold appeal for citizens experiencing the opposing responses—of hope and fear—to modern life. For peasant-workers in particular, conforming to an implied consensus of taste in commodities could provide a foundation and sense of security for those in the awkward transition from a still largely collective village society to individual choice fettered only by the limitations of discretionary income. At the same time, suggesting that consumption meant personal independence might assure the very same people, as well as others further up the social scale, that they were their own agents. As Walter Benjamin noted for Europe as a whole, with the rise of consumer culture by the late nineteenth century, freedom was equated with the ability to consume.[90]

To be an effective consumer demanded not only knowledge of what to buy and where, but also how to use the expanding choice of goods. The tone of many advertisements was scarcely distinguishable from the widely available how-to manuals that promised to teach late imperial Russians everything from cooking and etiquette to physical fitness. For instance, an advertisement for a household goods store in Red Square's trading rows urges a young housewife to come "straight to Zamiatin's. She may be a little inexperienced, but Zamiatin's will gladly help her with practical advice."[91] Not only would the store help with her housewifely skills, it would also provide transportation. When a new tramline opened in 1910 that stopped at Zamiatin's "very door," the owners offered to "give a hand" to customers by paying for their return fares if they purchased something in the store.[92]

Assistance in learning how to take care of the home may have been a real need for some women. Catriona Kelly cites sources showing that, until the twentieth century, most upper-class Russian wives left not just housework but also house management entirely to the servants, and many never entered their own kitchens. From around the 1910s, however, it began to seem shameful to neglect one's household. Advice literature and advertising alike offered to facilitate this shift in duties by educating housewives directly in the new expectations of running a home.[93]

As more goods became available, all classes needed training in consumption. Advertisers occasionally took on a tone of exasperation, as if the public was being unreasonably obdurate in not learning its lessons on commodities: "It is high time" (*davno pora*), exclaimed the Ermans food company, "for every housewife to know that the best seasonings for all dishes and preserves are only the Delikatess products of K. Ermans and Co."[94] Being a good consumer was thus something to be learned, a skill without which one could not take care of a family or even be a full member of society.

A knowledgeable consumer would know that the simple addition of a purchased item could open up new horizons for the entire family. Sellers of musical instruments and equipment particularly emphasized this notion. Not only could the gramophone "avoid boring evenings,"[95] but the auto-piano could bring instant talent into any family. "Each member of the family can immediately (not knowing music) play artistically on the FONOLA-PIANO."[96] The American auto-piano sold by the M.K. Grubesh store depicted the piano in a luxurious American domestic interior (helpfully labeled "America"), played by a wealthy woman with a mountainous vista beyond the veranda.[97] To bring the auto-piano into your home, it suggested, was to experience a vicarious whiff of the larger world, not to mention an instantaneous skill typically associated with the attainments of bourgeois leisure time.

The didactic tone of many advertisements deliberately suggested that those who bought their products were on some kind of inside track of useful information. Just as advertisers insinuate today, the "in" group knows what to buy; those on the outside were made to seem behind the times or even neglectful of their families' interests. "You really hadn't heard?" accused an advertisement for bicycles that were supposedly "ahead of the rest."[98] Clearly, those who had not heard were hopelessly out of touch. Such knowledge was assumed in a Shustov advertisement that began, "You know, of course, that rowanberry liqueur is the favorite drink of the Russian public."[99] Unspoken in this statement was the insinuation that anyone who did not know (or did not agree) was simply ignorant of an obvious and commonly accepted fact.

In advertising's classroom, knowledgeable consumption was tantamount to social responsibility. Advertising's ideal citizen was, naturally, a modern, consuming member of society—one who knew where to turn to fulfill his or her constant need for replenishment and satisfaction. This perfect consumer is portrayed at length in an advertising poem for Shustov cognac (here translated only in part). It is, significantly, entitled "The Modern Way" ("*Po sovremennomu*"):[100]

> Ivan Ivanych Milovzorov
> Lives the modern way.
> And without superfluous discussions
> He follows after progress.
> All the modern novelties
> For Milovzorov are law . . .
> Whatever has appeared on the market—
> He acquires in an instant.

In his apartment the furniture is in the "new style,"
For guests he always has a wide welcome,
There are no horses: Ivan Ivanych
Sees the use of the automobile.
Persistently following aviation
He is building a bold plan:
So that he can soar swiftly up to the heights,
He is getting an airplane!
* * * *

He know no melancholy,
He says that sadness is nonsense,
And to all wines prefers
Shustov's fine cognac!

Being modern here means buying the latest and the best; the goods define the life. Ivan Ivanych is happy because he wholeheartedly accepts the idea that material comfort, progress, and cutting-edge acquisitions are the point of existence. For him, consumption is a philosophy as well as a pleasure. This is consumerism before the term was invented.[101] To stress the point, Ivan's grumpy opposite appeared a month later in another advertising poem, "The Backward Man." This gloomy obscurantist rejected electricity, cars, and medicine, did not believe people could fly, and, of course, did not drink Shustov's cognac.[102]

Though the character Milovzorov exemplifies an exceptionally self-motivated consumer, he likes to share, or show off, his acquisitive prowess among friends. Depicting consumption as a shared activity suited purveyors of alcohol particularly well. As already seen, tobacco advertisements played on the phenomenon of *zemliachestvo* (fellowship based on shared roots) for lower-class customers. But the liquor industry appropriated this concept for a mixed clientele, especially in the case of Zemlianskoe beer, which co-opts the very term itself in the brand name (fig. 3.9).[103]

Even though zemliachestvo applied mostly to working-class urban immigrants, this advertisement depicts a rather well-to-do crowd of seemingly middle- and upper-class men and women. It is a motley gathering, intentional in its diversity. As the slogan "We all drink Zemlianskoe beer" demonstrates, enjoyment of a common product was enough to bring unlikely people together in a kind of consumerist camaraderie. Their choice of beer is reason enough for their happy commingling. In a similar advertisement for the Shustov liquor company, rows of people impatiently shout out their orders for cognacs, port wines, and liqueurs to go with their Easter pancakes. Under the slogan "Everyone demands [the various

FIGURE 3.9—"We all drink Zemlianskoe beer." Source: *Russkoe slovo*, September 17, 1909.

Shustov brands] for pancakes!!" this advertisement unites consumers less in carefree consumption than in united purpose and adamant demand.[104] In both cases people are portrayed as consumers first and foremost, brought together not by class or region, but by their common need and appreciation for a product.

Demonstrating mass demand, in addition to demand across social boundaries, was a key aspect of projecting the community of consumption. Mass production requires mass consumption, as has often been noted, but conversely, portraying mass consumption is a means of promoting mass production. Both parts of the process serve the other. Touting quantity of goods sold also boosted the image of advertising's modernizing agenda by suggesting the ever-improving mechanization of production. Firms wanted more customers not just to be able to sell more goods, but because quantity could be advertised as quality.

In 1899 the La Ferme tobacco factory was already boasting about the number of cigarettes sold in a day with the slogan: "By quantity judge quality."[105] The company continued this tactic into the 1910s. In what might seem an ironic foreshadowing of McDonald's presence in Moscow after the fall of communism, a La Ferme campaign of the 1910s depicts a man holding up a sign that reads, "More than 500,000,000 sold in 1911!"[106] Other tobacco companies entered the advertising race for declared sales increases. The Shaposhnikov firm proclaimed, "Not by the day—but by the hour! The demand for Eva cigarettes grows."[107] And the Shapshal tobacco firm depicted the stampede-like demand for its Kumir cigarettes with a mob made up of mixed social classes rushing the gates of the factory, while the watchman shouts, "Go away! Back!!! You're too late!!! All the

Kumir for today have been sold!!! Ten million!!! There are no more!!!" (fig. 3.10).[108] If deprivation of this brand-name product was cause for a riot, the suggestion was that consumption of it was as necessary as bread and as universal as breathing air. To be human was to be a consumer.

In advertising's vision consumption did more than bring people into a community of consumers in the same city, it also unified the nation as a whole. An advertisement for the Einem company depicts this graphically as its cocoa forms a river flowing from its Moscow-based cup down through Ukraine and "throughout all Russia" (fig. 3.11).[109] Similarly, the cosmetics factory Brocard symbolized the 2.5 million boxes of Swan's Down powder produced in 1914 as a road of packages snaking from one city to another. Claiming empire-wide popularity, the company states that its brand "has sales in all the cities of the Russian Empire, beginning from both capitals down to the smallest population points in our wide native land."[110] Through universal consumption, the empire is made one.

FIGURE 3.10—"The tobacco company of the Shapshal Brothers. The issue of the new cigarettes, Kumir. 20 for 6 kopeks." Watchman: "Go away! Back!! You're too late!!! All the Kumir for today have been sold!!!" Source: *Russkoe slovo*, November 5, 1911.

FIGURE 3.11—"Einem's Cocoa throughout all Russia." Source: *Russkoe slovo*, February 15, 1912.

The projected diffusion of advertising's consumerist new world stretched not only from city to village but also beyond the boundaries of Russia. In this process Russia was both recipient and distributor, villager and urbanite. The transfer of goods throughout the global market by the early twentieth century effectively integrated Russia into the web of international commerce, a fact that forced manufacturers to compete with Western rivals. Foreign businesses advertising in Russia stressed the country's incorporation into the world market as an opportunity for Russians to enjoy quality consumer products equally with the West. In figure 3.12, the fingers of the giant hand indicate some of the countries where Cupid (Amur) records and gramophones were made, linking Russia with Germany, France, England, and America—all reigned over by a gramophone player as mighty as the rising sun. "We know," reads the text, "what the public of the whole world wants in the field of gramophones."[111] Russians thus belonged to this global community of gramophone owners—they could feel they were part of the international consumerist vanguard.

Russian manufacturers responded to the international market in various ways. The centuries-old dilemma of Russia's identity vis-à-vis the West found its contradictory expressions also in advertising. Some companies appropriated and imitated Western styles as the ideal, while others proclaimed Russian goods as superior to any in the West. In the field of fashion, it had long been and remained acceptable openly to admire and adopt Western trends; in other industries accustomed to the standards of domestic production, Russian manufacturers tackled the international competition with bravado, claiming their goods were superior and beloved the world over.

The tobacco industry was most brazen in its assurances of premium quality worldwide. In a verse entitled "Truth," the Dukat company boasts:

FIGURE 3.12—"The Gramophone Company. The fingers of this hand indicate several countries where we make our records and Amur Gramophones." Source: *Russkoe slovo*, November 21, 1912.

Go around the world,
Inquiring everywhere,
But nowhere will you find
A sweeter cigarette than Ira.
And now everyone loves it
For its magical aroma
And everywhere they only smoke
Ira from the factory of Dukat.[112]

Few firms, however, were loath to appropriate the aura of Western sophistication in naming some of their brands. The untranslated names "Adorable," "Select" (Chepelevetskii perfumes), and "Sir" (Kolobov and Bobrov cigarettes, purporting to "answer to modern taste"[113]) imparted a touch of cosmopolitan refinement that, it was hoped, would appeal to a distinguished clientele.

Foreign and Russian companies alike seized upon Western fads that reached Russia and incorporated them into their marketing so as to present products in the light of the very latest fashions. At the end of 1913, newspaper pages were full of the newly popular tango, and several manufacturers jumped on the bandwagon, from record companies to perfume and champagne firms. "The latest word in fashion" (*krik mody*), proclaimed the Khristoforov company, was to "meet the New Year with Tango champagne."[114] And the Rallet company announced its new line of perfume in time for Christmas with the following lines:

The fashionable dance–
the fashionable scent
"Tango"
intoxicating
exciting.[115]

Through such enthusiastic assimilation of international trends, businesses promoted the vision of Russia as a country in step with cosmopolitan fashions and included in the evolving consumer culture of the West.

International integration did not mean losing step with Russia's own cultural rhythm, however. Those same manufacturers of Tango champagne and perfumes would as enthusiastically advertise new product lines for Orthodox Easter, saints' days, celebrations of Pushkin's birth, or the tercentenary of the Romanov dynasty, as seen in chapter 5. Cumulatively, such juxtapositions promoted advertising that surpassed the purely imitative. The blending of tradition and innovation,

Western and Russian, spoke to a population that constantly bridged similar divides. Simply through their responses to everyday life, advertisers and consumers alike were forging a peculiarly Russian version of consumer culture.

THE MYTHIC MUNDANE — COMMODITIES' MAGICAL TRANSFORMATIONS

In order to speak with any authenticity to the Russian population, advertisers had to acknowledge that the experience of modernity was not all tango dancing and champagne. As we have seen, the imagined community of consumption promised a sense of belonging in the potential alienation of the industrial-age city, but it also proffered solutions to sickness, depression, and nervous malaise. Urban progress entailed noise, overcrowding, anxiety, and frustration, as evidenced by the alarming spread of nervous illnesses in late imperial Russia. In the burgeoning medical marketplace that emerged in response to this crisis, doctors offered advice literature and treatments, while manufacturers offered products for every problem.[116] Consumers could splash on a dab of eau de cologne to refresh themselves in the "heavy, stifling atmosphere of the big city with its vast, nerve-shattering street traffic."[117] If they were troubled instead by a vaguer sense of unease, then patent medicines and electrotherapy could come to the rescue: "Just as the past hundred years have been called the age of discoveries and inventions, the twentieth century could justifiably be named the nervous century," began a typical advertisement for a patent medicine.[118] So when modern life sapped human psychic and physical strength, modern science and industry could restore them, if not through the ubiquitous cure-alls, then with ingenious inventions such as the Rejuvenator electrical belt, touted as the "savior of mankind" for a "nervous and sickly age."[119]

More mundanely, the correct choice of cigarette might be enough to rescue a consumer from ill health, as suggested by the visual imagery in figure 3.13.[120] The Dukat company advertisement contrasts the healthily plump, self-satisfied man on the left to his sunken, sickly-looking counterpart. Dressed almost identically, the difference, it appears, lies in the former man's wisdom as a consumer. He asks his colleague what he smokes, to which the answer is, "Whatever comes along." "That's no good. I smoke only Novost' (Novelty) from the Dukat factory, and I can't praise them enough. I advise you to do the same. You'll thank me for it." Clearly, the reader was to believe that the sallow man would also become jolly and healthy if he followed

FIGURE 3.13—"What kind of cigarettes do you smoke?" Advertisement for the Dukat Company's Novost' brand. 10 for 4 kopeks, 25 for 10 kopeks. Source: *Russkoe slovo*, January 17, 1910.

his friend's advice. And similarly, the reader himself could expect to enjoy robust health if he chose the recommended cigarettes. As the brand name implied, progress and health went hand in hand with newness.

Whatever a person's problem—health, family relations, or personal crisis—there was a product for his or her salvation. A 1909 advertisement for the Katyk company captured this tongue-in-cheek fashion (fig. 3.14).[121] A man with a gun to his head cries, "It's not worth living! There's nothing perfect in the world!" "Fool!" answers the advertisement, "Stop and remember that there *are* Katyk's cigarette tubes." Despite the rather off-color attempt at humor (not the Katyk company's first—this was the same firm that depicted the female worker with amputated arms discussed earlier), this advertisement was nonetheless tapping into a real dilemma of modern life, as Russian suicide rates were rising dramatically, especially after 1905.[122] The mass-circulation press commonly reported ten or twenty a day in the decade before World War I, accompanied by "lurid and sensational exposés, woodblock prints, scholarly analyses, updates on the latest figures, regular columns, readers' letters, and even satirical humor."[123] The dark humor of the Katyk advertisement was therefore not without context. It was also addressing the issue in a peculiarly Russian way, poking fun at the existential crises of the intelligentsia in their search for utopian perfection. The suggestion that utopia could be found instead in a cardboard tube shows that this advertiser was also mocking his own hyperbole.

Hyperbolic claims were not the only way that advertisers aggrandized their products, often humorously. If the purpose of an advertisement is to grab the public's attention, then showing larger-than-life commodities

FIGURE 3.14—"It's not worth living!" Advertisement for Katyk's cigarette tubes. Source: *Russkoe slovo*, November 25, 1909.

FIGURE 3.15—"Give the road to Zonofon!" Advertisement for gramophone records. Source: *Gazeta-kopeika*, January 25, 1909.

literally stopping traffic might do the trick. Thus, as a story-tall can of tooth powder is rolled down the street in an advertisement for the Maevskii firm, people peer from balconies and gape in the street, and a mother pulls her child to safety out of its path.[124] As noted in chapter 1, merchants throughout the nineteenth century had hung oversized models of their merchandise over doorways to draw customers' attention to their shops, but in the print illustrations of modern advertising, the purpose of giant scale went further—to make the ordinary extraordinary, to lift consumption out of the daily routine and prove the centrality of goods in contemporary life. In figure 3.15, Red Square is cleared by police escort for the arrival of a new, ten-foot-tall gramophone record.[125] "Give the road to Zonofon!" cry the police, as the crowds part like the Red Sea in front of this independently mobile creation. Here, the commodity dwarfs the consumers, who can only stand back in awe as it passes. The product has taken on a life of its own. Functionally useless at this size, this is commodity fetishism writ large. The record manifests the allure of modern material culture, its very advent promising to transform daily life from the mundane to the magnificent. The gramophone record here is as much a monument to the times as the newly restored architectural edifice of Red Square's trading rows in the background.[126]

In advertising's projected world of consumer culture, goods heralded and embodied modernity. They also offered solutions to modern life's problems. For those adrift in the anonymous and uprooted modern city, commodities would furnish life's anchor, fulfillment, and purpose. Where reality failed, the promise of consumption bridged the abyss of anxiety and uncertainty. The sum of advertising's messages amounted to far more than its parts; in its totality consumption was promoted as tantamount to a material faith for the excited, yet often bewildered, neophytes of the modern age.

In this material "religion" it is interesting to note how rarely the actual realities of current events entered into the picture. Beyond major holidays and national anniversaries, always commemorated with special novelties, advertisers were loath to complicate their material utopia with developments of a political nature. Before 1914 war and politics only occasionally appeared in Russian advertising. The tobacco companies made the bravery of the Russian soldiers a theme in some of the advertisements during the Russo-Japanese War of 1904–1905, and the Brocard company advertised a line of products especially "for those setting off for the Far East."[127] But when it came to the Revolution of 1905, the advertisers acted as if the social upheavals and strikes had not occurred. From the perspective of business interruptions, most tradespeople and manufacturers may have preferred it if they had not, even though many supported limited political reform. One interesting exception to this silence was a January 1906 advertisement for A. Strit's Moscow cigar store, which celebrated "THE RESTORATION OF ORDER AND QUIET."[128] After the blaring, capitalized headline, the copy itself decrescendos with ever-smaller print, and the accompanying illustration depicts an employee whispering confidentially into the ear of a monocled, top-hatted gentleman about where to buy the best foreign cigars. That luxury goods might be advertised in hushed tones perhaps reflects the very recent nature of the struggle for civil rights across classes. The magazine supplement to the same paper in which this ad was printed was still full of pictures from the December uprising in which Moscow workers were massacred; thus, the consumer desires of the elite seemed, even to this cigar seller, better whispered than trumpeted.

Manufacturers incorporated some references to postrevolutionary politics into their advertising because many were more in sympathy with the new parliamentary system than they had been with mass revolt. By 1905 even the most reactionary of the commercial and industrial leaders were beginning to see autocracy as an obstacle to economic prosperity and to side instead with the constitutionalists.[129] Around the time of the elections to the Second Duma in 1907, the Shapshal tobacco company brought out a brand of cigarettes called Duma (Parliament), with an accompanying illustration of a naked man struggling with a large snake (fig. 3.16).[130] The depiction is reminiscent of a Greek statue, perhaps that of Hercules, who battled serpentine foes more than once in his life. In many other contemporary advertisements the snake represented venereal disease or alcoholism. Satanic tempter or mythological assassin, the evils the snake symbolized could be overcome through a restoration of masculine strength and vigor.

Here, perhaps the snake stood for all society's ills, with the muscular Hercules representing the people's deputies in their struggle for social well-being and justice. In any case, given the Second Duma's rapid dissolution, the manufacturers not surprisingly discontinued this brand shortly thereafter. Five years later, after the parliament had proved ineffective as

FIGURE 3.16—"Duma cigarettes. 20 for 6 kopeks. The Shapshal Brothers Company." Source: *Russkoe slovo*, February 23, 1907.

an independent body, the same company advertised its long-established Kumir (idol) brand with a verse dedicated to the Duma, but rather more cynical in outlook:

> *"D'umny sovet"*[131]
> Be you "left" or be you "right,"
> "Trudovik" or "Kadet,"
> I give you all, not cunning,
> But honest advice.
> Throw down your squabbles, forsake your arguments,
> Talk only of business,
> And having finished your conversations,
> Smoke Kumir to your heart's content!!!

The zemstvo activists, widely respected for their dedication to social welfare and political progress since the Great Reform after which they were named, fared somewhat better than the Duma deputies under the advertisers' pens, but even here the message was ambiguous at best.[132] In 1907 the Shaposhnikov company put out a brand of cigarettes called Zemskiia, "in honor of all zemstvo activists."[133] Yet the border design of this advertisement might be interpreted as undermining a primary faith in human powers: it features drawings of charms and their appropriate "cabbalistic" meanings. Underneath in small print is written, "Cut this out as a memento. If it doesn't come in handy for you, then give it to someone else." The zemstvo activists were all well and good, but it did not hurt to offer them a little help from lucky charms.

Despite such sporadic intrusions of political events, the contemporaneity of advertising's world rested in currently available commodities, not reportage. Linked as it deliberately was to images of modernity and pressing issues of urban life, Russian consumer culture's reality was nevertheless more one of promise than realized experience. To adopt Michael Schudson's fitting phrase, advertising represented "capitalist realism," an unwitting precursor to socialist realism in that both portrayed a vision of progress through an imaginary prism of what would or should be, given the fulfillment of the respective dream.[134] And yet advertising constituted far more than a chimera. It was the voice of a consumer culture that was one of the real driving forces behind Russia's urbanization. By the very fact that advertising promoted the desirability of modern, city life with its promised fruits, it helped reshape the social landscape and expectations of tsarist Russia's last generation well beyond the urban population. As Burds states:

It was not just the signs and the stores . . . but the whole urban experience—even just secondhand accounts from neighbors and family members who had experienced the city directly—that stimulated the senses of country folk, luring them in a host of different ways to buy, to consume, to spend money in pursuit of the better life.[135]

The lessons of consumption suffused Russian society throughout the last decades of the imperial era, and in that sense, Russians were indeed becoming modern.

CONCLUSION

Advertisers encouraged an agenda of modern living that lauded mechanized production and new consumer goods, urged refinement of the common people through such things as improved hygiene and urban tastes, and portrayed a world in which modern commodities solved all modern problems. They vaunted all of this on a daily basis, in the process remaking their own image from petty cheats to civilizing colonizers and proponents of both modernization and modernity, the material and experiential boons of progress. But while advertisers could control what they put into their messages, they could not control the effects of those messages on the subjective reality of consumers. The desired effect overall was to offer satisfaction through whatever goods consumers could afford and to create ongoing demand for more. Consumption certainly rose, but we may never know the extent to which the rhetoric and promises of advertising also contributed to popular frustrations over the socioeconomic status quo. If, in advertising's vision, the pleasure of a cheap cigarette could make an individual worker rich and "tsar-like" for a moment, then the language of consumer culture introduced the concept of class transcendence, or even class irrelevance. This was a potential trajectory that would suit neither imperial industrialists nor the revolutionary opposition. The unease of tobacco advertisers with their own paternalistic campaigns to peasant-workers was rooted in a vague sense that modern consumer culture implicitly encouraged a subjective self-definition, something not easily contained within a fixed and supposedly objective class structure. What if people believed in the consuming dream too much? Promoting the illusion of a community of consumers sought to mitigate this risk by evoking a mirage of equally shared pleasures. Uncertainty about consumer culture's social implications was one reason for advertisers' often didactic tone; as teachers who offered guidance and had the best interests of their students at heart in the classroom of consumption, they could hope to set their own parameters on the lessons learned.

Advertising across the socioeconomic spectrum posed challenges, but class was only one of the shifting social and cultural characteristics that advertisers needed to keep in mind while addressing their customers. Gender categories appeared more solid to them, but here also they had to tread with care as the implications of consumer culture brought into question traditional perceptions of male and female identities.

FOUR

BEAUTY AND BRAVADO

Gender Identity on the Advertising Page

Can anything for men's use be found in nine-tenths of these shops?
All the luxuries of life are demanded and consumed by women.
—From "The Kreuzer Sonata" by Leo Tolstoy[1]

Tolstoy's protagonist in "The Kreuzer Sonata" presents us with an extreme view of female acquisitiveness, but it was hardly a radical opinion in the spectrum of commonly accepted notions about women and consumption during the late nineteenth and early twentieth centuries, either in Russia or the West. However, this chapter challenges the general assumption, both of the time and in much subsequent scholarship, that advertising and consumer culture during this period were overwhelmingly directed at women.[2] Consumption proved an alluring force for both men and women in Russia, despite the flawed perception that it tempted women far more.[3] When we shift the study of gender in consumer culture from the more usual focus on fashion, department stores, and magazines in Western societies to look instead through the lens of the mass-circulation press at the particularities of late imperial Russia, then men join women center stage in consumption, mitigating the prevalent perception that this was a heavily feminized arena.

It might be noted that newspaper readership was more male than female, and thus the daily press presents a source base that could slant conclusions about the gendered targeting of advertising in the opposite direction from those derived from fashion journals. However, the specific context of late imperial Russian society offers more than newspaper advertising as evidence to support the argument that, in contrast to the West, men were initially the target of consumer culture as much as, if not even more than, women. Once consumer culture expanded to include the lower classes, men were in the forefront, desiring modern goods. Most of the migrant laborers who more than doubled the size of Russia's major cities at the turn of the century were men. It was a disproportionately male population (sixty-two percent in 1900 St. Petersburg) that urban advertisers needed to address. While this gender imbalance lessened over time as more women migrated from the villages for work, by 1910 there were still 110 men for each 100 women in the nation's capital.[4] Male workers became the primary vectors of city fashions and tastes to the countryside, inspiring rural women and men with dreams of urban commodities on their periodic visits back home to the village.

Given the predominance of male urban consumers, the study of Russian advertising contributes to emerging scholarship on masculinity in the late imperial era.[5] On a daily basis newspaper advertisements reinforced (in often intimate detail) what it meant to be a man. In this period when men were entering the supposedly feminine domain of consumption and women's traditional roles were being challenged by activists and the forces of modernization, advertisers found themselves walking a cultural tightrope through gender issues. They downplayed the potentially destabilizing influence of consumer culture on traditional gender roles by emphasizing stereotypes of masculinity and femininity. Yet they also brought to the surface fears and anxieties about gender identity for both sexes as they offered products to preserve and sustain manhood and womanhood. And most fundamentally, Russian advertisers implicitly contradicted the strongly held notion that consumers were necessarily female by targeting men as well as women.

The historiography of consumer culture traces the association between consumption and women to industrialization's removal of paid work from the home. In this perceived split, production now required wage labor, which was (however problematically) primarily linked with male workers in workshops or factories. Therefore, production was seen as male. Work in the home was unpaid and was consequently seen as domestic, unproductive, and female. But the home (as well as nonproductive leisure activity outside it) remained the locus of consumption. Deprived of their status as productive partners in the household economy, women's main activity was now seen as consuming the products of male labor. However, this shift in attitudes about female labor is more applicable to western Europe than to Russia, where peasant culture had always regarded women's work, even in the fields, as unproductive.[6] Nevertheless, with growing urbanization and the rise of wage labor after the emancipation of the serfs, by the late nineteenth century the identification of men as producers and women as consumers spread in Russia as it had in the West. These perceived roles played into preexisting gender assumptions: modern production is rational, efficient, and thus male; consumption is irrational, subject to whim or passion, and thus female.[7]

The association of women with consumption strengthened and spread beyond the home as new retailing practices emerged in late nineteenth-century Russia. In part this was because women were more likely to take their time and browse in the modern, western-style *magaziny* (shops with window displays and fixed prices) and spacious department stores. Traditional Russian shops (*lavki*), in contrast, created a more masculine than feminine atmosphere, with aggressive sales tactics and the expectation of bargaining. Once inside these small, dark shops, mere browsing was not acceptable or even possible, since most goods would be kept behind the counter. Having stepped across the threshold, the customer must be pressured to buy, and some women expressed distaste for such intimidation.[8] While many women confidently held their own in the bargaining contests, it was men who were more likely to express pride in their bartering skills and to actively enjoy the challenge of winning a bargain. The lavki coexisted with modern stores throughout the imperial era, and men continued to engage in the contests of traditional commerce well into the era of modern retailing. For many women, however, such shopping was not an experience to be savored, unlike the atmosphere of department stores, with their elaborate interiors and comforts such as seating and rest areas.[9] Not only did the encouragement of browsing stimulate women's desire for fashionable goods, but the new arenas of consumption also rendered female consumers more publicly visible than they had formerly been. The shoppers were, in a sense, part of the display, their presence and attire implicit affirmation of the merchandise's feminine appeal. Yet department stores remained a tiny proportion of shops overall, both in Russia and the West before World War I. Their glamour and novelty has tended to exaggerate their place in the experience of shopping during this time.[10]

The perception that women were the primary consumers is rooted in more than the new locations and styles of trade. Being fashionable was decidedly more complex and expensive for upper-class women than for men, entailing as it did several changes of clothing a day, as well as diverse accessories such as gloves, ribbons, and hats.[11] The finery and ostentation of women's fashions contrasted sharply with the sterner lines and colors of men's appearance, as Russia followed the late Victorian male repudiation of the eighteenth century's sartorial flamboyance.[12] While men's clothing might still be expensive, the elaborate nature of women's fashion in contrast to men's naturally heightened the association of female consumption with useless frivolity. The fact that women's domestic and personal ornamentation served both sexes (as Thorstein Veblen pointed out in 1898) by providing the expected markers of class distinction and respectability could be conveniently ignored by contemporary critics of female consumption.[13] Instead, the cultural and social emphasis on female fashion, combined with its greater variety, promoted the perception that women were the primary consumers in modern society.

That much female consumption was ultimately for men goes beyond Veblen's point about presentation of family status. Women's varied adornments were seen as essential in luring men; such goods were a means for women to market themselves as commodities for male consumption, both as single women in search of husbands and as married women seeking to keep them. Men expected that women would and should dress to heighten their appeal to the opposite sex. Women's purchases served purposes beyond their own satisfaction and were re-commodified in the competitive process of sexual attraction in which men were the ultimate consumers. This observation is, of course, part of the standard feminist critique of consumer culture's objectification of women, which has come under fire in recent years as revisionist scholars point out that many women find their own pleasure and individual empowerment in fashion and self-beautification.[14] Such was no doubt the case in late imperial Russia also, but the fact remains that, in the rhetoric of the advertisements themselves, women beautified themselves for the sake of men. This is true even in those ads purportedly written by women, as in the examples for breast enhancement discussed later in the chapter.

The perception that upper-class women generally spent more time and money on personal adornment than their menfolk, even if true, is not basis enough to define consumption as primarily female. Cost is not the most important identifier of active involvement in consumer culture. If it were, then only the rich would be worthy of study. Modern consumer culture is in part defined by the fact that it encourages universal participation in dreaming about and purchasing commodities. Taking the anthropological perspective, goods have social and personal meaning often irrespective of price.[15] The meaning attached to a humble item such as a certain brand of cigarette can be as strong an indicator of a person's psychological investment in consumer culture as that attached to a Parisian ball gown. As Douglas and Isherwood note, goods that cater to physical needs such as food (and cigarettes) are "no less carriers of meaning than ballet or poetry."[16]

The commonness of the objects of much male acquisition rendered their purchases less visible symbols of the new consumer culture, associated as it was with frivolity and irrationality. For instance, a fashionable woman's hat embodied notions of feminine consumer culture, while tobacco was simply accepted as a given requirement for male comfort and hardly a whimsical phenomenon. Yet, choosing a cigarette brand was as much a matter of consumer taste as coveting the latest style in hats. Nonetheless, the hat exemplified capricious consumption while the cigarette did not. A shot of liquor was as unrelated to production as a spray of perfume, but the drink did nothing to undermine a man's perceived role as producer, despite the fact that it might reduce his rational faculties, while the harmless scent relegated a woman to frivolous consumer. In the popular mind female fashions fit definitions of irrationally acquisitive consumer culture more readily than did liquor and cigarettes. This is despite the fact that by the late nineteenth century tobacco products were increasingly subject to brand-name marketing and manufactured as items of mass production, making them in effect more typical of consumer goods than the hand-sewn hat. When consumption is seen as the opposite of production and is simultaneously associated both with nonessential whim and with women, then the assumption that women's purchases will be frivolous (while men's will not) becomes automatic.

One of the ironies of the perceived exclusion of men from consuming activity is that mass consumption is an accompaniment of modernity, which has often been gendered as male. As Rita Felski points out, many modern thinkers essentialized woman as natural and ahistorical, and therefore as antithetical to the forward march of progress. In this view women in modern society would be left behind in their traditional roles as homemakers and mothers. Yet, with the advent of mass consumption, housewifely duties were themselves changing, with new goods and marketing practices. Modern consumption brought women more visibly into the public arena, thus partially liberating them. In this sense it was seen as a threat to proper womanhood. Some also feared the corrupting influence on families of unrestrained female desire for goods.[17] In addition, consumer culture imported the objects of mass production into the domestic sphere, further blurring the perceived division between public and private.[18] What was most to be feared, however, was that consumption would seduce and thereby emasculate men.[19] As Felski notes, critics feared the feminizing influence of consumer culture's pull toward irrational, "inchoate desire."

Men were in danger of the "castrating effects of an ever more pervasive commodification."[20] Consumer society could thus be doubly threatening, both to the safe assumptions of traditional gender roles and to the virility of modern progress. Consumer culture was ambiguous, unsettling terrain. Small wonder, then, that even though Russian advertisers appealed to the vanities and anxieties of both men and women, they rarely challenged gender stereotypes overtly. Nevertheless, advertising's content suggested that men were full partners with women in the passion for consumption.

FASHIONING MEN

Men have likely been more overlooked than absent in the history of western consumer culture, but in Russia it is clear that traders intentionally addressed them.[21] No historian of late imperial Russian advertising could state, as has Lori Anne Loeb for the same period in Britain, that "the male voice was rarely an important feature of the Victorian advertisement."[22] While Loeb's study is explicitly based in an examination of family magazines and ladies' journals, thus prejudicing her findings toward women, she also cites a British trade journal of 1913, making the broader assertion that ninety percent of advertisers designed their ads with women in mind, leaving men almost entirely out of the picture.[23] Given that advertisers addressed men as much as, if not more than, women in the Russian daily press, what might explain the difference?

First, as already mentioned, the male urban population in late tsarist Russia was substantially higher than the female, making the need to appeal to male consumers obvious to any rational business owner. To further weight the gender imbalance in terms of probable readers for ads in the popular press, literacy rates among women in Russia remained low. Working-class women in particular would be far less accessible targets than men via primarily textual media such as newspapers. Although literacy among women factory workers was higher than among their village sisters, in Moscow province it was still only twenty-six percent by 1908, up from less than five percent in the 1880s. Literacy rates for male workers, in contrast, rose from thirty-three to seventy-six percent in the same period.[24]

Second, despite growing demands for women's rights in the late tsarist era, Russian patriarchy remained strong, and the ideology of domesticity may not have brought as much financial influence to Russian women within the home as it did to their Western counterparts. While Russian women enjoyed more legal rights to their property than in the West, the familial dynamics of their restricted world remained more authoritarian.[25]

A study of the Russian mass-circulation press shows that Russian merchants and manufacturers saw both men and women as likely customers. This is true even in the matter of clothing, usually associated with female consumption. In 1909, for instance, the advertising agency of Nikolai Gol'din put out a single advertisement for multiple clients—a tactic that allowed small storeowners to be part of a larger advertising spread than they might otherwise afford (fig. 4.1).[26] Under the caption "I Shop in Moscow," the central illustration is the consumer himself, the full-length figure of a well-dressed gentleman. This image of the well-to-do male consumer is surrounded by a list of diverse goods including (counterclockwise in the order printed) fashion magazines, cigars, children's clothing, cigarette tubes, stationery, gramophones, fashionable cloth, tea, Crimean wine, cigarettes, diamonds, women's clothing, saddles and harnesses, chocolate, shoes, tobacco, and men's clothing.

FIGURE 4.1—"I Shop in Moscow." Composite advertisement for multiple businesses. Source: *Russkoe slovo*, March 3, 1909.

A female version appeared the following month, and both ads were repeated several times.[27] It is significant, though, that the depiction of the male consumer appeared first, suggesting that men were targeted as purchasers of a full range of goods for the family. The inventory was as mixed for both versions, with the slight difference that corsets and toys were advertised beside the woman, although fashion magazines (and cigars) were missing from her list. Gender roles were clearly not the deciding factor in storeowners' decisions to participate in these ads. In the eyes of advertising agent Gol'din, and by implication of his clients, men were considered as natural a target for consumption as women, at least for luxury items beyond the family's basic groceries.[28]

Indeed, Russia's consumer market sometimes overtly depicted men as the primary shoppers. They were decidedly in the forefront of a 1907 advertisement for a clothing store (fig. 4.2), in which three men speak to the audience: "We three [in large letters] and our wives [in smaller letters] attire ourselves stylishly, in the latest fashion and, most important, inexpensively at the Fashion Bazaar (*Bazar mod*) shop."[29] These men were shown leading the way in their households for both consumer taste and financial decision making. The emphasis on cost suggests that this storeowner wished to reach not just the well-to-do, but also lower-middle-class customers who aspired to fashionable bourgeois respectability.

Despite the tendency to see concern with dress as a feminine foible, by the late nineteenth century men's demonstration of sartorial style had become a marker of masculinity and status across the social spectrum in Russia. During the 1820s European dandyism had spread among certain members of the nobility (Petr Chaadaev being a notable example).[30] As Olga Vainshtein notes, the desire of some men to express themselves through their attire outmaneuvered even Russia's authoritarian insistence on uniforms for most state servitors, with officers padding their shoulders and suffering corsets in order to cut a trim figure in the tight-fitting trousers of the early nineteenth century.[31] By the end of the century, fashion journals such as *Dandy* (*Dendi*) had spread the desire for male fashionability to the middle classes, with many young men tapping into the "code" of the dandy—the "well-polished stereotype of masculine elegance."[32]

The association of men's fashion and masculinity did not stop with the middle classes. Male urban workers focused on dress and accessories (pocket watches were a favorite) to express their style and independence, spending a significant proportion of their wages on clothes and footwear.[33] Another 1907 *Fashion Bazaar* advertisement promoted clothing for all men, "from worker to millionaire," depicting a working-class and a wealthy man sharing a mutual glance of dignified respect. Although

FIGURE 4.2—"We three and our wives." Advertisement for *Bazar Mod clothing store.* Source: *Russkoe slovo*, March 11, 1907.

dressed according to their stations, each projects a pride in appearance regardless of status.[34] As the *Fashion Bazaar* ad promises, "All will find clothes in accordance with their means (*soobrazno sredstvam*)." Thanks to the availability of ready-made clothing, a smart appearance was affordable for everyone.[35]

Despite the theme of affordability in many ads for men's clothing, images more often depicted wealthy sophistication than working-class outfits. Since many young, especially single, workers shared with the better-off population a desire for European-style suits and shoes, such portrayals guaranteed a broad appeal, even if aspirational. The aspiration was not necessarily for membership in a different social class. Mark Steinberg has suggested that some workers wore suits as a silent claim for human dignity.[36] Perhaps even more consciously they did so for style. These ads were not really selling class, but classiness. So it did not matter if the image was of a top-hatted gentleman out and about with his walking cane and optional monocle or of suavely relaxed male friends talking over a smoke; the appeal was as much in the masculine poise—the slant of a hat, the attitude of confidence—as in the clothes themselves. In figure 4.3, for instance, the casual, conversational poses contrast with the blaring declaration, "Know this!! That you can dress beautifully and inexpensively only at A.M. Lisianskii's."[37] It is the air of masculine nonchalance that makes this ad stand out, rather than the slogan. These men are not so much showing what to wear, as how to wear it. The inclusion of a cigarette added a tone of savoir faire in this era when smoking spelled confident coolness rather than addiction and cancer. Although male appearances of this period have often been described as dull and standardized (with the exception of the dandy), they were nonetheless imbued with nuanced codes of masculinity, codes that advertisers helped to create and perpetuate.

FIGURE 4.3—"Know that you can dress beautifully and inexpensively only at A.M. Lisianskii's, Moscow." Source: *Russkoe slovo*, March 17, 1907.

Even some ads for women's clothing employed masculine status (as well as susceptibility to feminine wiles) to tempt customers to buy. A Lodz ready-made clothing manufacturer depicted a wife using her powers of persuasion on her husband: "My darling! Order something again for us from Lev Rubashkin's firm in Lodz. I will be very grateful; after all, we are already both convinced that everything that firm sends is superb" (fig. 4.4).[38] The form the wife's gratitude would take is insinuated by her seductive embrace of the husband, whose play of resistance, standing hand on hip, is belied by his responsive smile. The ad leaves little doubt that the woman will get her new clothes, and the man his reward too. Such a message reinforced the image of woman as temptress of consumption, but it also perpetuated the male image of powerbroker in the home. He could fulfill or deny her wishes, and conceding meant his sexual gain.

FIGURE 4.4—"My darling! Order something again for us from Lev Rubashkin's firm in Lodz. I will be very grateful." Source: *Russkoe slovo*, March 10, 1910.

Images of control constituted the overarching appeal to male consumers in clothing advertisements. The fashioning of men offered the self-projection of social awareness and domestic power—fiscal, cultural, and sexual. Far from feminizing, it was assured that men's purchases of fashion would affirm their masculine identity and strengthen their standing in public and at home. The clothes made the man, but the man also made the clothes.

CONSUMING WOMEN

Male control remained at issue even as advertisers employed feminine allure both to associate goods with sexuality and to sell goods directly to women. Whether being consumed or consuming, the final target of many female images in advertisements was male. When women were the objects of consumption, they were portrayed along a spectrum of male attitudes from desire to denigration. While the denigration and marginalization of women was a particularly striking theme in Russian advertising and the subject of a later section, the association between male-targeted goods and the "seductive woman" was by far more common.

Tobacco manufacturers were among those most apt to connect their products with a fantasy world of young female beauties. Variations of the exotically draped woman appeared in many brands, from a seductively statuesque beauty dreamily lifting her hair to mix with the emerging smoke of an eastern hookah in Shaposhnikov's advertisement for Albanskii tobacco (touted for its "genuine eastern taste and aroma"),[39] to La Ferme's Godiva-like beauty, long hair covering bare breasts on the Chudo-Tsvet (miraculous bloom) cigarette package,[40] or La Ferme's bare-footed, smoking Diushes (duchess) embodying her brand in reclining pose (fig. 4.5).[41] All promised sensual delight for the male smoker through orientalist images of odalisque-type fantasy. Even the biblical mother of humanity was appropriated for the purpose of promoting her namesake Eva cigarettes (fig. 4.6).[42] "It is a sin not to smoke!" proclaims this poster, depicting bare-breasted Eve reaching for the apple. (The original sinner is thus doubly sinning here, for there is no cigarette in sight.) In other tobacco advertisements female beauties, like ghostly fantasies of desire, take shape in the undulating smoke rising from a man's cigarette (fig. 4.7).[43]

But why stop at fantasy? Manufacturers also claimed an actual connection between product choice and success with women, as in the following conversation:

FIGURE 4.5—*(above)*
"Diushes cigarettes. La Ferme
Company. 20 for 6 kopeks."
Source: *Russkoe slovo*, November
12, 1913.

FIGURE 4.6— *(right)*
"It's a sin not to smoke! Eva
cigarettes. 10 for 6 kopeks.
A.N. Shaposhnikov Tobacco
Company, St. Petersburg.
Source: Russian State Library
poster collection.

FIGURE 4.7—"No. 6 cigarettes. 10 for 6 kopeks. La Ferme Company." Source: *Russkoe slovo*, February 16, 1914.

He: "What drew you to me, dear Mia?"
She: "You smoke Havana cigars from the firm of A. Strit, Stoleshnikov Alley, Titov House, and that is evidence of your good taste."[44]

Just as the right product could attract women, the wrong one would repel them. In an advertisement for Viktorson's tobacco tubes, well-dressed women hold their noses in repugnance while they pass a man smoking "good tobacco in bad tubes." But when he switches tubes, they hang on his arm and compete to breathe in his alluring smoke, proving that "any tobacco in Viktorson the Elder's tubes attracts."[45] In the realm of consumer culture, the measure of the man lay in his market choices.

Conflating commodities and sex, such ads were ultimately about men consuming women through goods. But what of advertisements that addressed female consumers, women seen as subjects rather than objects? Products such as perfume and cosmetics traded primarily on women's desire to be attractive—to men—and thus, even when women were the target audience, they still remained the ultimate object of consumption. Unlike ads for men that traded on the sexual allure of goods by portraying seductive women, advertisements for women's products did not portray female fantasies of men, but rather depicted the woman herself in seductive or naturalistic settings. Perfume brand names such as Love Me, Caress, and Coquetry implied seduction even without their accompanying illustrations. This tendency to speak to women through reflected male desire should not surprise us since it prevailed also in Western consumer culture throughout the twentieth century, as demonstrated by the shock value of a 1990s television commercial that broke the mold by depicting several women ogling a young, Pepsi-drinking, bare-chested worker on the street below their office window. The one-sided nature of sexual objectification in advertising, largely a function of the passive role reserved for women in traditional gender relations, held on long after women's political and sexual liberation.

The exception proves the rule, and, as Erving Goffman's study of gender roles in American advertising showed in the late 1970s, the jolt of the exception exposes the often-unconscious cultural norm.[46] In his study of magazine advertisements, Goffman notes the typical poses of men and women when featured together; the man usually stands higher than the woman, whose head is often tilted to look up at him. To demonstrate the degree to which late twentieth-century culture absorbed and accepted such standard depictions, after a series of typical examples Goffman presents a few exceptions, with the man in subordinate position. The effect is jarring and revelatory. If we apply this tactic in various ways to Russian advertising of the early twentieth century, certain gender norms also appear.

Poses and settings in perfume advertisements presented women as sensual and dreamy, or flirtatious, intrinsically at home in nature, or happy in the role of flighty socialite. In any case, they remained within the accepted notions of femininity, more elemental, yet more superficial than men. In light of these prevailing norms, an advertisement for the St. Petersburg Chemical Laboratory's eau de cologne (fig. 4.8) appears striking indeed.[47] This female mountain climber may have been in nature, but in the decidedly male role of intrepid adventurer. She is more an interloper in nature than a part of it, painting an advertisement on the rock face, no less! The mixture of daring, as she dangles from her precarious foothold, and risk-taking entrepreneurship makes the gender choice in this advertisement highly unusual—a choice no doubt prompted by the desire to make readers stop and take a second look, yet also reflective of the changing ideas of progressive thinkers (both men and women) about female potential. The pioneering spirit of the female is mirrored by the company's trademark of Peter the Great's equestrian statue in the left-hand corner. Even the two figures' poses echo each other, arms extended to indicate progress toward the future.

FIGURE 4.8—"Eau de cologne. St. Petersburg Chemical Laboratory. First in quality!" Source: *Russkoe slovo*, December 4, 1912.

Changes in the gendered nature of the consumer market itself led to some disjunctures in advertising imagery when cultural norms lagged behind actual practice. We have already seen that tobacco was targeted primarily to men. In the nineteenth century a woman who smoked was seen as rebellious, especially if she flaunted social custom by doing so in public. Barbara Alpern Engel notes that young women who joined the nihilist movement in the 1850s and '60s declared their independence by cropping their hair, dispensing with crinolines, "wearing blue eyeglasses and smoking in public."[48] In an 1851 story by Evgeniia Tur, an adolescent girl dreaming of liberation from parental discipline counted smoking among her yearned-for freedoms: "When I'm married I'll go to all the balls, all the parties, masquerades—I'll have many bouquets—and I'll try to have more lovers—in a word, I'll do whatever I want. I'll smoke cigarettes and ride horseback. I've thought about this for a long time."[49] It was a sign of both naïveté and/or realism (depending on the compliancy of her future husband) that the girl could only imagine attaining these liberties, such as they were, through marriage.

Despite the persistence of such attitudes toward female smoking, some respectable women were beginning to take up the habit, at least in the home. From as early as the 1890s, tobacco manufacturers produced a few brands of cigarettes for women, taking care to market them in a feminine way. In 1892, for instance, the owner of the Ottoman company advertised its Vizitnyia (Visiting) cigarettes as "a pleasant and useful novelty for ladies who smoke or are beginning to smoke. I have put out these thin cigarettes made from ten-ruble tobacco especially for the ladies. It is entirely possible to substitute them for candies, to give the ladies a surprise."[50] This advertisement was consciously venturing into unfamiliar territory, as far as the gender of its intended consumers. In spite of the fact that the cigarettes were expressly for women, the advertiser could not help but address men as the intermediaries between the tobacco market and female consumers. A decade later tobacco advertisements for women, in the rare cases they appeared at all, were still clearly establishing a tentative foothold in the market. In 1903 a St. Petersburg tobacco warehouse announced a new brand called Pioner for "elegant ladies."[51] The choice of name was hardly coincidental, and the advertisement made a great point of the product's lack of dust and odor—elegant ladies need not fear soiling their feminine appearance with this tobacco. Neither of the above advertisements actually depicted a woman smoking.

As the new century progressed, more advertisers began to show women holding cigarettes, although in Bogdanov's poster for Mechta (Dream) cigarettes, the lady in question is decidedly refined and upper class, even though enjoying one of the cheaper brands (fig. 4.9).[52] The association of femininity with the women's brands, it seems, was only realizable through an upper-class image. By the 1910s some advertisers embraced the rebellious nature of female smoking. In the mass-circulation press, however, such images remained extremely rare, and newspaper tobacco advertisements were so predominantly male that what may have been the first ad featuring a woman with a cigarette actually in her mouth still retains a jarring quality for the present-day peruser of Russia's prerevolutionary press. For about two years the Shaposhnikov company had been picturing a man with weathered, bohemian appearance to advertise Krem cigarettes; at the end of 1910 the company suddenly substituted genders, using a female version of the same picture for Eva cigarettes (fig. 4.10).[53] The switch took on a positively daring aspect in light of the almost total absence of such images up to that point. As with Goffman's superordinate female, this woman was transcending an invisible, yet entrenched boundary between the sexes, a boundary that coincided less and less with reality but still reflected mainstream notions of gender.

FIGURE 4.9—"Mechta cigarettes. 20 for 6 kopeks. The tobacco factory of A.N. Bogdanov, St. Petersburg." Source: Russian State Library poster collection.

FIGURE 4.10—"Eva cigarettes. 10 for 6 kopeks. A.N. Shaposhnikov Factory." Source: *Russkoe slovo*, November 28, 1910.

Despite such occasional deliberate testing of social limits, the promoters of consumer goods were usually eager to stay within the strictures of accepted cultural standards. This is probably more true of advertisements in the daily press than of posters, since newspaper ads were often printed repeatedly in a medium that depended upon paid subscriptions and street sales. In order to sell goods, advertisers sought a favorable response from as many people as possible, and for the most part this meant appealing to popular cultural standards and tastes. Advertising thus tended to trade on accepted notions of gender roles, counting on the power of stereotypes more often than shock value to reach customers. Images of consuming women, both as subjects and objects, tapped into deeply engrained expectations about the aspirations of women and men alike.

MARGINALIZING WOMEN

Given the prevalence of patriarchal, sometimes verging into misogynistic attitudes in imperial Russian society, advertisements that today might shock an audience with their marginalization and denigration of women were actually situated well within the range of accepted gender norms. In such ads women were seen as distractions or detractors from manliness. Consumer goods, in these messages, proved far worthier of male devotion than the fairer sex. An ad for Shapshal's Deia cigarettes exclaims:

> I am angry! Furious! I'm trembling all over!!!
> Vengeance! Death to the villain!!!
> He's stolen my dress coat, lured away my wife
> And smoked up all my Deia!!!
> The wife and the coat . . . that's neither here nor there,
> But . . . to be without Deia—now that's disaster!![54]

Such attitudes about wives reflected a dismissiveness toward women that was a common theme of Russian culture, especially among the lower classes. Despite women's essential roles in the peasant household, the patriarchal social structure relegated them to the lowest rungs of the family hierarchy. Indeed, if the much-cited proverb, "A hen is not a bird, and a woman is not a human being," is given any cultural weight, they might be seen as even lower than the bottom rung. While other proverbs acknowledge women's importance, it is undeniable that Russian peasant and urban lower-class popular culture embodied a strong vein of misogyny. Denigration of wives, stereotypes of old hags, and lewd innuendo about loose women were the stuff of many a comic routine in the popular entertainments of St. Petersburg and Moscow.[55] Although choice of marriage partner was legally voluntary for all classes, arranged marriages were still the norm, and a certain pragmatic cynicism seems to have prevailed in men's expectations about relations with their wives (this was far less the case for women, who tended to have more romantic hopes, at least before marriage). Another proverb states, "A wife is very dear to her husband twice: the day he marries her and the day he buries her."[56] Such sayings suggest that advertisers' marginalization of wives was nothing new. Tobacco and liquor constituted far more manly attachments than a spouse.

Thus another Shapshal advertisement for Kumir cigarettes depicts love-making as a means to an end—the procurement of tobacco:

> The sweetheart whispers [to his] date:
> "With you I have forgotten the whole world!"

And then himself at parting begs
"Six kopeks for Kumir!?!"[57]

The transcendence of love proves short-lived in the face of potential
tobacco deprivation. Ultimately, women provided less long-term fulfillment than cigarettes.

It was Shustov cognac advertisements, however, that most often played
on this theme of marginalizing women. In one of the firm's multitudinous
advertising anecdotes, entitled "Don't Forget to Do (from the notebook
of a 'true' Russian)," a traveler's to-do list includes detailed instructions
for each point on his itinerary. Near the end appears: "In Voronezh—get
married. Don't forget! Strawberries for Ivan Ivanovich."[58] A "true" Russian man was obviously supposed to take marriage lightly. He had more
important things to think about, like errands for his friends. This reflects
expectations for male bonding patterns in Russia: in contrast to girls,
young men were encouraged to maintain ties to male peer groups at the
expense of their spousal relationships.[59] For women, their husbands were
to come first.

Shustov's advertisements perpetuated the idea that romantic love was
something for men to outgrow. An advertising poem called "Whom and
What I Have Loved" traces a man's evolving attachments as he grows up;
as a child he had loved his nanny, as a schoolboy his story books, as a thir-
teen-year-old his bicycle, as a seventeen-year-old his neighbor's daughter,
Mania. But as a mature twenty-five-year-old he proclaims:

Now I have already become
Quite like a man:
Now alone I love—
Only Shustov's cognac.[60]

Here, romantic love is superseded not by male friendships, but by commodities. Indeed, the commodities are the friends.

Many Shustov advertisements went further than marginalization of
women to demonstrate that, if a man should be so foolish as to fall in love,
he would soon discover the fickle nature of female loyalty and be forced
back for solace to his more trustworthy cognac. The poor male lover,
betrayed by the heartless object of his affections, was a common Shustov
theme.[61] Gender roles were never reversed in this campaign for the male
market. As in the tradition of Russian folk songs, exclusive love on the part
of a man always led to tragedy.[62] All in all, a man was better off directing
his devotion to a good drink in the first place, as in the following verse:

"To the Shot Glass"
(Not a parody)
Friend of my harsh days,
My clean little dove!
Alone in the dark of the pine cupboard
For a long, long time you wait for me . . .
But don't be sad. The time will come,
You will hear my cheerful step,
Melancholy, suffering—all will be appeased
With fragrant Shustov's cognac.[63]

This anthropomorphized shot glass experiences the pangs of an abandoned wife or lover but remains a source of comfort without recrimination, ready to respond to her man's arrival whenever it might be. Beloved because she delivers his true contentment—liquor—the vessel of consumption becomes the perfect companion, superior to a flesh-and-blood spouse.

Women were not only diminished in many male-oriented advertisements, they were disparaged as well, in some cases even demonized. In a campaign for the La Ferme company's Iar cigarettes, which featured a series of ads based on the theme that tobacco trivializes the burdens of daily life, one variation depicts an image of a witch-like hag shaking her fist. She is the threatening mother-in-law of the poor man with whom the accompanying poem sympathizes as he comes home from work to a topsy-turvy home that is full of washing from morning till night. As if domestic labor were a deliberate female conspiracy designed to torment him, it is the man who suffers—and who is offered escape through the transcendent experience of tobacco.[64]

In another Shustov ad, entitled "How to Live to Be a Hundred," two pieces of advice relate the perils associated with women. Each contains the built-in pauses of a comedy routine, designed to give the punch lines more effect. The first advises, "Avoid pretty women, in order not to hang yourself . . . on their necks." This makes a play on the phrase "to run after someone," which in Russian translates literally as "to hang yourself on someone's neck." The second piece of advice warns, "Do not argue with your wife, so as not to receive . . . a blow."[65] Echoing the comic themes of popular entertainment, these advertisers were capitalizing on jokes they already knew many consumers would enjoy, and in the process they were perpetuating gendered stereotypes engrained in popular culture.[66]

The common disparagement of women facilitated their objectification in what are to modern sensibilities shocking images, such as the armless peasant woman seen in figure 3.5. Her amputated state was designed to demonstrate the hygiene of a product manufactured "without the touch of human hands"; her unenviable condition was not supposed to evoke pity. In another such example an advertisement for a book of magic tricks asks: "How can you spend long winter nights without boredom?" The depicted answer to that question shows a man cutting off a woman's head (fig. 4.11).[67] Clearly the purpose of these advertisements was to attract attention by presenting a startling image; that does not alter the fact that in both cases it was a woman's body that was portrayed in mutilated form.

Some advertising campaigns did focus on male physical torment, such as those promoting treatments for neurasthenia or venereal disease. In addition, a series of ads for rheumatism cures depicted agonized men undergoing medieval tortures like the rack. However, the pictures in such ads, though sensational, were not offered for humor but rather for sympathy

FIGURE 4.11—"The secret of magic!" Advertisement for a book of magic tricks. Source: *Russkoe slovo*, November 23, 1907.

and the promise of treatment.[68] The depictions of these suffering men also showed very human responses to physical pain. Conversely, the decapitated and armless women in the examples mentioned above both remained expressionless in their disembodiment. They were blank objects upon which to demonstrate the magical or technical prowess of male skill and industry. Whether dehumanizing, demeaning, or reducing to irrelevance, the gendered advertisements discussed in this section deprived women of full personhood, using them rather as foils for the consuming male.

DOMESTICATING MEN

One topic on which advertisers' sympathies lay firmly with women, however, was the devastation caused by alcoholism. In contrast to the common themes of male self-reliance and control, advertisements for curing drunkenness depicted men as dependent on women and in dire need of domestication. Alcohol-induced domestic abuse and neglect were perennial problems in Russian society that had long proved resistant to state attempts at reform.[69] In the modern consumer age, it was affirmed, commodities would succeed where regulation had failed.

Advertisers of patent remedies for alcoholism unashamedly highlighted drunken men's debility and abuse of their long-suffering wives. If other products' advertising sometimes denigrated wives for the benefit of male readers' misogynistic funny bone, in these ads women were elevated as the traditional mainstays of domestic life. (Implicitly reductionist, stereotypes always allow for contradictions.) It was thought that, despite the inherent weaknesses of their gender, women would inevitably sacrifice themselves in order to keep the home intact. In one advertisement, entitled "Why Do Men Drink?" a redeemed alcoholic assures "mothers and wives" that he now understands how "the whole weight of drunkenness lies on the weak shoulders of a woman; she pays for it with broken happiness and health."[70] Or with broken bones, as drink worsened the long-normalized practice of wife beating in many homes.[71] Female alcoholism, while it existed, was a social ill invisible to the purveyors of patent remedies, or more likely ignored by them as outside the comfort zone of cultural norms.[72]

The overall message of the anti-alcoholism ads, however, was that women's sacrifice was not enough, or the problem would have been solved long before. Ultimately, it was a consumer product that turned the drunken husband around and ended the family's suffering. Likewise, commodities facilitated the creation and maintenance of a contented home. In portrayals of domestic happiness, cigarettes (a less destructive addiction, perhaps) were also instrumental in cementing relationships and keeping harmony between couples. A maiden might secure her young man's love if she remembered to give him his favorite tobacco every day;[73] a young couple in love would find a lifetime of happiness if they just bought Tary-Bary (Tittle-Tattle) cigarettes,[74] and even Shustov allowed the possibility of an "ideal pair" if both partners shared a love of cognac.[75] In terms of marital concord, advertisements commonly depicted before and after images of misery and happiness—due to the better aroma of a superior cigarette not driving the wife out of the room,[76] or patent medicine's transformation of an inadequate husband and father into a strong and confident man participating enthusiastically in a house full of children.[77]

In its semi-imaginary world advertising was free to promote such social ideals in black-and-white terms. By grounding their messages in stereotypical notions of (and aspirations for) exemplary domestic life and personal happiness, all the advertisers had to do was insinuate the role of consumption into the picture to suggest that life's success or failure rested on a simple choice of goods. Wherever human inadequacies and vices appeared, the appropriate remedies were available.

BODY ISSUES

The realm of personal inadequacy in the face of the gendered cultural ideals that consumerism perpetuates and helps to create has long constituted fertile territory for advertisers. When it came to anxiety over physical appearance and personal flaws, Russian advertisers were quick to humanize and amplify the fears of both men and women. Despite shared concerns over facial blemishes, graying hair, and crooked noses (all requiring the appropriate creams, tonics, and corrective devices for both sexes), advertising nevertheless emphasized very different physical qualities for manliness and for femininity. Sufficient height and hair emerged as the main requirements for male beauty, while strength and sexual virility were the indispensable characteristics of manhood. Smooth skin quality was important for feminine allure, but more essential still, a large bosom combined beauty and womanhood. These contrasts in the essential qualities of gender are congruent with the health brochures that formed part of Russia's advice literature in the late imperial period. Catriona Kelly's survey of this material finds also that men's health literature focused on physical fitness over looks, while women's brochures saw female appearance "in Social Darwinian terms."[78] The latter emphasized not physical health but personal attractiveness—in particular a generously sized bust. The rhetoric of advertising was scarcely distinguishable in this regard from that of health manuals.

Appearance was not entirely neglected for men, of course. Although advertisements for increasing height (the method by which this would be attained was never explained up front) technically addressed men and women, it was the short man who was seen to suffer social and sexual disadvantage. A 1912 advertisement, entitled "How to Become Tall," graphically depicts the short man's predicament. His uplifted face barely reaches his dance partner's décolletage.[79] The image projects social embarrassment and sexual inadequacy on the part of the man, polite toleration on the part of the taller woman.

Even more than height, full hair was bruited as a sign of virility for men. The quality of a man's moustache took on phallic importance in many advertisements: "Even the smallest moustaches can be made big and thick," assures a purveyor of Ustanin, a product that would endow moustaches with "a surprisingly elegant form."[80] "Beautiful moustaches are the best adornment of a male face. If instead you have only a little fluff of hair, don't lose heart," comforts one advertiser.[81] Another writes with empathy that the youth dreaming of beautiful moustaches would, within only a short time of using Peruin-Peto, have "long, luxuriant moustaches and beard."[82] That hair was associated with sexual attractiveness is made even more evident in a different advertisement for the same product: "The beauty of a husband consists of luxuriant hair growth on the head, dandyish whiskers (*shchegol'skie usy*), and a stylish beard."[83]

The advertising promises of hair growth tonics were so prolific in the press that they became the subject of cartoonists. "Before and after" advertisements were lampooned in *Peterburgskaia gazeta*'s magazine supplement *Our Time* (*Nashe vremia*) as early as 1903. Figure 4.12 shows "the secret exposed," in which a man's full head of hair was first photographed for the "after" shot, then cut and shaved to provide the "before" and "during" treatment pictures.[84] That such satirical exposés in no way curtailed hair tonic advertising probably says more about the hopefulness and persistence of male vanity than about the efficacy of the formulas, in which case the advertisers had successfully tapped a raw nerve among the male population.

While for men appearance was a matter of personal vanity and attractiveness to the opposite sex, for women it was couched in terms of almost literal life or death. Beauty was to be preserved at all costs from wrinkles and age spots. Face creams and cosmetics were the weapons against aging and fading into obscurity. With melodrama worthy of the era's popular novels, the promoters of Krem-Emal face cream set forth an aging woman's fateful dilemma:

The beauty of a woman is her mighty and authoritative power, beauty subjugates and hypnotizes, but old age is the grave of beauty. . . . Going through the twilight of life, that satanic age, when your poor heart is deceived by the lying signs of youth, gratifies itself with the illusion that it can still experience the joys of love, but senses too late that no one will answer it with love—have recourse to the saving palliative for you: Krem-Emal.[85]

This advertisement makes explicit the underlying implications of many milder exhortations to preserve feminine beauty: in the mirror of advertising, a man was simply unattractive without a healthy moustache and a full head of hair, but a woman practically ceased to exist without her looks.

As important as a woman's face was her figure. Although diets were advertised for overweight men as well as women, females of regular size

FIGURE 4.12—"The secret exposed." Caricature of hair growth treatments. Source: *Nashe vremia*, May 1, 1903.

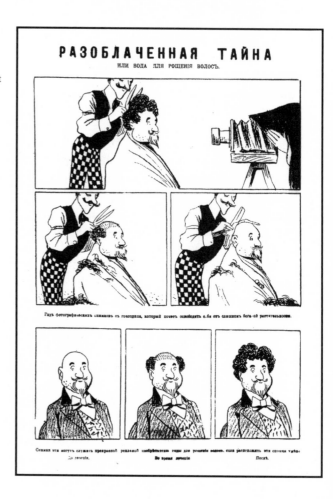

were still subjected to the rigors of the much-advertised corset. Pinching the waist and distorting the body to emphasize bosom and bottom, this undergarment was considered an essential part of an attractive female form. The dangers of corsets for women's health had become a matter of public concern by the turn of the century, but newspapers continued to carry numerous ads promoting severely pinched waists. A supposedly improved "anticorset" of 1907, lauded by doctors for its harmlessness (so the advertisers claimed), still resulted in unnaturally slim waists and a distorted stance.[86] Such was the necessary arsenal of female beauty that a 1911 caricature, entitled "The Anatomy of the Modern Woman," depicted the natural female as a defenseless, naked waif without the deployment of her full cosmetic armor (fig. 4.13).[87] At the top, the socially acceptable woman strikes the typical pose of the corseted woman in advertisements, more unnatural than a drill soldier on review. Few images better demonstrate gendered ideals as cultural constructions.

The promise that consumer products could overcome the deficiencies of nature to meet the man-made requirements of beauty was commonly stated in the abundance of advertisements for breast enlargement (as with height enhancement, the methods were never specified). Lack of a full bosom, "that main prerogative of femininity,"[88] was explicitly described as a physical defect for those who had been "so cruelly offended by nature."[89] One thus deprived could hardly hope for male attention: "Even a pretty woman or young lady with a bad chest and thin shoulders loses all her attractiveness in men's eyes, and therefore we must remember that perfection of the bust is power for all of us."[90] A woman's selfhood and influence were seen to lie only in her ability to interest a man in her physical charms. In the absence of this power, she led a joyless existence and even questioned her own feminine identity:

> I know very well that terrible feeling of complete dejection that every flat-chested woman experiences; it is perfectly familiar to me what you have to go through, conscious of the fact that you have a woman's face but a figure like a man's. . . . With what pity every man must look at a woman who is as flat-chested as himself. Can such a woman really arouse in a man that ardor and cause in him those feelings that the sight of a real woman awakens in him? . . . Of course not.[91]

This fellow sufferer, Margarita Merlen, attested that her joy at finally expanding her chest six inches was (ironically) like "a stone fallen from [her] heart." Not only did she no longer feel that she was "neither man nor woman, but something in between," she also found herself the center

FIGURE 4.13—"Anatomy of a modern woman." Satire on women's corsets and cosmetics. Source: *Peterburgskii listok*, October 27, 1911.

of attention among both men and women, who previously had studiously ignored her. Figure 4.14 represents the thousands that Mme. Merlen claimed to have helped—a veritable bevy of busts.[92]

The messages of Mme. Merlen and others like her might well have found their mark in the hearts and minds of young women raised with the primary life goal of marriage. Despite the development of higher education for women in the late nineteenth century and the presence of a significant minority of liberal or radicalized women who rejected the traditional female trajectory, the matrimonial ideal still predominated across female society, from the finishing schools of the elite to the folk customs of the peasantry.[93] Even in arranged noble marriages, where a woman's wealth and status might play decisive roles in finding a husband, it was rare for looks to be ignored altogether.[94] As for girls of peasant and working-class origins, many of the rituals and songs they participated in from adolescence focused on their future husbands and the singular importance of marriage. As Anne Bobroff points out, girls were conditioned by folk customs to see their primary commitment and loyalty to their spouse, at the expense of their female peer groups.[95] In light of such conditioning, Mme. Merlen's contention that a blossoming figure had restored her to both male and female attention suggests the possibility that women also judged each other by male values.

In any case, the dire melodrama of the language that advertisers addressed to women's physical appearance was intended to exploit fear of failure—failure to acquire the recognized niche and any semblance of influence that traditional society allocated to women as wives. A woman's existence was validated through her husband. According to laws that remained virtually unchanged throughout the imperial period, a Russian wife "had almost no separate civil identity; without her husband's express permission, she could not work, study, trade, or travel. . . . Before marriage, the girl's movements and activities were similarly guarded by her parents, particularly the father. In many ways, the wife-daughter's status under the husband-father was analogous to that of the landlord's serf."[96]

Without the ability to acquire a husband, she was invisible and powerless.

FIGURE 4.14—"A magnificent bust, guaranteed within a month." Advertisement for Madame Merlen's breast enhancement. Source: *Russkoe slovo*, August 15, 1913.

It was no accident that advertisers repeatedly connected female appearance with power, because without the capacity to attract, a woman had no importance, no role to play. Thus her appearance was her existence. That Russian society was changing at the time these advertisements appeared and that women in fact found a great variety of roles to play did not deny the prevalent stereotype of the old maid, nor did it remove the fear that the stereotype could arouse. These advertisements counted on such fears and on women's hopes for marital happiness.

In contrast, advertising reserved men's existential fear not for looks, but for sexual impotence. Although a big moustache was important as a signifier of virility, far more important was the actual ability to perform sexually. In the realm of patent medicine advertising, the impotent man faced self-annihilation. Remedies saving men from impotence went beyond restoring their sexual prowess to rescue them from "complete despair," which could have led to suicide or insanity.[97] Good looks were less crucial for men because appearance was less central to their social and sexual role. In contrast, strength and potency represented the essence of manhood, and it was for this arena that advertisers reserved their most melodramatic rhetoric addressed to male consumers.

Sexual potency was the predominant issue in patent medicine advertisements. For instance, although Dr. Poehl's widely advertised potion claimed to cure everything from hysteria to arteriosclerosis, its very name, Spermin (whose connotation is exactly the same in Russian as in English), shows that its primary target was the man worried about his virility. It promised to cure impotence and the rampant condition of "neurasthenia," a term invented in the Victorian era that became a medical buzzword by the turn of the century throughout Russia and the West.[98] Indicating a vague psychological unease involving easy fatigability and loss of motivation, the word neurasthenia was also often used in the sexual sense. Spermin was only one product in a crowded market. Another remedy of the same name but different manufacture was even more specifically subtitled in impressive-sounding Latin, "extractum testiculorum."[99]

In addition to neurasthenia, the euphemistically coined "mistakes of youth"[100] were another regularly cited source of sexual problems. Youthful mistakes comprised illicit promiscuity and, perhaps even worse in the contemporary mindset, masturbation. Laura Engelstein has documented the prevalent dread of these practices in late imperial Russia, paralleling similar fears in Western countries. Doctors and public health officials alike believed in the dire consequences of young people's sexual activity: "Spermatorrhea, impotence, constipation in girls, abnormal menses, neurasthenia, neuroses and psychoses, and many other functional disturbances are the results of masturbation, early sexual activity, sexual excitement—in short, of physical and psychological depravity."[101] In the classified pages of the mass-circulation press, the high number of doctors promising to treat the "painful consequences of masturbation" also testifies to the perceived seriousness of this "depraved" habit, which was seen as a disease in itself.

Advertisers readily jumped on the bandwagon of male sexual insecurities, putting out many variations of the "before" and "after" pictures: men in despair versus men in their muscular glory.[102] Purported testimonials from grateful clients who had been redeemed through patent medicines were common and often quite explicit in their detail. Under the heading "Much wasted seed," a G.P. Barankov wrote that he was sending the Biola-Lasley company his photograph as a sign of his salvation from twenty-two years of sexual weakness and "derangement" to which he had previously seen no end. V.G. Pavlov showed similar gratitude to the same firm after suffering for twelve years with his sexual organs: "Now I can boldly tell anyone you please that I feel a completely different person; my limbs, and especially noticeably, my sexual organs are strengthened, the spermator-rhea has stopped, and I have been literally reborn."[103]

Ironically, by discussing men's sexual inadequacies so openly in print, advertisers (particularly those of patent medicines) gave voice to the emasculating effects some feared from consumer culture itself. In so doing, advertisers were able to bring male anxieties out into the open, divert them by blaming them on the stresses and moral influences of modern life in general, and assert their products as the solution. Consumer culture was thus deftly turned from seducer to savior. Indeed, the rhetoric of salvation and rebirth was commonplace in patent medicine advertisements, which offered the regeneration of real manhood. Figure 4.15 depicts the struggle against male debility in mythic proportions: with the help of Validolin, the empowered man could be restored "to a new life" and could hold at bay the vicious snake that would otherwise sap his strength.[104] The positioning of the snake in this image suggests that the phallic symbol could be both the satanic cause of debility and the heroic proof of virility when properly controlled.

Without strength and sexual energy, the advertisers warned, any man was a hopeless case, destined to lose out in every aspect of life:

> The stronger always celebrate victory not only in a fight, but also in life. The strong, healthy man does not know failure, the whole world opens up for him and few things seem impossible. . . . If you suffer from general and sexual weakness, neurasthenia, and its consequences, timidity, a weak memory, the consequences of ugly habits, sleeplessness, headaches; if you are nervous, irritable, overtired, DON'T WAIT A DAY—DON'T WAIT AN HOUR.[105]

FIGURE 4.15—"Validolin restores to new life." Advertisement for patent medicine. Kosta and Company, Moscow. Source: *Russkoe slovo*, October 7, 1911.

As accompanying illustrations demonstrated, if this man rushed to restore his potency, he would transform from a helpless and solitary, head-in-hands wreck into the center of female attention.

In another testimonial for Biola-Lasley, G.K.T. refers to the social consequences of his eighteen years "suffering" from masturbation: "I lost a lot of strength, could never be cheerful. . . . I was shy with women, dissatisfied with myself." Now he claimed to be part of a wonderful social circle and loved by everyone.[106] The return to sexual "normality" and virility rendered him socially visible and sexually eligible. In this sense virility was to masculinity as buxomness was to femininity; they represented the sine qua non of the male and female image and essence. An advertisement for Aurolin medicine, a cure for male impotence, brought these essentials of gender together: addressed to men, it pictures a full-chested woman as the apex of womanhood, accessible to her counterpart ideal of manhood.[107] Only the paragons were worthy of each other.

Other products in addition to patent medicine traded on the male ideal of strength and stamina. The sun would "begin to shine again" for those who realized that the Iuvenator electrical belt would help where despair and dejection would not.[108] This advertisement (one of a series for this device) did not even deem it necessary to explain the causes of said despair. Any of the usual litany with which readers of the popular press were quite familiar would no doubt apply. More specific in its use was the "scarcely perceptible" Erektor, purportedly recommended by the Austrian psychiatrist Richard von Krafft-Ebing, whose work on sexual psychopathology had been available in Russian since 1887.[109]

Products not explicitly connected with sexual performance were also promoted through images of virility. Usually these were items consumed mainly by men, but such was not always the case; van Houten's cocoa illustrated its benefits through the depiction of a burly weightlifter, even though the cocoa was hardly an exclusively male drink.[110] Shustov's cognac, in contrast, was marketed almost entirely to men, and many of its advertisements carried more than a hint of machismo. For instance, in a poem entitled "How to Become Brave," the reader is asked what he should do in order to overcome all rivals and attain success among the young women, "so that everyone all around should marvel aloud: / 'Where did he get his strength?' / So that a *bogatyr*'s spirit should live in [him] / And a noble ardor."[111] The "secret" of such power was predictable—cognac would do it all.

Cigarettes could be similar sources of vigor, as exemplified in a 1909 advertisement for Krem brand, in which a wrestler cheers his victory, brandishing lit cigarettes in both hands.[112] "The idols are overthrown, the ideals smashed!! By the quality and stylishness of Krem. Whoever will smoke them once—will not start to smoke others!!" The triumphant hero holds the new leading brand aloft, his foot on the chest of his rival, who is out cold on the floor. Even though the real rivals in this ad are other cigarettes, the image draws directly upon the popular passion for wrestling, which became a professional sport in Russia in the late imperial period. Its celebrities combined the "village strongman" ideal with the discipline of Greco-Roman athleticism and were described by the popular press as modern-day versions of the bogatyr (medieval folk hero).[113] Images of victory in personal battle would appeal also to workers who had brought the love of fistfighting from the villages to the city streets. In peasant culture fistfighting served several social functions beyond just letting off steam: it entered into courtship as a means to win female approval, it established individual bravery among peers, and it demonstrated group loyalty in fights between villages.[114] To associate a commodity with victory in one-on-one combat was to tap into both recent popular culture and age-old, deeply held values of masculinity.

Consumer goods could also be associated with virility in less direct ways than by simply depicting muscular bodybuilders and wrestlers. As Louise

FIGURE 4.16—"The very best cigars from the factory of A.G. Rutenberg. Factory founded in 1839." Source: *Russkoe slovo*, April 29, 1914.

McReynolds argues, brawn was not necessary for masculinity among educated, urban males.[115] Nevertheless, sexual potency was essential, no matter what the social background or physical strength. This is suggested phallically in figure 4.16, an ad promoting the "very best" cigars from A.G. Rutenberg's factory.[116] All we see of this man are his well-dressed legs and the gigantic cigar protruding from behind an armchair. He is sedentary and clearly used to a life of luxury; whether his torso is corpulent or muscular is irrelevant and hidden. All we need know of both man and product is their exaggerated sexual virility.

In some advertisements the commodity itself was anthropomorphized into a symbol of belligerent heroism, as in the La Ferme tobacco company's 1900 poster, "The fight of the miraculous bogatyr, Trezvon cigarettes, with the heathens (*basurmanami*)" (fig. 4.17).[117] "Father Mikhei," the future Uncle Mikhei of the Shaposhnikov company before he changed his company allegiance, is here depicted as a packet of cigarettes (the face is an actual portrait of the copywriter), successfully slaying the competition with his cigarette-spears. The poem below describes Trezvon's victory in gory, if caricatured detail, limbs torn from sockets and heads "twisted like buttons." This imagery is not only bellicose, it is nationalistic into the bargain, with rival goods taking on the role of non-Orthodox enemies. Both the name Trezvon (ringing of bells), evocative of Russian churches, and the beautiful woman decorating the cigarette packet represent the purity of the cause and the concomitant moral strength of the weapon. It is significant that the creator of Uncle/Father Mikhei, Sergei Korotkii, was himself a proud veteran of the Russo-Turkish war and continued to live out his days of combat in imaginative battles for the tobacco market.

Examples of advertising's reinforcement of ideals of femininity and masculinity go beyond simply demonstrating that consumer culture appealed to both sexes. By highlighting admired gender traits and trading on the fear of losing gendered identity, advertisers were speaking to a culture of anxiety that they clearly saw as inherent in the modern experience. These advertisements brought into sharp relief the centrality of gender to an individual's sense of place in modernizing society. That they so fiercely reinforced traditional norms despite the transformations afoot in turn-of-the-century Russia suggests a double intent: to assuage each sex's fears of losing their respective powers by offering commodities as a means of holding back the tide (of age, modern life, physical and psychological inadequacy, etc.), and to reassure people that consumption secured rather than threatened masculinity and femininity. Advertisers sought to contradict the contemporary perceptions of consumer culture as inessential, unproductive, and destabilizing by asserting their products as invigorating and restorative for both men and women—indeed for society as a whole.

FIGURE 4.17—"The fight of the miraculous bogatyr, Trezvon cigarettes, with the heathens." Poster for La Ferme Tobacco Company. Source: Russian State Library poster collection, 1900.

CONCLUSION

The perceived division between production and consumption as male and female, as if women did not work and men did not wish for stylish clothing or a good brand of tobacco, created a false cultural dichotomy that Russia's advertisers deftly overrode. The universal "she" in consumption was as flawed and incomplete a notion as the universal "he" in industrial production. Just as advertisers needed to draw all classes into the market, they could not achieve a consumer culture without men as well as women. Nevertheless, they had to tread carefully in encouraging men to consume, assuring male customers of the possibilities for projecting masculinity through the correct selection of goods. Fashion, claimed for men, exuded confidence and control. Products from hair tonics to cigarettes added sex appeal and vigor, just as liquor could demonstrate men's aloof independence from women.

Implicitly, however, advertising carried more challenges to accepted male than female roles. In commercial representations it was women who were least often allowed to escape their allocated place. Images of the liberated female explorer or smoker remained rather isolated on the newspaper pages, and women continued to exist largely as a reflection of the male gaze. Rather, it was men whose traditional status was more in question on the marketing stage. Consumer culture at its most forceful has to create needs, not just acquisitiveness. To do so, it must evoke fears and anxiety, in addition to desires. Where advertising appealed primarily to men's desire—for a sharp suit or a good smoke—masculinity could remain unthreatened. But where there was need, as in ads that played on men's worries about impotence, inadequacy, or weakness, manliness was opened to doubt. Neediness was definitely not part of the accepted repertoire of masculinity. Advertisements selling products that sought to preserve and restore lost manhood exposed and commodified the most intimate details of men's personal lives in public. Their private concerns about appearance, sexual potency, and fulfillment were now proclaimed daily in the popular press. Women's intimate fears were also broadcast, but as the perceived weaker sex, grounded in the private realm of home and family, they were supposed to be more caught up with personal concerns. Advertising commercialized the personal for men and women alike, but the threatening inversion lay in personalizing the public man.

In this light, the sexist bravado of much rhetoric for the male market takes on added significance. Men might be shoppers, but the goods they bought only heightened their distance from women by providing superior pleasures. They might be weak and needy, but the right products would restore their true essence of manhood. Advertising thus promised to enhance and preserve masculinity, even as it drew men into the supposedly feminine values of consumption.

Advertising's greater focus on male consumers in Russia than in the West was based in the social context of the country's industrializing cities. This characteristic made up just one of the factors distinguishing Russian commercial publicity from its Western counterparts in the early twentieth century. The cultural context also offered unique depths to sound for symbolic resonances with the Russian public. Just as advertisers stretched accepted gender roles while overtly affirming tradition, they found fair game in commercializing the sacred canons of Russia's cultural heritage in the name of honoring national identity. Values of gender and nationhood fell subject to the manipulations of marketing, but they also provided essential frameworks for a specifically Russian consumer culture.

FIVE

MODERNITY THROUGH TRADITION

Advertising's Appropriation of Russian Culture

"The Sights of Moscow"
Beautiful old lady Moscow!
She charms everyone in a glance . . .
There's the tsar-bell, tsar-cannon,
And long lines of boulevards.
The ancient Kremlin, with its tsar's palace,
Gardens over the Moscow river,
Pushkin, Minin, and Pozharskii,
Ranks of grandeur.
****

And on Sadovaia Street—
The old Shustov enterprise.
Who in Moscow doesn't know it?
—Advertisement for Shustov cognac[1]

If modernity, in the words of Baudelaire, is the transient and the fleeting, advertising is doubly ephemeral.[2] Not only does it tout the new, but in the era when its predominant medium was the mass-circulation press, advertising appeared with the shelf life of a day. Yet in Russia many of its daily attempts at self-reinvention were clothed in the guise of "eternal" elements of national culture, reflecting the Romantic (and Slavophile) perception of national character and traditions as timeless and inherent. Whether it be through the multivalent images of Mother Russia or the invented traditions of historical jubilees, advertisers linked their commodities to a presumably shared heritage that suggested permanency in a world changing too quickly for comfort.[3]

It was natural for those creating the advertising to draw upon their own cultural context in searching for appeals that would resonate with the public. But the tactic of cultural appropriation also served further purposes. It could both soften and heighten the shock of the modern. A new brand may be more striking and noticeable when anachronistically placed in a cultural context that predates it. Such a juxtaposition simultaneously enhances the impact of the new while defusing its threat. Drawing upon Russian heritage was an act of contrasting and bridging old and new cultures by demonstrating the persistence of tradition within modernity. As Lotman and Uspenskii propose in their discussion of change in Russian history, connection with the past makes itself felt most acutely when people sense a "predominant orientation towards a total break with it." And yet, at such times, it is not the actual past that looms large but rather "chimerical constructs of the past."[4] It was out of chimerical constructs, the myths and iconic images of Russian tradition, that advertisers built reassuring linkages from the premodern past to their envisioned future of capitalist consumption.

The appeal to Russia's heritage also bridged material and spiritual cultures. As we have seen, advertisers had to counteract embedded prejudices among the intelligentsia, not just against trade but any emphasis on *byt* or the conditions of material daily existence. What better way to attempt this than by connecting commodities to emblems of "the Russian soul"? If the objection to the material world lay in its "transience without transcendence,"[5] advertising would link goods to permanence and meaning.

As cultural producers, advertisers drew from the national signifiers and myths they thought would be most evocative for the Russian population. "Myths," notes Svetlana Boym, "are sites of a shared cultural memory, of communal identification and affection."[6] This definition is laden with significance in assessing the potential for advertisers casting a cultural net. It was not just a question of triggering recognition, but emotion, a shared memory held in affection. If an advertisement could activate such a visceral response, it was no longer preaching consumption at its audience, but drawing people into an inclusive circle, identifying consumption with an imagined community of cultural meaning.[7]

The community of consumption was, like the imagined nation, not necessarily a reflection of social or historical reality. Well ahead of his time, Frenchman Ernst Renan astutely pointed out that national identity relies on selectively shared memory and meaning. It is as much about forgetting as remembering.[8] Similarly, in its own cultural constructions advertising could both simplify and complicate what it meant to be Russian. As we will see, advertisers often ignored the geographic and ethnic complexities of late imperial society, especially the multinational empire, emphasizing instead cohesive myths of Russianness. Yet they also challenged those myths, by undermining the intelligentsia's agenda of unifying Russian culture through the classical canon and in general by commodifying cultural themes that many Russians cherished as central to their national being.

In turning to the cultural motifs selected by advertisers, we see a broad range of appeals to belief in a shared national identity, from foundational myths such as Mother Russia to aspects of folk culture, mainstream Orthodoxy, historical symbols, and the classics of Russian art and literature. Associating goods with icons of culture is what advertisers now call "borrowed interest," in other words, adding value by association.[9] But the practice evolved before there was a term for it. It just made sense to draw on recognizable symbols, whether by placing a commodity against a backdrop of the Kremlin or simply appealing to patriotism. Many of advertising's cultural borrowings were actual national monuments such as the Kremlin, but in the Russian context appropriations of literary and artistic themes might also be called borrowed national monuments. The Russian term *pamiatnik* is more flexible than the English word "monument," as Lindsey Hughes points out. It includes not just physical structures, but key examples of "visual, built, or literary culture, as in such combinations as *pamiatnik kul'tury* (monument of culture) or *pamiatnik zhivopisi* (monument of painting)."[10] The Russian word *pamiatnik* is rooted in the word for memory; in its appropriation of *pamiatniki*, advertising was invoking the collective memory of Russianness.

Lest this all seem rather lofty for the profit-oriented strategies of marketing, there was also a prominent aspect of play and parody in advertising's cultural appropriations. Advertisers were acknowledging what they perceived as central elements of shared Russian identity, but they were also playing with those elements, sometimes in homage, quite often in jest. Drawing on high and low, mixing genres, and adapting the literary and artistic canon for humorous effect, advertising was no respecter of cultural boundaries. As such, it implicitly challenged the very traditions it seemed to elevate.

Using a very loose definition, these aspects of advertising might be called creations of popular culture. They were popular in that they drew threads from the widest possible fabric of cultural meanings shared across the ethnic Russian population and with those threads created new patterns and even crazy quilts. This "bricoleur effect," to borrow Stuart Hall's phrase, took "fragments and emblems . . . from one cultural discourse and reassembled [them] in another."[11] Especially in its use of literary and artistic themes, advertising was carnivalesque in the Bakhtinian sense, not simply as a reversal of "low" and "high" cultural hierarchies, but in demonstrating a disregard of the binary division altogether.[12] By commercializing the sacred (both in terms of religion and culture) and ignoring lines of genre and audience, advertising was transgressive even as it seemed to affirm tradition. Transgressing traditional boundaries, after all, is what modernity is all about.

The irony here is that most Russian advertisers were believers in the civilizing mission of consumption, as we saw in chapter 3. Few industrialists would have wanted to turn society upside down. Each individual advertisement that commercialized valued symbolic terrain was simply an attempt to reach the Russian audience through a shared Russian culture, often using humor to capture attention. The cumulative effect, however, was a disregard for traditional boundaries and a transformation of landmarks of Russian history and culture into commodities used to sell other commodities. In Hughes's phrase, advertisers were promoting "consumable Russianness."[13] Nevertheless, although advertising was implicitly and playfully transgressive, its intent was normative, seeking to inculcate market values, attract and mold consumers, and make consumption a natural part of Russian culture. In cultivating consumers, advertisers found the traditions and myths of tsarist Russia a rich field to sow.

FOLK NOSTALGIA

In one of the peculiarities of Russian urban history, the majority of the two capitals' populations at the turn of the twentieth century were peasants. Peasant migrant workers who maintained active links with the village (often leaving their families there) constituted most of the population growth in the burgeoning cities. For example, seventy-three percent of Moscow's 1.17 million population in 1902 had been born elsewhere, and sixty-seven percent were categorized as peasants. In that same year, ninety-three percent of Moscow's factory laborers were migrants and thus urbanized in culture only to varying degrees.[14] In 1910 St. Petersburg similar figures applied, with sixty-nine percent of the city's 1.9 million population classified as peasants.[15] Scholars of the prerevolutionary working class have recently emphasized the level of nostalgia among these people (mainly men, although increasingly women as well) whose lives were split between village and city.[16] While the lure of city life was undeniable, in its entertainments, freedoms, and higher incomes, the harshness of working-class conditions often rendered idyllic the memories of rural life. This effect was heightened by the tendency of villagers to treat migrant laborers as special guests when they returned home. The suppliers of essential cash from factory wages, these mostly absent husbands, fathers, and sons were to be given time to rest when they returned and excused from the hardest labor. They were also the center of attention in the village, admired for their city refinements and fashions.

Advertisers were responding to real longings, then, when they depicted idyllic visions of country life in promoting goods affordable to a workingman's pocket. For instance, the Bogdanov tobacco company's 1903 poster for Malina (raspberries) cigarettes shows a young peasant girl, plump and pretty, delighting in the berries of the season, freshly plucked (fig. 5.1).[17] The incongruities of this poster's real and imagined contexts could not be sharper: the overcrowded, dirty city, where this advertisement would have been posted, versus the open-air naturalness of the image; the unspoiled health of the peasant and her berries versus the product itself (the cheapest brand of cigarettes); the predominantly male society of the urban workers versus the alluring young women left at home. Similarly, the La Ferme company depicted dancing peasants in its poster for another cheap brand of cigarettes, Mazur (from "mazurka"), suggesting a joyful return to distant loved ones and the pleasure of village entertainments.[18] Such images offered not just rural nostalgia but a means to negotiate the pain of urbanization through the release experienced when smoking brand-name tobacco. The city caused separation, but it also provided compensations.

Increasingly popular in the late nineteenth-century countryside were the *lubki* (chapbooks) sold by peddlers. Originally illustrated with woodcuts, by the end of the century the modern commercial versions of lubki were keeping publishers busy supplying rising demand. In his study of popular literacy in Russia, Jeffrey Brooks finds that the greater mobility of late imperial society was reflected in the pervasive themes of the lubki: exotic adventures in strange lands, adaptations of the medieval heroic epics (*byliny*) with a growing tendency for the hero to be portrayed as an everyman rather than a knight—in other words, an emphasis on the individual overcoming difficulties to achieve success.[19] Tales in which the common hero must strike out alone and face all obstacles in his path challenged the

FIGURE 5.1—"Malina cigarettes from the A.N. Bogdanov tobacco factory, St. Petersburg. 20 for 5 kopeks." Source: Russian State Library poster collection, 1903.

traditional village emphasis on collective responsibility and discouragement of individuality but spoke to the rise in migrant labor (*otkhod*) which saw one-third of all adult peasant males in the Central Industrial Region forced to find work in the cities in the 1890s.[20]

Individual success stories fit the agenda of consumer culture perfectly. And if the obstacles on the journey seemed too great, consumer goods could come to the rescue. We see these themes in an advertisement for Bauer's Sanatogen tonic (fig. 5.2).[21] Two kindly warriors (bogatyry—the heroes of medieval folklore) dismount to administer the restorative to a peasant who, like many of us, has "fallen on life's path, weakened by daily cares in the struggle towards intended goals." The magnanimity and transformative powers of legendary heroes, the notion of life as a path with definite and individual goals, the motif of the journey through difficulties, all these were prominent themes of lubok literature. It is also noteworthy that this ad appeared in *Russkoe slovo*, the newspaper most widely read in the countryside, as well as enjoying the largest circulation in Moscow.[22]

In promoting their cheapest goods to peasant-workers, several leading tobacco manufacturers sought to make their advertisements appear like lubki. They did this either by naming brands after fairy tale characters such as the Snow Maiden (*Snegurochka*) or by turning their advertising into miniature adventure stories. To heighten the similarity between advertising and lubki, some companies went a step further than printing single lubok-style ads. After a certain number had been issued separately in newspapers, they would compile these ads into booklets to be sold along with the regular trade in popular literature. One such compilation from the Shapshal factory was published under the title, "The Public's Favorite Cigarette Kumir in Songs, Stories, and Sayings." In one of the fantasy stories contained in the booklet, printed complete with accompanying woodcut-style illustration, the undersea ruler "Tsar Triton" takes a fancy to the appropriately named Kumir ("idol," here in the sense of a pagan god) cigarettes (fig. 5.3).[23] The makers of Kumir, the Shapshal Brothers, must find a way to deliver their goods underwater to Triton himself. The brothers overcome all difficulties, building a submarine to reach the ocean kingdom.

This story is clearly derived from the Novgorod *byliny* centering around the medieval merchant hero, Sadko. In the folk tale Sadko so charms the sea tsar by playing his *gusli* (a stringed folk instrument) that the monarch enriches him with gold-finned fish. Later, he must pay tribute by going underwater to play for the tsar. Expecting to die, he survives beneath the sea, marries the tsar's daughter, and returns to a wealthy life back

FIGURE 5.2—"Many fall along life's path." Advertisement for Bauer's Sanatogen tonic. Source: *Russkoe slovo*, April 17, 1914.

in Novgorod.[24] In the Shapshal version, it is Kumir cigarettes that have charmed the tsar, rather than folk music. And the undersea mission is accomplished by the decidedly modern means of a submarine. However, once outside the vessel, Shapshal's modern-day Sadko finds himself similarly able to breathe in water. The motive of exploiting folk nostalgia is explicitly stated in this advertisement, which declares that "a fairy tale is a creation of the folk community (*detishche mirskoe*)!! Our people (*nash narod*) love a story!" This appeal is deceptively folkloric, however. The modern elements—submarine craft, modern industrialist in urbane top hat and tails—intrude on the original folk creation. But that fact makes it all the more reflective of the actual changes occurring in late imperial popular culture and in society as a whole. Commerce and culture, as well as city and village, increasingly overlapped.

FIGURE 5.3—"Here is your Kumir! Take your order!" Source: Shapshal Brothers advertising booklet, "Liubimitsa publiki papirosa 'Kumir' v pesniakh, skazkakh i pribautkakh," 3rd ed. (St. Petersburg: 1913), 11. "The public's favorite cigarettes, Kumir, in songs, stories, and sayings."

APPROPRIATING APPROPRIATIONS OF THE "FOLK"

As Russian society was rapidly transforming and industrializing, it was far from only the peasant-workers who were experiencing folk nostalgia in the modernizing city. Educated society also found a sense of continuity and identity in retrieving the customs and imagined values of premodern folk culture, and advertising capitalized on this trend. The discovery of the "folk" by intellectuals throughout the nineteenth century was a Europe-wide phenomenon triggered by the erosion of traditional culture in fast-changing societies. Assuming that folk culture was pure, timelessly national, and "artless" (in the sense of "genuine"), scholars gathered and preserved (and in the process often changed) folk songs, stories, and crafts as collective representations of their national traditions.[25] In Russia, as in the West, a national arts and crafts movement sought to "capture the still living creative spirit of the people and give it the opportunity to revive."[26] This movement developed to rescue native folk art, not simply from neglect but from already encroaching exploitation, as machine production was replacing traditionally handmade crafts.[27] It is one of the ironies of the period that industrial magnates have been among the major preservers of preindustrial culture; in the Russian case, the founder and sponsor of the artists' colony designed to promote the arts and crafts mission was industrialist Savva Mamontov, whose money came from the very processes of modernization that were threatening what he wished to save.

At Abramtsevo, his estate outside Moscow, Mamontov hosted and supported the Wanderers (*peredvizhniki*), the late nineteenth-century school of realist artists named after their traveling exhibitions. The Wanderers turned to specifically Russian subjects, often focusing on the plight and innate nobility of the peasantry in the wake of the disadvantageous terms of serf emancipation in 1861. Dismissing the neoclassical emphasis of the Petersburg Academy of Art, they sought "to arouse compassion and sympathy for the common man" and to preserve authentic (i.e., folk) culture.[28] Even the early twentieth-century avant-garde, who rejected the national focus of their realist predecessors as too inward, rendering Russian painting irrelevant to the international art world—even they included artists such as Natalia Goncharova and Mikhail Larionov, who found inspiration in the primitivist styles of Russian folk art. Musicians also formed part of the movement to reclaim folk culture, incorporating folk themes into their compositions, as in Rimsky-Korsakov's operas. Indeed, for nineteenth-century composers including such motifs was seen as an essential measure of their Russianness.[29] And in literature the author Tolstoy most fully embodied the belief that the peasantry represented the essence of Russian culture, to the extent that later in life he rejected the novels that had made him famous in favor of writing religious-philosophical tracts, moralistic stories, and tales for peasants.[30]

For Tolstoy and for the Wanderers, the point was to preserve traditional culture and values unsullied by the postemancipation market and industrial forces that were diluting and polluting genuine Russian traditions. Yet, the popularity of their works ironically rendered their efforts more susceptible to commercialization, as they created more accessible targets for appropriation. Advertisements that adapted the paintings of the Wanderers or the image of Tolstoy transformed the artists' intended nobility of purpose into commercial gain, undermining and subverting their original meaning. Leo Tolstoy, for instance, preferred peasant dress because it brought him closer to the culture he wished to preserve, but this fact provided the Gabai tobacco company with a multivalent image for its new brand of cheap cigarettes in 1905 (fig. 5.4).[31] Under the brand name The Glory of Russia (*Slava Rossii*), this deceptively simple ad simultaneously links the cigarettes with folk culture, the literary classics, the Russian countryside (in the leafy border as well as Tolstoy's peasant outfit), and national prestige. The author was effectively made to serve the very commercialization he despised.

Artists Ilya Repin and Viktor Vasnetsov were two of the Wanderers whose works were best known and also most appropriated by commerce.[32] Both were prominently represented in the collections of the Russian Museum in St. Petersburg, newly opened in 1898 to display the work of Russian artists to the public. Their works were familiar to the gallery-visiting population, and perhaps beyond that through reproductions, but even a worker who had never set eyes on either would be familiar with the Russian themes that were the subject of the paintings. For instance, in an example from each artist, we turn to two images that hearkened back to the heroic past: the intrepid bogatyr of medieval folk epics, and the freedom-loving Cossacks. To associate a product with a bogatyr was analogous to Anglo-American advertisers capitalizing on King Arthur's knights of the round table. And the image of the Cossack had represented an ideal of fierce independence for Russians since at least the seventeenth century—indeed many Cossacks were descended from escaped serfs and impoverished landowners who had joined the multiethnic hosts on the southern steppe.

FIGURE 5.4—"The Glory of Russia. L.N. Tolstoy. New cigarettes, 20 for 5 kopeks. S. Gabai Company." Source: *Russkoe slovo*, May 7, 1905.

The bogatyr was a favorite subject of Viktor Vasnetsov in his evocations of the Russian medieval epics, the byliny. *Bylina* (sing.) is an invented term, coined in the 1830s by folklorists who began collecting the epic songs in the nineteenth century. The word comes from the verb "to be," i.e., "something that was." The peasants themselves referred to the epics as *stariny* or *starinki,* meaning "old tales."[33] In the (perhaps rather inflated) words of Soviet folklorist Sokolov, "these ancient songs . . . [reflect] the most diverse aspects of the historical and everyday life of the Russian people"; their characters "incarnate in themselves the heroic features of the Russian people, their dreams and hopes."[34] The hero of the byliny was not the medieval prince, but his warrior knight, the bogatyr, who through strength and wit would overcome all difficulties in service to his lord. One of Vasnetsov's most famous paintings was his 1882 *Warrior at the Crossroads,* which depicts a lone bogatyr approaching a bewitched plain, strewn with the bones of the fallen. He considers the dire warnings engraved on a stone marker as he must choose which way to go:

> As for going straight
> You won't remain alive.
> There's no path
> Not for one walking across
> Nor riding across
> Nor flying across.

Hidden under the grass and thus invisible in the painting are the last two lines: "Go right—be married/Go left—be rich." Vasnetsov thus creates a single choice for his warrior: to tackle the difficulties ahead, a familiar byliny motif.[35]

Stories of success in the face of such impossible obstacles have ensured the bogatyr's persistence as a resonant image of Russian masculinity and invincibility to the present day. In a recent anthology on Russian visual culture, Helena Goscilo discusses the multiple appropriations of Vasnetsov's bogatyr paintings for commercial, satirical, and political purposes from the imperial through the post-Soviet periods.[36] Instantly recognizable for all Russians, Vasnetsov's *Warrior at the Crossroads* was first commercialized as a prerevolutionary advertising poster by the Weiner (Veinerovskii) beer factory in Astrakhan (fig. 5.5).[37] In the poster, both warrior and steed bend their heads before an oversized bottle of beer that covers the now nondescript stone marker.

FIGURE 5.5—The Weiner beer factory in Astrakhan. Source: Russian State Library poster collection.

This poster is a tongue-in-cheek homage to both folk literature and fine art and as such would resonate with workers, peasants, and educated elite alike, albeit on different levels. The choice of subject could suggest all kinds of possible interpretations. Is the beer magical, part of the mysterious landscape of the painting? Is it an eternal fixture of Russian culture, like the byliny themselves? Is drink the answer to the knight's dilemma, the only guide through the dangerous maze ahead—the modern equivalent of a bogatyr's heroism? In Goscilo's interpretation, the company's sales strategy was based "not only on the safe assumption that Russian machismo equals alcohol intake, but also on viewers' familiarity with Vasnetsov's painting." The advertisement, like the painting, "eliminates choices . . . confidently asserting that for drinking heroes, Weiner beer 'is the only way to go.'"[38]

In all its potential meanings, the manipulation of this folk image became a visual joke. Perhaps, given that the beer stands in front of a marker with such fatal warnings, there was also an element of dark humor at play, a taunt to male bravado to proceed and consume, those who dare. If the poster's humor succeeded in jolting a passerby into stopping to take a second look (and whether or not the person had seen Vasnetsov's painting the folk theme would be universally recognizable), it had achieved its aim. Humor works, in anthropologist Mary Douglas's estimation, because it attacks something formal with something informal. If a joke is a play on form, the Weiner poster rearranged the culturally sacred forms of byliny and high art into something as informal and profane as a beer promotion. It was funny because it leveled the cultural hierarchy and produced a liberating sense of "freedom from form in general."[39]

In the Ottoman tobacco company's appropriation of Ilya Repin's famous painting, the *Zaporozhe Cossacks* (*Zaporozhtsy*, 1880–1891), the very name of the company creates an inversion of meaning (fig. 5.6).[40] Repin's grand-scale original depicts the Zaporozhe Cossacks writing to the seventeenth-century Ottoman sultan, composing with great hilarity a mocking and insulting rejection of his offer to take them into his service. The irreverence and humor in the painting as a whole symbolize the Cossacks' fiercely held independence and raucous defiance of authority. On the simplest level the Ottoman poster associates the pleasure of smoking with the freedom of Cossack life. But for those familiar with Repin's painting, there is more going on here. The advertisement singles out two of Repin's most prominent figures and rearranges them with props from various parts of the composition to form an image, not of defiance, but of complicit enjoyment in smoking Ottoman's cigarettes and pipe tobacco. Who has the last laugh in this adaptation? Have the Cossacks finally been tamed by consumption? Or have they rendered the power of the Turks into an enjoyable commodity? Ultimately, the company's name is an appropriation itself, since the Ottoman factory was Russian, capitalizing on the popular association of Turks with smoking and turning Russia's oft-time foe into a source of merriment and satisfaction. Such an appropriation is all the more significant given that the Ottoman company was founded in 1882, shortly after the conclusion of the Russo-Turkish War.

FIGURE 5.6—Ottoman Tobacco Factory, St. Petersburg. Source: Russian State Library poster collection. No date.

Both of these examples show how advertisers played freely with folkloric and historical themes in art and how they incidentally spread familiarity with those works of art. For many passersby in the street, the original form of the image would be the commercialized version, rather than the painting hanging in the museum. In our own times people often become familiar with a piece of classical music through an advertising jingle or movie sound track and are then surprised to learn that it was written by Beethoven or Mozart. In his famous essay on art in the industrial age, Walter Benjamin points out that modern techniques of reproduction have rendered the work of art transportable and separable from the original. One of the consequences of mechanical reproduction is that, although the art loses its "aura" of originality, it becomes accessible to everyone instead of only the elite few.[41] But advertisers went far beyond faithful reproduction of the type seen in museum gift shops. Instead, they transformed the work of art into a parody of its original. The effect was a mischievous wink, rather than a tip of the hat to the artistic world. To encourage the enjoyment of consumption, they turned the lofty goals of the Wanderers into representational vaudeville.

While appalling for purists, these commercial manipulations were not necessarily antithetical to folklore and popular culture in general. The byliny evolved over centuries of oral tradition and survived in multiple versions. In folklore there is no single, uncontested "original." Flexibility and variability have always been the crux of folklore's longevity, and even in the industrial age of mass media, the major criteria for what constitutes folklore still apply: it is "socially relevant, based on tradition, and applied to current needs."[42] All three of these criteria apply to an example such as the Weiner beer poster. There is much to be said for folklorist Linda Dégh's argument that mass media, and commercial advertising in particular, do not spell the death of genuine folklore but rather keep it alive by popularizing it at all levels of society.[43] Thus the "magico-animist worldview" of folk tales was perpetuated in Shapshal's underwater audience with the sea tsar just as it is in a genie emerging from a bottle of cleaning fluid in television advertisements today.[44]

Dégh highlights a key paradox of consumerism. It is a component and formative part of modernity, and yet it is itself irrational since it promises that goods will solve all problems and fulfill all desires. An essential accompaniment of rationalized and efficient mass production, consumer culture nevertheless creates a world of "modern legends, modern magic, modern irrationalism."[45] It is in this sense that Russian advertising achieved the seemingly irreconcilable as regards tradition: it simultaneously perpetuated and undermined, honored and poked fun.

ORTHODOX RUSSIA

In Orthodox festivals advertising found fertile ground for magic. For the majority in prerevolutionary Russia, to be born Russian was to be born Orthodox, regardless of one's level of personal piety. While historiography has tended to essentialize contrasts between Russian Orthodoxy and Western Christianity, there is still truth to the general assertion that Orthodoxy emphasized mystical and sensory experience over intellectual theologizing.[46] In this regard its holidays and popular rituals served the dream world of consumption well. Advertisers' lively engagement with religious celebrations (and often increased expenditures for holiday publicity) demonstrated the vitality of Orthodox festivities for much of the Russian populace.

Over the last century in the West, the commercialization of religious holidays has become the lifeblood of retail industries, especially surrounding the gift-buying frenzy of Christmas. In prerevolutionary Russia, too, the popular press bulged with advertisements for trees, presents, and holiday refreshments in the days leading up to Christmas. At Easter candy firms showed peasants in national costume offering traditional Easter delicacies (fig. 5.7)[47] and bakers advertised cakes with the initials XB (Kh. V.) for *Khristos voskres* (Christ has risen) baked into them.[48]

The Orthodox calendar, however, gave even more regular opportunities than Western Christianity for religiously justified consumerism. Imagine the potential Hallmark moments if all people of the same name shared the same birthday. Orthodoxy's tradition of celebrating name-days—the day of one's sainted namesake—more than birthdays created just such opportunities for Russian merchants. Particularly popular for a flurry of ads for perfume and other feminine gift ideas was the multiple saints' day of Vera (Faith), Nadezhda (Hope), Liubov' (Love), and their mother Sofia (Wisdom) on September 17 each year.[49]

Enchantment and magical representation abounded leading up to the most important holiday in the Orthodox calendar, Easter. Department stores set up "fantastic holiday landscapes" to display their goods, and Easter prompted many firms to transfigure unrelated goods into the shape of eggs, in honor of the popular custom of egg-giving.[50] Perfume and soap were packaged in decorated eggs made of china, bronze, wood, or crystal. The cosmetics firm Brocard, for instance, fused popular and court consumption by offering a replica of one of Fabergé's most renowned pieces—the Lilies of the Valley egg, presented by Nicholas II to his mother, Maria Feodorovna, in 1898.[51] Just like a Fabergé, the Brocard egg opens to reveal surprise gift items hidden inside, in this case

FIGURE 5.7—"The Einem Company is taking orders for *kulichi* and *paskha* [Easter sweets]. A large selection of Easter gifts." Source: *Russkoe slovo*, March 19, 1909.

not diamond-studded portraits of the royal family as in the original, but eau de cologne, perfume, and soap. In a more incongruous example of gift-bearing eggs, the Gramophone Company Trading House depicts gramophone records emerging from an oversized egg to celebrate "the exultant sound of bells and the marvelous church singing of the most famous choirs in Russia" (fig. 5.8).[52]

But it was the holiday leading up to Lent, Shrovetide, that became most magical. One contemporary described her childhood memories of this holiday as a whole week without school, when "Holy Russia became the land of pancakes, of swift horses pulling sledges of every type through town and countryside, of fancy dress balls and parties and of little children tobogganing in villages and backyards on homemade chutes."[53] Folklorist Yuri Sokolov suggests that the magical aspect of this Shrovetide revelry lay in the fact that it was not just a celebration of what was presently available but also wish fulfillment through representations of joyful abundance.[54] Such an interpretation is evident in advertising for the occasion. In response to the general festivities, many advertisers splurged on half-page ads or joined forces with other firms (through the

mediation of an advertising agency) to fill a page with goods that literally danced in the pre-Lenten merriment. Figure 5.9 shows Shrovetide greetings against a Russian winter landscape peopled with sleigh riders, a woman in traditional costume, and anthropomorphized goods.[55] A pair of liquor bottles dance together like fairy-tale characters; a jar of sour cream carries its own spoon and smiles from its flat-lid face; caviar, herring, and furniture ads, resembling giant snowballs with heads, arms, and feet, jovially toast the season. Living commodities mix with religious holiday and the popular imagination in a tableau that goes beyond commodity fetishism. When goods take on a life of their own, the ordinary becomes magical and the magical purchasable. This is taking Marx's theory one step further, as Walter Benjamin described. It is not just that fascination with commodities leads consumers to ignore their use value in favor of their exchange value, but that both exchange and use value become invisible in place of "purely representational value."[56] The dream world comes to life. In Benjamin's view, the more rationalized mass production becomes, the more irrational must be the seducing of consumers to see widely available goods as uniquely desirable. Benjamin's focus on consumer culture led him to perceive in modernity a "reactivation of mythic powers" rather than Weber's "demythification" and "disenchantment" of society.[57] For Benjamin, the modern cage that binds us is made of magical dreams, not iron.

FIGURE 5.9—Composite Shrovetide advertisement for multiple companies. Source: *Russkoe slovo,* February 7, 1906.

The mingling of magic and the marketplace is of course not unique to Russia and continues in Western advertising to this day. Jackson Lears traces the phenomenon back to the days of medieval fairs, when trade was associated with "a carnival atmosphere, with fantastic and sensuous experience, perhaps even with the possibility of an almost magical self-transformation through the purchase of exotic artifacts in a fluid, anonymous social setting."[58] What better fluid, anonymous social setting than the modern city? And especially in an imperial Russian city, with its semirural working population, what better environment for advertisers to promote the easy coexistence of folkloric and religious representations with rational civilization? Like the gramophone records inside the egg, modernity could exist within tradition, and vice versa.

MOTHER RUSSIA

As old as was the identification with Orthodoxy, the shared identity of Russianness found even deeper roots in its symbol of common origin, Mother Russia. To employ such a timeless signifier in aid of modern consumption was highly effective in linking modernity to the myth of eternal Russia. The foundational mother myth goes back to pagan times as the Mother Damp Earth of Russian folk belief. Mother Earth and Mother Russia represent the coming together of the natural and historical aspects of the motherland.[59] The fruitfulness and sacredness of the land is evident in peasant customs, such as securing an oath by eating a mouthful of soil, rather than swearing on the Bible, as we might expect centuries after the acceptance of Christianity.[60] According to historian Joanna Hubbs, the peasants perceived "*Matushka Rus'* (Little Mother Russia) . . . as 'married' to *Batiushka Tsar* (Little Father Tsar)." It was the steadfastness of Mother Russia that provided the continuity behind the changing power of the tsars.[61]

Yet Mother Russia was not just relegated to peasant mythology. In many cultures the myth of motherland implies belonging to a single, natural, and timeless family. As Elena Hellberg-Hirn points out, "Its symbolic domain lies outside social hierarchies; it embraces and is embraced by the whole population, high and low, old and young. In short, the myth of the Motherland ultimately refers to the nation seen as a metaphorical family, whose time, of course, is non-historical."[62] In the hands of advertisers, Mother Russia could reach across time and social space to the community of consumers, reaffirming national identity in the process of adapting it to the modern market.

An 1884 poster for the Maria Vasilevna Sadomovaia yarn factory in Moscow richly conveys the symbolism of Mother Russia (fig. 5.10).[63] This advertisement combines several binary opposites that encompass the nation: rural/urban, male/female, young/old, motherland/fatherland, peasant craft/modern industry, and in the sweep of the figures in the foreground, the movement from tradition to modernity. The mother figure, standing atop a pedestal inscribed "Russia," is as alive as her people, flesh and blood, not stone. She wears a red silk, fur-lined traditional costume and holds to one side a shield bearing the symbol of the fatherland and imperial power, the double-headed eagle. To the other side of her stands the male, phallic symbol of industrial power, the smoking factory chimney. This triumvirate brings together ancient and modern emblems of national might with the eternal feminine presiding over all.

Even the medals awarded to the factory at the 1882 All-Russian Manufacturing Exhibition illustrate the marriage of Mother Russia and Father Tsar: Alexander III adorns the front, while Mother Russia sits on the reverse in miniature, holding a shield and orb and surrounded by the fecund imagery of Russian agriculture (a sheaf of wheat and cornucopia of fruit and vegetables), industry (machine parts), and science (the caduceus, medicine's symbol of winged, intertwined serpents).

At the feet of the central Mother Russia image, her children reflect the changing times. The left of the picture depicts a village scene, with thatched cottages, trees, and peasants dressed in rural garb. In the center women, a man, and a child sort their yarn to make their own clothes, such as the traditional embroidered apron of the woman facing us. At center right sits a man, half peasant, half worker, wearing the leather boots that

FIGURE 5.10—"The first Russian factory for knitting and embroidery yarn." Poster for Maria Vasilevna Sadomovaia yarn factory, Moscow. Source: Russian State Library poster collection, 1884.

reflect the influence of city fashions. And to the right, walking away and turning their backs on the village, we see men dressed in ready-made and increasingly dapper city clothing. Yet, even in the village scene there are signs of encroaching urban life, as the peasants surround men sporting city waistcoats and long coats—perhaps their migrant laboring kin. Behind Mother Russia, the long factory building also forms a unifying link between old and new. The mother figure blesses and supplies both, but the basic directionality in this ad is over the hill toward the future—modern industry and commodity goods.

While the female namesake and probable founder of the Sadomovaia factory might play a role in the emphasis on Mother Russia in this advertisement, plenty of male-owned businesses also employed iconic representations of feminine Russia to sell their goods. More often she was brought down from her pedestal in the form of the *krasavitsa,* or beautiful woman in traditional dress. Whether or not such images were intended to represent Mother Russia per se, they evoked a similar confluence of time-less tradition and feminine Russianness and were at least deliberate echoes of the Mother Russia trope in Russian culture.[64] For instance, in another explicit juxtaposition of modernity and tradition, a 1905 advertisement for the Joint-Stock Gramophone Company depicts a krasavitsa representing "all Moscow" as she listens to her modern gramophone player with a selec-tion of records arrayed beside her (fig. 5.11).[65] Through her window we catch a glimpse of that most ancient of Moscow views, the Kremlin. In this promotion of consumerist leisure, the caption asserts, "All Moscow listens to the gramophone," but it is a decidedly traditional Moscow enjoying the pleasures of modern entertainment. Such images suggested that consump-tion amplified rather than threatened Russian traditional identity.

An 1886 poster produced by the Chepelevetskii soap company also plac-es the Russian beauty against the traditional backdrop of golden cupolas and Kremlin walls (fig. 5.12).[66] In this image we see not only the use of tradition to endorse the products of industry but also the simultaneous processes of production and consumption. Sitting elegantly on her veran-dah, the krasavitsa implicitly endorses the giant packet of soap (which has no doubt enhanced her beauty) by resting her arm upon it, while beneath her a cutaway to the basement reveals humble workers industriously manufacturing and packaging soap bars by the crate (note that the bricks of the wall are made of soap). While most definitions of Western consumer society hinge on the increasing separation between the spheres of produc-tion and consumption beginning in the second half of the nineteenth century, advertisers often proudly combined the two, as noted in chapter 3. Certainly in Russia, the parallel developments of mass production and mass consumption rendered both aspects worthy of display.[67] Production is not hidden but deliberately exposed as part of the underpinnings of Russian power, as well as its cultural beauty. Indeed, if the viewer's eye fol-lows the flow of this composition from the basement workers through the oversized product to the woman's right hand touching the soap, through her left hand pointing across the water toward the Kremlin, the connection between industry, commodity, tradition, and power is made explicit. The inclusion of the company's medals, won in an Italian exhibition, also add international prestige to the Russian symbolism of this poster.

Representations of the krasavitsa were keenly appropriated by foreign companies, as well as Russian. The French-owned Brocard toiletries firm used her in its posters, and the Singer sewing machine company, as was its custom in its international marketing campaigns, depicted a woman in

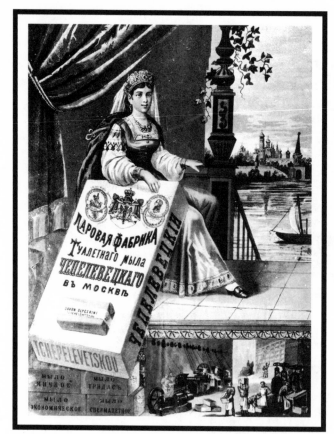

FIGURE 5.12—"Chepe-
levetskii's toilet soap steam
factory in Moscow." Source:
Russian State Library poster
collection, 1886.

national costume in posters and trademarks.[68] Both long-time manufacturers in Russia, employing Russian workers, they recognized the importance
of speaking to the cultural identity of their public. The symbolic terrain of
Russianness was open territory.

This poses the question, how could foreign enterprises present themselves as Russian, especially in a culture that tended to see modern retailing as a Western influence to begin with?[69] To consider how advertising's
projected world could paper over the actual non-Russianness of many
firms requires looking at Russian identity in more depth and thinking
about how Russians have seen and used their own history. Far more than
for any other European nation, Russian identity has for centuries been
an ongoing source of individual searching and public debate, among the
educated population, at least. To ask what is Russianness, as the editors
of a recent anthology on the subject assert, is not a question that has an
answer. "Russian identity is and has been a topic of continual argument,

of conflicting claims, competing images, contradictory criteria."[70] It is one of the largest underlying themes of imperial Russian history. The most catalytic fault line in this historical geology is the reign of Peter the Great, who forcibly redirected almost every aspect of Russian society to face the West. The reforms of Peter the Great formed a chronological divide in the mindset of Russians, on each side of which the partisans of tradition and modernity were often respectively arrayed. In the central intelligentsia debate of the nineteenth century, Peter represented the crux of the division between the conservative (if not reactionary) Slavophiles and the reform-minded Westernizers. To admirers of the modernizing, Westernizing tsar, Russia was and should be firmly a part of Europe. Western European influences were not contrary to Russianness, they felt, but rather enhanced Russia's true nature.[71] In contrast, for those who saw Peter's reforms as a betrayal, pre-Petrine customs, styles, and institutions constituted the essence of true Russianness.

Yet, even for the nostalgic Slavophiles, in one regard foreignness was essential to preserving a pure Russian society: their idealized vision of the organic, peaceful, and voluntaristic unity of the Russian people required an imported ruling dynasty to take care of the state business of governing. The story told in the Primary Chronicle, one of the major written records of medieval Kievan Rus', is of the Slavs inviting in Varangian leaders from Scandinavia to rule what would become the first Russian state. This account created a basis for the myth of voluntarily accepted foreign rule over a society that could thus itself remain unsullied by state power.[72] The embrace of foreignness in Russian rule, Richard Wortman argues, was seen as a crucial aspect of tsarist power going back to the fifteenth century. The tsars derived their aura of superiority, elevated above the common people, from their association with foreign images of political power, be they Viking, Byzantine, French, or German. This foreignness was "the animating myth of Russian monarchy" up to the late nineteenth century.[73] Thus, even the promotion of Russian tradition could incorporate elements of foreignness.

The integration of foreignness into Russianness, both at the level of traditional rule and of modernization, allowed the foreign companies manufacturing on Russian soil to capitalize on Russianness as much as their native counterparts. As noted in chapter 1, by the late nineteenth century the Russian business community was made up of a complicated mix of traditional Russian merchants, Russian entrepreneurs not born into the merchantry, descendants of European emigrants born in Russia, foreign entrepreneurs living in Russia, and international companies owned abroad but with Russian branches. Although Moscow, with its long connections to the traditional Russian merchantry, maintained a tendency toward geographical separation of Russian and foreign retail enterprises, on the advertising pages of the most popular newspapers no such divide appeared.[74] In consumer culture's vision foreign companies could advertise Russianness as successfully as any Russian manufacturer, and Russian manufacturers could advertise goods of foreign provenance as if they were samovars or vodka. Despite some nationalistic claims that Russian goods bested the international competition, the complexities of foreign entrepreneurship faded in the realm of commercial publicity.

We might take one famous example to illustrate the extent of multicultural influences in products that could still be seen as icons of Russianness. Fabergé Easter eggs are among the most well-known artifacts of Russian decorative arts. A symbol of Russian imperial culture, they are infused with French art nouveau styles, the brainchild of Carl Peter Fabergé, of French Huguenot descent and Russian birth. Fabergé eggs achieved fame because they were beloved of the Russian tsars, who had more German than Russian blood in their veins.

Foreign products, like the Slavophiles' view of political power, did not taint the Russianness of the consumer market in advertising's view. And just as foreign goods could become Russian, so could non-Russian consumers, as the ethnic diversities of the market audience were largely ignored. The culture that advertisers appropriated and projected was overwhelmingly *russkaia* (Great Russian), not *rossiisskaia* (empire-embracing Russian). The tendency to see the whole empire as Russia goes back to the sixteenth century, when Muscovy began its expansion beyond ethnically Russian territories. The gradual incorporation of contiguous lands over succeeding centuries, combined with the assimilationist policies of the tsars, created a perception among Russians that the whole empire was the Russian homeland. This vision was fostered in the art, literature, and textbooks of the nineteenth century, despite arguments from non-Russians for separate identities. Mother Russia embraced the whole land.[75] While Russian peasants continued to see the non-Russian borderlands as hostile, the forces of industrialization and consumption increasingly drew them into urban society's vision of a unified, all-Russian culture also.[76] Advertising's selective iconography played a key role in this process. As Svetlana Boym points out, "Cultural specificity is not synonymous with cultural or national purity; most cultures, including the Russian, are inventively eclectic."[77] Also "inventively eclectic" were the proponents of commodity culture in Russia, whether disseminating representations of timeless and all-encompassing Mother Russia or more historically concrete symbols of the fatherland.

FATHERLAND

As Mother Russia and Orthodoxy drew upon feminine and spiritual aspects of Russianness, certain emblems of autocracy, historical triumphs, and straightforward appeals to patriotism evoked the state-centered, masculine side of Russian identity. In the commonly perceived dichotomy between the two Russian capitals, Moscow is the heart of the nation and St. Petersburg the head. The gendered implications of this perception render the ancient capital of Moscow susceptible to associations with both Mother Russia, as the female heart, and the fatherland, as the origin of state power. Located in the geographical and metaphorical heart of old Russia, Moscow represents "the ideal model of a centralized state . . . embodied in the concentric structure of the national territory, with the city of Moscow in the centre of Russia, the Kremlin in the centre of Moscow, the Tsar . . . in the centre of the Kremlin."[78]

Also located within the Kremlin are two artifacts that provided overt links with the fatherland for advertisers marketing goods primarily for male consumers. The Tsar-cannon and the Tsar-bell symbolize the grandeur of the premodern state. The Tsar-cannon was forged in 1586 but proved too large to be fired and so stands as symbolic guard to the residence of the Muscovite tsars. The Tsar-bell was commissioned by Tsar Boris Godunov at the turn of the seventeenth century and is the largest bell in the world; it also proved too large to be played. In the cases of both these monuments, the epithet "Tsar" relates to size as well as their dedicated position at the center of Muscovite autocracy. In an ironic echo of the state they glorify, the very size of these structures undermines their practical effectiveness, but as symbols they successfully evoke power and royal determination.

By linking their products with these landmarks, manufacturers were clearly seeking to suggest the centrality and permanency of their decidedly nonessential goods. "The three sights of Moscow," claimed the Dukat tobacco company, sounding like one of the guide books that served the late-imperial growth in sightseeing, are the Tsar-bell, the Tsar-cannon and Diushes (Duchess) cigarettes (fig. 5.13).[79] Leaning against the giant cannon balls, the oversized Tsar-cigarettes become a fixture of the historic site. Adding to the existing irony of the monuments, this cigarette brand name, although royal, is French. Given the date of the advertisement—the centennial year of Napoleon's invasion—the juxtaposition is clearly intentional. Perhaps the products of the old defeated enemy are an offering at the fortress he plundered, a belated acknowledgment of Russia's superior power. The Russian capital proved the downfall of the

would-be French conqueror, and resting against the symbols of Russian military and cultural might, the French-named commodities are playfully tamed into Russianness.

More straightforwardly Russian in its appeal, and even more blatant in its appropriation of historical sites, is the Shustov liquor company's use of the Tsar-bell as a company image. How better to claim legitimacy and permanency for the widely advertised cognac brand than by adopting as its trademark the Tsar-bell, with the words "Favorite brand. Shustov's cognac" embossed in bronze traditional Russian lettering on its side (fig. 5.14)?[80] This is the equivalent of Budweiser laying claim to the Liberty Bell.

In the unlikely event that people did not grasp the association themselves, the company's advertisers occasionally made it explicit, as in the following advertising anecdote:

"At the Examination"

Teacher: Good . . . now tell us, how many famous cannons do you know?

Pupil: One.

Teacher: Which one?

Pupil: The Tsar-cannon.

Teacher: And how many famous bells do you know?

Pupil: Two.

Teacher: Which ones?

Pupil: One is the Tsar-bell . . .

Teacher: And the other?

Pupil: The Shustov bell.

If this association was ingrained in a schoolchild, then the implication was that it was part of the general culture shared by everyone. And if not, then it was to be taught, as the school setting suggests.

In appeals to patriotic consumption, the tsar most commonly appropriated was Peter the Great. Several companies incorporated Peter's equestrian statue, the Bronze Horseman, into their advertising from time

FIGURE 5.14—"Favorite brand. Shustov's cognac."
Source: *Gazeta-kopeika*, January 9, 1910.

to time. However, it was a foreign-owned firm that adopted Peter's statue as its trademark—the St. Petersburg Chemical Laboratory, a toiletries firm of French ownership. Having named their company after the capital, they naturally wanted to capture the spirit of the city. The Bronze Horseman statue (so named after Pushkin's 1833 poem) is as emblematic of St. Petersburg as St. Basil's Cathedral is of Moscow. St. Basil's—almost an exaggeration of traditional Russia's idiosyncratic architecture—symbolizes Moscow's history and connection to Orthodoxy. In contrast, the Bronze Horseman represents the new Russia of Peter's turn to the West and progress, an apt choice for a Western chemical company. In addition to representing the reformer pointing to water, his portal to western navigation, the statue itself reflects the secularizing influence of the Enlightenment. Statuary was a break with traditional Orthodoxy inasmuch as the church formerly frowned upon sculpture as sacrilegious. Catherine the Great's homage to her illustrious predecessor, unveiled in 1782, was the first such public monument in Russia.[81]

Although companies could appropriate images of Petersburg's most famous statue with impunity, attempts to lay claim to Peter's portrait as a trademark faced official opposition. In 1912 the Dukat tobacco company tried to take out a trademark for one of its cigarette brands showing the Tsar wielding an ax. The Department of Trade and Manufacturing ruled that exclusive rights could not be given "to the depiction of Emperor Peter the Great's portrait on a label."[82] The issue was not that it would be disrespectful to portray the Tsar on a packaging label but that his image could not be claimed by any one firm. Commercialization of royalty was not seen as inappropriate; rather, the Tsar-Father belonged to everyone.

In 1907 the Ottoman tobacco company capitalized on Peter's pioneering reputation in verse: "The great Peter cut a window through to Europe, / Pushing Rus' far onto a new path; / And Ottoman has opened the eyes of smokers / By putting Oko cigarettes on sale."[83] As the founding of St. Petersburg was to Russia, so Ottoman's Oko (an archaic term for "eye") was to smokers; both would allow Russians to see and experience greatness, even if in tobacco's case only as an effect of nicotine. An irony of this particular case of value by association lies in the fact that the Ottoman Turks were second only to the Swedes among Peter's enemies. In advertising's reservoir of cultural references, however, such inconvenient details did not have to matter. Advertisers selected elements of Russian history that suited their purpose, combining them into new narratives.

While Peter's appearance in the advertising pages was occasional, historical references became widespread during the years of official jubilees. Nicholas II staged several major jubilees during his reign, but the commercial world did not wait on royal promptings to profit from these occasions. In August 1912, the tsar commemorated the centenary of the major battle against the French at Borodino, but advertisers were gearing up with allusions to Napoleon's invasion already in 1910.[84] In that year, the Moscow Dukat company began advertising the arrival of its new Napoleon brand cigarettes in the rival capital of St. Petersburg. In a play on the theme of invasion, an advertisement published in St. Petersburg went as follows: "Alarm and fear / Gripped the manufacturer here, / As soon as he heard the news / That from Moscow Napoleon / Had come to take Petersburg."[85]

In the centennial year itself several more firms named new products in honor of the great event. Interestingly, the companies were both French- and Russian-owned, yet neither denigrated the French invader. This is in stark contrast to the derogatory caricatures of Napoleon that filled the popular prints at the time of the invasion.[86] In the intervening century the rise in national spirit as a result of the victory of 1812, as well as Tolstoy's nuanced depiction of both sides in *War and Peace*, allowed Russians to feel a reluctant admiration of Napoleon mixed with patriotic pride at his defeat. Thus, in 1912 the French-owned Rallet company felt no compunction about putting out a line of perfumes and eaux de cologne called Napoleon's Bouquet, which claimed to be made from "essences of the Great Emperor's favorite flowers"![87] Another French firm, Siou and Company, named its latest eau de cologne "1812" and included portraits of famous generals in each purchase (unspecified in the ad was whether these generals were Russian, French, or both).[88] Leading into 1912 the Russian cosmetics firm Ostroumov commemorated Russian patriotism and acknowledged national sacrifice with its free advertising calendars and books dedicated to the "year of horror and glory."[89]

The war of 1812 and the sacrificial burning of Moscow prompted, in many minds, the awakening of national feeling in Russia. Another watershed year that can lay claim to such influence had occurred two centuries earlier, as a national army fought off other invaders and brought an end to the Time of Troubles' chaotic interregnum by electing a new dynasty, the Romanovs. The tercentenary of that event in 1913 was the greatest jubilee of the late empire.[90] Both historic events helped forge national consciousness and as such were fruitful sites for commercial patriotic allusions.

Again perfumers were prominent in appropriating the occasion, with the same mix of Russian and French companies. Chepelevetskii announced a new Jubilee eau de cologne, and Ostroumov distributed a special book about the Romanov dynasty with any purchase of three rubles or more. The French companies were most brazen in placing themselves in the seventeenth-century context, however. Brocard put out a whole line of jubilee products, advertised in the old script and featuring the imperial symbol of the double-headed eagle (fig. 5.15).[91] In an overtly anachronistic borrowing, Rallet promoted a new line of soaps and perfumes named "Russian Boyars." The underlying company slogan went so far as to rewrite history by proclaiming: "A. Rallet and Company: the perfumer of the Russian boyars."[92] Considering that the company was not founded until 1843, the suggestion that it had supplied fragrances to the seventeenth-century Muscovite nobility was something of a stretch. Accuracy was not the issue; evoking the Russian past was.

Perhaps the most interesting use of the tercentenary theme was not for perfume but for liquor. The Ivan Smirnov liquor company (not the same as the famous Smirnov vodka firm) published an advertisement in which a boyar representative of the 1613 aristocracy faces a gentleman of

FIGURE 5.15—"Jubilee eau de cologne, soap, perfume. Brocard Company, Moscow. 1613–1913." Toiletries in honor of the Romanov tercentenary. Source: *Russkoe slovo*, May 25, 1913.

FIGURE 5.16—"Jubilee Rowanberry Liqueur. 1613–1913. Ivan Smirnov and Sons." Liqueur in honor of the Romanov tercentenary. Source: *Russkoe slovo*, March 3, 1913.

1913 across a bottle of Jubilee Rowanberry Liqueur (fig. 5.16).[93] The elite representatives of Muscovite and modern Russian society join each other in a toast across the centuries. Their difference demonstrates progress, and yet their shared gaze represents an essential Russianness that remains unchanged in their mutual approval. No matter that the actual boyar of 1613 would have stared in unrecognizing disbelief at his modern descendant, here tradition and modernity are explicitly united in the pleasure of consumption.

The elitist appeal of this advertisement is additionally intriguing in light of ongoing public discourse about the meaning of the Romanovs' 1613 election. The selection of the new dynasty by representatives of the people in the seventeenth-century *zemskii sobor* (assembly of the land) was seen by moderate opinion in 1913 as a national rather than elite or divine mandate and as a model for the alliance of state and society.[94] In official publications and the mind of Nicholas II, however, 1613 represented the divine sanctioning of a monarchy not apart from but embodying the nation.[95] Nicholas felt more in tune with the seventeenth century than the twentieth, and he commissioned a commemorative album of the tercentenary that opens with portraits of the royal couple facing their Muscovite counterparts[96]—unintentionally echoing Smirnov's aristocratic juxtaposition across time.

Of course, it did not require major historical events to evoke patriotic consumption. It could be as simple as choosing a brand name, such as the Russia (*Rossiia*) bicycle of the Moscow Leitner company, or Our Glory cigarettes from the Shaposhnikov firm.[97] "Our Glory" is conveniently left undefined. It might apply to the product itself, or to the nation as a whole, but the implication was to tie one to the other in an inclusive suggestion of shared greatness. A more heavy-handed appeal to Russianness suggested that purchase of any other brand than the one advertised was unpatriotic. The Bogdanov tobacco company in early 1905 exhorted "you Russian people . . . you Moscow citizens" not to be captivated by French names but rather to smoke "our Russian cigarette—Strekoza (Dragonfly)." "Whoever smokes this native one, / Believe me, will not repent it."[98] This heightened exclusiveness might have been a result of the country being at war at the time, even if with Japan, not France.

Differentiation between Russian and foreign consumption was a recourse of the Shustov cognac campaign from time to time, perhaps to counteract the fact that cognac is a French term for a French drink, although this brand was made in Russia. In a poem entitled "Nations and Their Drinks," the Shustov company defined national character by tastes in consumption, proclaiming that, although a Spaniard might drink Malaga wine to "feel courage, / like a true patriot," and a German drinks only beer, the "good Russian / drinks Shustov cognac!"[99] Other nationalities' preferences were right and proper for them, but Russians should be Russians.

If Russian national character could absorb the contradiction of being defined by a French drink, it was also flexible enough to incorporate many other oppositions. We can look again to a Shustov poem describing the Russian man, entitled "Portrait" (translated here in part):[100]

> There he is, all as painted,
> The Russian man,
> Sometimes calm, sometimes agitated
> In our twentieth century.
> Well-proportioned figure and light brown hair,
> And shoulders broad as a barrel . . .
> Voice powerful as a trumpet,
> Keen wit in his eyes.
> Sharp-minded, simple-hearted,
> In love with his native land,
> Hardly indifferent either
> To progress he.
> To live in a civilized way, differently,
> Attracts him all the time,
> He is streets ahead
> Of any "European"!
> . . . .

He is passionately hospitable
(He learned it from his ancestors),
He loves to cram his table
Full of appetizers.
And as a sign of kindness,
He always lovingly offers
To his guests, of course,
Shustov's cognac.

The poem demonstrates the tension between native character (idealized as a combination of strength, wit, warmth, and the valuing of ancestral traditions) and adaptability to change—even pioneering progress. Strong as a bogatyr, simple-hearted and embodying the ancestral quality of hospitality, this paragon is yet more modern than any "European"—the quotation marks suggesting pompously self-styled Russian Europeans, perhaps. This portrait manages to combine the xenophobia of the Slavophiles with the open-mindedness of the Westernizers. The Russianness of this true Russian (who also knew no laziness and delighted in the arts) lay as much in his love of progress as of tradition, in his choice of liquor as in his love for the fatherland. Indeed, the latter two were practically equated. The messages of consumption confirmed and embraced the myths of Russianness, even as they drew Russians into the modern world of commodity culture.

LITERARY RUSSIA

One of the most prominent myths of Russianness, writes Boym, is "the myth of the national unity of Russian culture based exclusively on the heritage of the great literary classics" of the nineteenth and twentieth centuries.[101] The literary canon formed one of the prime targets for commercial appropriation. From the golden age of Russian literature in the first half of the nineteenth century, national identity became more and more linked with classic authors such as Pushkin, Gogol', and Lermontov, rather than the earlier primacy of church and tsar. Jeffrey Brooks traces this development to literary critic Vissarion Belinskii, but the movement was later heightened by the broader postemancipation agenda of the intelligentsia to spread their values among the common people through the literary classics.[102] For many in the intelligentsia, used to seeing themselves as the creators of Russian culture as well as the moral conscience of the nation, the rapid rise in mass-produced commercial print culture from the 1860s on was tainting the national heritage with market values and literary hackwork. Among the urban population especially, mass-circulation newspapers carried serialized potboilers full of adventure and intrigue, and successful publishers catered to the popular taste for detective novels and romantic melodrama.[103] As Brooks points out, even those liberal members of the intelligentsia who supported the rise in commercial, popular literature as a necessary phase in the breakdown of "backward" peasant culture, assumed that good books would soon follow, to "integrate the common people into a unified high culture."[104] Thus they promoted the movement to include favored writers in "the national pantheon of Russian national heroes with generals, tsars, and church fathers."[105]

What began as an intelligentsia mission became official state policy by the turn of the century. The centenary of Pushkin's birth in 1899 was declared a national holiday, probably by the tsar himself, and at the beginning of the new century the Holy Synod told parish teachers to honor Gogol' and the poet Zhukovskii by combining readings of their works with liturgies, hymns, and patriotic songs.[106] By the late nineteenth century, commercial publishers such as A.S. Suvorin were producing inexpensive editions of the classics in the millions for mass distribution.[107] To intelligentsia dismay, the literary canon also "circulated in bowdlerized chapbook editions with flashy new titles and bright covers," and peddlers hawked verses by classical poets such as Nekrasov in lubok-style prints and popular songbooks.[108] Manufacturers jumped on the bandwagon too, with packaging featuring famous Russian authors and composers, such as V.I. Asmolov and Company's 1903 series of packets for their Glory of Russia cigarettes (fig. 5.17).[109] No doubt the manufacturers hoped that consumers would try to collect the whole set, like present-day baseball cards.

If we combine the increasing accessibility of the classics with the growth in literacy in the late imperial period, it is clear that Russian literature was no longer a preserve of the elite.[110] Even the illiterate might absorb famous passages of Pushkin or Gogol', given the fact that schoolteachers, priests, and literate fellow villagers read them aloud. Advertising capitalized on this accessibility of Russian literature with frequency, commercial license, and often humor. As Lawrence Levine points out, one cannot successfully parody what is not familiar.[111]

A glance at the pages of such newspapers as *Gazeta-kopeika*, the penny gazette of St. Petersburg, shows also that the boulevard press promoted the classics not just by advertising cheap editions of books but also by printing commercial advertising's own types of bowdlerization. Since the readers of *Gazeta-kopeika* were the working poor and semiliterate, there was clearly an expectation that some literary references were so widespread as to generate recognition among the broadest spectrum of the urban popula-

ISSN>

Apolog

FIGURE 5.17—"The Glory of Russia. V.I. Asmolov and Company in Rostov-on-Don, 1903." Uncut sheet of cigarette packet designs. Top row: Zhukovskii, Glinka, Krylov. Second row: Derzhavin, Goncharov, Nekrasov. Bottom row: Lermontov, Griboedov, Gogol'. Source: State Historical Museum Archive.

tion. Indeed, one does not have to have read a text directly for certain passages to strike a chord. In our own culture "to be, or not to be" suggests Shakespeare even to those who have not read *Hamlet*. Similarly, among the best-known lines in Russian literature are these from Pushkin's "Bronze Horseman," about St. Petersburg, the creation of Peter the Great:

> I love you, Peter's creation,
> I love your stern, harmonious aspect,
> The majestic flow of the Neva,
> Her granite banks,
> The iron tracery of your railings,
> The transparent twilight and the moonless gleam
> Of your pensive nights.[112]

A 1912 advertisement for a St. Petersburg clothing warehouse was intended to draw a wry smile of recognition (or perhaps a cringe):

> I love you, Peter's creation!
> I love your stern, harmonious aspect,
> I love that at house number eight,
> On Panteleimonskaia Street there is a warehouse!!
> Haberdashery, cloth
> For women, men and children,
> In everything there the world of culture reigns,
> In everything—believe it, really and truly!!![113]

This advertisement seems designed to convince the better off that it was not beneath them to shop at a warehouse, especially one that specifically offered merchandise "for poor as well as rich" (*dlia bednykh i dlia bar*), because, as the imitation of Pushkin proves, "there the world of culture reigns." That assertion is somewhat belied, however, by the exclamatory insistence of "believe it, really and truly!!!"

More adept at literary manipulation were the advertisers for the Shustov liquor company.[114] The series of advertisements for Shustov cognac constituted one of the most vigorous marketing campaigns in the prerevolutionary press. In attempting to sell a single product to a broad audience, the company deliberately turned advertising into popular entertainment, drawing from as great a diversity of genres as newsprint would allow. The campaign ran for years in many major newspapers but never more intensively and creatively than from late 1910 through 1912 in *Gazeta-kopeika*, where scarcely a day went by without a new cognac advertisement. It is a rare ad campaign even in our own hypercommercial culture that brings out a new message every day. Usually disguised as noncommercial contributions to the newspaper, these advertisements carried no illustrations but appeared in various forms: verse, story, advice column, riddle, fairy tale, bylina, and comical or historical anecdote.

Many of the poems and stories in the Shustov campaign were based on classic works, references which, for the poorly educated readers of *Gazeta-kopeika*, were often explained in subtitles such as "An Imitation of Lermontov," "A Parody of Chekhov," or "A Free Imitation of Nekrasov." Such helpful hints suggest that the Shustov company intended to join the intelligentsia crusade to disseminate a unifying Russian culture, and the ads contained enough of the original works to achieve such a goal. Yet they also carried deliberate mischief. Humorous in tone, these advertisements were far more parody than homage, adjusted as they invariably were to include a punch line about Shustov's cognac. This campaign mocked the very process of "enlightenment" that it seemed to foster.

Shustov's advertisements showed no compunction about playing fast and loose with literary references, as in one of their cleverest ads, a conflation of two of the most famous satirical short stories by Nikolai Gogol', "The Nose" (1836) and "The Overcoat" (1842). Gogol' had become one of the most popularized classic writers through the dissemination not just of his stories but also of his biography. The intelligentsia saw publishing biographies as a means of spreading the classics by tapping into the common people's familiarity with saints' lives (*zhitie*). "Through the process of popularization," Stephen Moeller-Sally notes, "Gogol' became a freely appropriable self-validating cultural symbol."[115] His stories were also "freely appropriable" for commercial gain.

In the original version of "The Nose," the socially ambitious and vain Collegiate Assessor, Kovalev, wakes up one morning to find his nose missing and ends up chasing it around St. Petersburg, amazed to see it posing in full dress uniform as a higher ranking bureaucrat than himself. In "The Overcoat," the impoverished clerk, Akaky Akakevich, scrimps and saves for months to replace his threadbare overcoat, only to have the prized possession stolen from him by thieves—a blow that leads to his insanity and death. In the Shustov amalgamation, entitled "The Nose," the hero is Collegiate Assessor Akaky Akakevich, who gets up one morning to find the button of his overcoat missing.[116] In a direct paraphrase of Gogol"s passage in which Kovalev discovers his flat face, the Shustov mix-and-match character feels his coat, "but the place was completely smooth and flat, there wasn't even a trace of threads: the button had disappeared without a trace." On his way to work, the Collegiate Assessor recognizes and accosts his button, which is walking down the street as an old woman. Just as Gogol"s story "The Nose" ends with the bumbling narrator waffling about the improbability of such an occurrence as an independently mobile nose being lost and found, the narrator of the

Shustov version also breaks into the story to explain the appearance of a walking button by declaring that the reader would not have forgiven another anthropomorphic nose, even if Gogol' himself had risen from the grave. What has all this to do with cognac? In good absurdist style, absolutely nothing, until the last, throwaway line. At the end of Gogol''s story, the narrator finally decides that such things as walking, talking noses do happen—"seldom, but they do." Again paralleling the original story's structure, the Shustov narrator similarly injects a suggestion of fact as he states that he may have just seen a giant tuft of hair carrying a bottle of Shustov's cognac down the street. This last is the only mention of the product in the entire, lengthy parody. Late twentieth-century advertisers did not invent the practice of selling goods through irrelevant association of product and message!

Mikhail Lermontov's poetry was a favorite target of Shustov's literary machinations. For instance, the first verse of Lermontov's poem, "How Dreary, How Sad" ("*I skuchno, i grustno*," 1840), about the futility of life and love, was reproduced verbatim in an advertisement of 1911. However, Lermontov's closing lines, in which he decides existence is an empty, stupid joke, became "And if fate hadn't given us Shustov's cognac . . . life would have been an empty and stupid joke."[117] In "The Rock" ("*Utes*," 1841), Lermontov's evocation of loneliness, a golden cloud settles for the night on a desert rock, only to fly away across the sky in the morning, leaving just a trace of moisture in a crevice of the old rock, which stands crying, alone again in the desert. With commercial rather than poetic license, the image is transformed into a lonely shot glass, standing alone in an empty restaurant and dreaming wistfully of the golden youth who had filled it with Shustov's cognac the night before.[118] This is imitation at the expense, rather than in flattery, of the original. The shot glass image would, of course, be more immediate than the metaphor of a weeping rock to the readers of *Gazeta-kopeika*; but perhaps the intention goes further, to a deliberate mocking of elite pretensions for the enjoyment of a down-to-earth, working-class audience. Such an interpretation would certainly be in tune with the taste for social satire in the popular entertainment of the day and a natural reaction to the condescension of the upper classes.[119] Shustov's advertisements contain the central prerequisite of jokes: they are potentially subversive in that they carry an "element of challenge" to the social and cultural hierarchy.[120]

If we broaden the definition of the cultural canon to include art for a moment, mockery of the educated elite seems at first to be clearly intended in a Shustov anecdote entitled "Modern Connoisseurs," in which two friends "from good society" are visiting the art museum and assessing Karl

Briullov's famous painting *The Last Day of Pompeii* (1833). As they survey the depiction of people dying and a grand building crumbling under volcanic destruction, we eavesdrop on their conversation:

> "How do you like it?" asked one.
>
> "There was a big shot living there, but . . . I don't see Shustov's cognac," answered the other.
>
> "Apart from that, although the figures are good, still it's difficult to say which one is Pompeii."
>
> "And I'll tell you what's surprising to me," said the other, "the city is in flames, and there isn't a single fire pump!"[121]

If we take at face value that these "connoisseurs" are from "good society" and still do not know that the Pompeii in question is a place, not a person, then the joke is on the elite's appreciation of their own culture. However, taking this anecdote as a whole, it is clear that the description of the characters is an ironic and mocking reference to those members of the lower classes who aspired to an identification with "high" culture—the worker intelligentsia. A significant minority of the urban labor force, these largely self-educated workers were often the target of hostile ridicule from their less intellectual peers.[122] The Shustov characters betray their humble roots both in their language—the term "big shot" (*tuz*) is a slang expression, unlikely to be used by actual members of "big shot" society to describe their peers—and in the focus of their concerns: the preoccupation with fire pumps suggests a pragmatic literalism (well-grounded in the vulnerability of villages to fire), rather than an educated artistic sensibility. This time the joke is on the elitist pretensions among the working-class audience's own ranks. Nevertheless, the selling point surreptitiously included is a dig at the rich: the suggestion that the high life cannot be all that high if it doesn't include Shustov's cognac.[123]

The Shustov campaign did not simply parody the Russian cultural canon and the pretensions of high art's admirers. The overall effect of the campaign was to blur the perceived lines between "high" and "low" culture by including the whole range of genres in a grab bag of accessible references. In her argument against the usual "divorce" of advertising from other cultural productions, Jennifer Wicke finds that early Western advertising "plucked at will" along "the literary spectrum from Mother Goose to Shakespeare," often without regard to target audience.[124] Described by Wicke as a primarily nineteenth-century phenomenon in the West, the equivalent range of fairy tales to Pushkin offered prime pickings for literary borrowings in Russia well into the twentieth century.

The Shustov campaign stretched the spectrum further, however, to include most of the categories of Russianness addressed in this chapter: sentimental evocations of motherland, images of the fatherland, traditional folk tales, the old chronicles and imitations of the classics—all with the incorporation of the inevitable cognac to give an irreverent twist to hallowed themes. Even the mother's lullaby was fair game. In a 1911 ad a mother coos her baby to sleep, wondering about his future, and concluding that he will grow up to drink Shustov's cognac, "according to the general example."[125] Jokes about children whose understanding of the world was colored by their father's love of liquor, as when a teacher asks a pupil to name Russia's liquid measures and receives the answer "by the shot glass," were mixed in with Nekrasov poems and Gogolian tales.[126] Lyrical odes to poetic inspiration (ultimately attributable to a stiff drink), gems of "practical advice" (including the necessity of cognac for an enjoyable life), riddles to which the answer was always Shustov ultimately allowed no difference between night club jokes and Lermontov's poetry. They all served the same commercial purpose.

This leveling process was hardly the dissemination of a unified Russian culture that the guardians of elite standards had in mind. And indeed its implications went beyond their nightmare of the classics drowning in a sea of pulp fiction. Advertisers were not simply adding to the volume of commercialized print. By adapting the classics and blending them with jokes and verses, they were creating a new cultural hybrid. Shustov's anecdotes and poems, and all the other advertisements that appropriated literary and artistic themes, helped to make advertising a genre in its own right—a textual and iconic vaudeville, the parodic canon of consumer culture, resting heavily on the spectrum of Russian culture but producing its own peculiar blend of irreverence and homage, mimicry and originality, entertainment and salesmanship.

CONCLUSION

Despite the mission of cultural unity promoted by an educated population, the traditional boundaries of late imperial Russian culture and society were stretching almost beyond recognition under the forces of commercial and industrial development, as well as changing tastes. This period saw an increasing diversity of cultural interests across society, with many members of the lower classes aspiring to high culture and members of the upper classes "slumming" in the burlesque houses. All this led to "a jumble of tastes and a proliferation of genres."[127] Advertising facilitated this mixing and also formed one of the new genres. By manipulating the icons of Russianness, advertisers helped tilt the foundations of traditional culture in favor of the modern market. In their adaptations of permanence, they promoted flux.

The reflections of Russian culture and society in the advertising pages of the late imperial press were both simplified and distorted. Advertising is not a mirror, unless (as Jackson Lears puts it) one of the fun-house variety.[128] Russianness was largely stripped of the complications of multiethnic empire, but it easily assimilated multinational commerce; seventeenth-century boyars coexisted with twentieth-century consumers in shared toasts; modern manufacturers became characters in medieval folk tales; commodities came alive and joined in Shrovetide festivities. Yet it was precisely this adaptability, this mixing of cultural references, that made Russian advertising peculiarly Russian. Shuffling symbols of national identity and commodities with purposeful abandon, advertisers could draw any card from their pack of goods to demonstrate the cultural rootedness of consumption. Like magicians, they could pull rabbits from hats—or in this case, gramophone records from Orthodox Easter eggs—but in the process they maintained the framework of tradition to contain the experience of modern consumer culture. They became creators of a folklore of the marketplace, proving the vitality and relevance of the national culture even as they reinvented it to serve commercial ends.

Russian advertisers borrowed from the West, but more importantly they rifled through their own cultural treasure house to create an imaginative collage that would not have worked anywhere else. Because of this creativity, advertising was more than an arm of commerce; it became a formative part of the shifting nature of what it meant to live in modernizing society, as a Russian, a man, woman, worker, or housewife, but most of all, as a consumer. In promoting the new identity of consumer, advertising helped to define—and to challenge—the meanings of individual, community, class, gender, and nationhood in the last decades of tsarist rule.

APPENDIX A

ADVERTISING CONTENT IN *PETERBURGSKAIA GAZETA*
(PUBLISHED FROM 1867 TO 1917)

The great variety of advertisements makes categorization difficult and somewhat artificial. The table is thus intended as an indication of trends over time and not as an exhaustive analysis of a newspaper's daily advertising content. The size and location of advertisements, features that cannot be included in a table such as this, were as important as the number of advertisements, from the points of view of both the newspaper and the advertisers.

The table categories are defined as follows:

Retail traders includes all merchants selling goods not produced by themselves from established business premises. Those manufacturers who also operated shops are not included in the retail section.

Small businesses represents perhaps the most varied category, including many kinds of services, from furniture movers and exterminators to piano tuners. It comprises agencies (employment, advertising) and law offices, as well as regular business conducted from the advertiser's home (anything from teaching to fortune-telling).

Manufacturers includes those who produced their own goods for sale. Toiletries and tobacco are included in the total but also listed separately due to their emphasis in this study.

Health is divided into commercial products such as patent medicines and nutritional items and listings of private doctors and clinics of all specialties.

Recreation and public events includes theater, cinema, restaurants, lectures, and all kinds of popular entertainment.

Publishers includes book and periodical publishers. Bookshops, unless they belonged specifically to one publisher, are listed under retailers.

Official includes announcements of governmental or official institutions, as well as the obligatory annual accounts of corporations and banks.

Travel includes recreational and passenger travel (foreign hotels and steamship companies) but not commercial shipping companies.

Artisans includes printers, tailors, and others who plied a craft.

Financial includes banks, credit societies, and insurance companies.

Education refers to institutions of learning offering complete courses of study, i.e., not including home tutoring.

Classified includes obituaries as well as all other personal notices of an occasional nature—e.g., personal belongings for sale, jobs wanted.

TABLE A.1 ——**Average number of advertisements in** *Peterburgskaia gazeta,* **1867–1912**

	1867	1872	1877	1882	1887	1892	1897	1903	1907	1912
Retail traders	3	4	4.5	13	17.5	18	18.5	19.5	18.5	33
Small businesses	1	1	2	7	10	10	10.5	13.5	17	50
Manufacturers (total)	0	.5	1	5.5	10	7	8	10.5	8	14.5
Manufacturers (toiletries)	0	0	.5	1	1.5	2	2	3.5	3.5	4
Manufacturers (tobacco)	0	0	0	2	2.5	1.5	2	2	1	1.5
Health (commercial)	.5	.5	3.5	2.5	1	.5	.5	1	2	4
Health (drs./clinics)	.5	0	2.5	11.5	16.5	12	30.5	51	63	87
Recreation & public events	1	1	2	5.5	6	9	12	14.5	19	18.5
Publishers	1.5	2	2	3	2.5	2.5	2.5	2.5	1.5	1.5
Official	.5	.5	0	1	1.5	1.5	1.5	1.5	1	3
Travel	.5	0	0	0	.5	.5	.5	.5	1	2.5
Artisans	.5	.5	0	.5	1.5	1	1	2.5	2	5
Financial	0	0	.5	.5	4	1.5	1.5	2	.5	1
Education	0	0	0	2.5	1.5	2	1.5	3.5	9	12
Classified	4	4.5	6.5	59	134	116	104	171	136	241
Other	0	0	0	.5	.5	0	.5	1	.5	1
Total	13	14.5	24.5	112	207	181.5	193	294.5	279	474

Note—Figures are daily averages taken from two weeks' worth of issues every five years when possible (issues for 1902 were under restoration) and rounded to the nearest half point. The weeks were selected from the first half of November and May to allow for seasonal differences. The heaviest advertising times were usually in December and March or April, coinciding with Christmas/New Year and Easter; the slowest time tended to be midsummer. I have avoided these months precisely because they were not typical. There were often also daily variations in the amount and type of advertising (e.g., more on Sundays, more entertainment advertisements on weekends), which is why a full week's issues were counted at a time.

APPENDIX B

NEWSPAPER STATISTICS

TABLE B.1———*Russkie vedomosti* income

Year	Subscription income	Retail sales	Advertising income	Misc. income	Total income	% Income from advertising
1883[1]	118,067	5,946[4]	58,160	8,691	190,864	30
1884	116,844	2,123	51,423	4,074	174,464	29
1885	150,688	2,090	63,946	6,134	222,858	29
1886	131,352	3,247[5]	67,976	27,910	230,485	29
1887	167,353	5,725	74,263	8,583	255,924	29
1888	192,870	9,995	88,454	6,555	297,874	30
1889	191,680	8,619	99,948	8,465	308,712	32
1890	201,109	5,620	103,682	10,691	321,102	32
1891	204,820	6,230	117,250	10,485	338,785	35
1892	213,817	7,246	129,357	9,010	359,430	36
1893	205,546	8,801	129,424	7,199	350,970	37
1894	213,308	4,935[6]	137,239	7,306	362,788	38
1895	221,409	3,279[7]	141,421	8,729	374,838	38
1896	226,203	3,935[8]	145,870	9,456	385,464	38
1897	227,479	7,547	147,506	12,941	395,473	37
1898[2]	219,691	10, 746	136,837	11,962	379,236	36
1899	232,780	11,271	160,231	14,998	419,280	38
1900	212,013	8,321	183,807	14,905	419,046	44
1901	217,914	11,044	181,655	15,382	425,995	43
1902	222,607	11,207	180,482	15,217	429,513	42
1903	231,154	7,262[9]	176,436	10,402	425,254	42
1904	329,309	50,319	172,050	13,807	565,485	30
1905[3]	444,661	66,643	156,513	20,778	688,595	28
1906	360,990	150,618	270,113	22,447	804,168	36
1907	309,160	108,654	326,513	20,678	765,005	43
1908	249,193	93,593	311,180	19,476	673,442	46
1909	220,366	85,389	277,267	18,250	601,272	46
1910	205,184	81,227	275,267	14,802	576,480	48
1911	202,434	84,555	267,215	15,612	569,816	47
1912	188,647	78,955	260,808	26,191	554,601	47

Source—RGALI, f. 1701, op. 2, d. 7, ll. 24–25. Figures are rounded to the nearest ruble and therefore may not add up exactly to the totals. Percentages are also rounded. Note that the sharp fall in relative weight of advertising income in 1904 and 1905 is explained less by a drop in advertising than by the great increase in sales (almost doubling subscription income between 1903 and 1905), which was due to public interest in the events of war and revolution. Circulation for 1905 was even higher than it appears, since the paper lost a month's publication due to the strikes that brought much of Russia to a standstill during that revolutionary year.

Notes—

1. From November 16, 1882, *i.e.*, 13 1/2 months.
2. Covers only ten months.
3. Minus one month due to strikes.
4. No street sales from June 11 to August 15.
5. No street sales from September 8 to December 4.
6. No street sales from October 30 to December 31.
7. No street sales January 1–28 and December 23–31.
8. No street sales from January 1 to May 10.
9. No street sales from March 2 to September 2.

TABLE B.2 ——*Russkoe slovo* income

Year	Advertising income	General expenses	Circulation on December 31	% of expenses paid by advertising
1900	49,700	208,000	28,400	24
1901	59,300	243,700	30,600	24
1902	72,700	274,300	30,100	27
1903	117,500	379,500	43,700	31
1904	199,700	843,900	117,000	24
1905	257,600	929,400	157,700	28
1906	344,700	959,100	98,100	36
1907	516,200	1,242,900	126,500	42
1908	679,300	1,442,800	117,500	47
1909	782,400	1,646,600	133,700	48
1910	897,800	1,874,900	156,000	48
1911	1,083,300	2,309,400	187,800	47
1912	1,236,800	2,648,900	266,600	47
1913	1,407,700	3,338,900	262,800	42
1914[1]	1,250,500	4,289,600	569,000	29

Source—ORRGB, f. 259, p. 4, e. kh. 1, l. 5. It is clear from their evenness that these figures should be taken as approximate. Other charts in the same collection also showed some discrepancies. However, the differences were not extreme, and this information can therefore still give a fair impression of financial developments.

Note—1. The sharp decline in percentage of expenses paid by advertising in 1914 reflects the onset of a decline in advertising quantity everywhere as war began to affect trade.

TABLE B.3 ——*Rech'* income

Year	Subscription income	Street sales	Advertising income	Misc. income	Total	% income from advertising
1908			84,125			
1909	162,200	205,560	109,554	2,150	479,464	23
1910			143,757			
1911	182,235	249,752	165,322	27,961	625,270	26
1912	176,979	214,544	199,654	46,805	637,982	31
1913	161,307	213,662	233,999	46,839	655,807	36
1914[1]	103,783	154,919	127,193	28,732	414,627	31

Source—RGALI, f. 1666, op. 1, d. 11, reel 1. Figures are rounded to the nearest ruble or percent.

Note—1. First eight months only.

APPENDIX C

TOILETRIES INDUSTRY ADVERTISING ACCOUNTS

TABLE C.1 ——A.M. Ostroumov advertising expenditures

Year	Sales	Net profit	Advertising expenditure	Advertising as % of sales	profit
1901	660,759	37,041	20,806	3.1	56.2
1902	609,505	28,641	27,502	4.5	96.0
1903	736,846	31,449			
1906	1,174,088	68,783	38,261	3.3	55.6
1913	2,006,440	67,343	50,989	2.5	75.7

Source—TsGIA g. Moskvy, f. 1828, op. 1, dd. 1, 3, 7. Figures for 1913 are from RGIA, f. 23, op. 28, d. 1554. All monetary amounts are rounded to the nearest ruble. Percentages are given to the nearest decimal point.

TABLE C.2 ——Brocard advertising expenditures

Year	Sales	Net profit	Advertising expenditure	Advertising as % of sales	profit
1893–94			39,351		
1901–02		191,315	114,598		59.9
1906–07	2,686,908	243,089			
1912–13	4,924,946	314,706	154,775	3.14	49.2

Source—TsGIA g. Moskvy, f. 51, op. 10, d. 169, 171; f. 429, op. 1, dd. 4, 9; f. 429, op. 2, dd. 1, 4, 6, 7, 8. Brocard's fiscal year began in May. Advertising figures for the years 1893–94 and 1901–02 were totalled from monthly itemized accounts under the headings of "Publications" and "Posters and price lists." TsGIA g. Moskvy, f. 429, op. 1, dd. 4, 9.

TABLE C.3 ——S. I. Chepelevetskii and Sons advertising expenditures

Year	Sales	Net profit	Advertising expenditure	Advertising as % of sales	profit
1913	1,256,919	93,283	41,159	3.3	44.1
1914	1,115,558	36,416	29,900	2.7	82.1

Source—TsGIA g. Moskvy, f. 51, op. 10, dd. 1289, 1290; RGIA, f. 23, op. 28, d. 2413. Clearly, the accounts for 1914 were affected by the outbreak of war.

NOTES

BE   Entsiklopedicheskii slovar' Brokgauza-Efrona (Brockhaus and Efron Encyclopedic Dictionary)

BSE   Bol'shaia Sovetskaia Entsiklopediia (Great Soviet Encyclopedia)

d.   delo (file)

e. kh.   edinitsa khraneniia (storage unit)

f.   fond (collection)

g. (plural gg.)   god (year, years)

GIM   Gosudarstvennyi istoricheskii muzei (State Historical Museum)

GTsTM   Gosudarstvennyi tsentral'nyi teatral'nyi muzei im. A.A. Bakhrushina (A. Bakhrushin Central State Theater Museum)

l. (plural ll.)   list(y) (page, pages)

MERSH   Modern Encyclopedia of Russian and Soviet History

ob.   oborotnaia storona (verso)

op.   opis' (inventory)

ORRGB   Otdel rukopisei Rossiiskoi gosudarstvennoi biblioteki (Manuscript division of the Russian State Library)

pk.   papka (carton)

PSZ   Polnoe sobranie zakonov Rossiiskoi imperii (Complete collection of the laws of the Russian empire)

RGIA   Rossiiskii gosudarstvennyi istoricheskii arkhiv (Russian State Historical Archive)

RGALI   Rossiiskii gosudarstvennyi arkhiv literatury i iskusstva (Russian State Archive of Literature and Art)

TsGIA g. Moskvy   Tsentral'nyi gosudarstvennyi istoricheskii arkhiv goroda Moskvy (Central State Historical Archive of the city of Moscow)

TsGIA SPb   Tsentral'nyi gosudarstvennyi istoricheskii arkhiv Sankt-Peterburga (Central State Historical Archive of St. Petersburg)

INTRODUCTION

1. On Soviet advertising, see Cox, "All This Can Be Yours!" and "'NEP Without Nepmen!'"; and Marjorie Louise Hilton, "Commercial Cultures."

2. The cultural experience of modernity in Russia has been the focus of an increasing number of works over the last three decades. Some important examples are Brooks, *When Russia Learned to Read*; Clowes, Kassow, and West, *Between Tsar and People*; Engelstein, *Keys to Happiness*; Frank and Steinberg, *Cultures in Flux*; Clark, *Petersburg*; Hoffmann and Kotsonis, *Russian Modernity*; Steinberg, *Proletarian Imagination*; and McReynolds, *Russia at Play*.

3. Cooper, *Colonialism in Question*. Cooper succinctly unpacks three such overburdened concepts: "identity," "globalization," and "modernity."

4. These terms are often conflated, which only serves to confuse already complex issues. While they certainly overlap, maintaining the distinctions facilitates clarity. "Modernity" is also a (much contested) term of periodization, but I use it predominantly in the cultural sense. See Gunn, "Public Sphere," 17.

5. David Blackbourn states that by the 1870s Germany possessed an "unmistakably capitalist market economy with a major industrial sector." *Long Nineteenth Century*, 178. However, the first department stores appeared only in the 1890s. See Barkin, "Crisis of Modernity," 31. Russia's first department store, Miur and Mirrielees, opened in Moscow in 1885.

6. Engels, *Working Class in England*.

7. Max Horkheimer and Theodor Adorno's 1944 critique, *Dialectic of Enlightenment*, laid much of the theoretical framework for the idea that consumer culture imposes passivity and conformity. For a useful overview of the many ways in which scholars have challenged this thesis, see Tiersten, "Redefining Consumer Culture."

8. On the growth of individual aspirations in Russia's traditionally collective society, see especially Brooks, *When Russia Learned to Read*; Steinberg, *Proletarian Imagination*.

9. Among others, see Naremore and Brantlinger, *Modernity and Mass Culture*, 12–13. Also see Raymond Williams on the complexities of the qualifier "mass" in many contexts, *Keywords*, 195–97.

10. See Frisby, *Fragments of Modernity*.

11. Quoted from Benjamin's *Das Passagen-Werk* in Frisby, *Fragments of Modernity*, 254.

12. Taylor, "Two Theories."

13. Quoted from *Das Passagen-Werk* in Frisby, *Fragments of Modernity*, 207.

14. In her study of cultural change in Petersburg, Katerina Clark aptly rejects the tendency to see continuity and discontinuity as a dichotomized "either/or." *Petersburg*, ix.

15. On consumption as part of the civilizing process, see Elias, *Civilizing Process*.

16. This paradox is convincingly analyzed by Torbjörn Wandel, "Too Late for Modernity," 261 and passim.

17. Berman, *All That Is Solid*, 13–15.

18. Burds, *Peasant Dreams*; Engel, *Between the Fields*; Brooks, *When Russia Learned to Read*; McReynolds, *News* and *Russia at Play*; Ruane, "Clothes Shopping" and *Empire's New Clothes*; Marjorie Hilton, "Commercial Cultures."

19. Loeb, *Consuming Angels*, 185.

20. Olga Semenova Tian-Shanskaia, for instance, observed this about Russian peasants in her nineteenth-century ethnographic studies. See *Village Life*, 144.

21. My thanks to Charles Halperin for pointing out this connection, which he traces to the sixteenth-century *Domostroi*. For descriptions of the blessing ceremonies, see Marjorie Hilton, "Commercial Cultures," chap. 2.

22. On questioning the centrality of class in modern western historiography, see Joyce, *Democratic Subjects*; and also, Joyce, ed., *Class*. In Russian history, Mark D. Steinberg has been at the forefront of examining subjective individual identities that often challenged class boundaries. See *Proletarian Imagination*.

23. Rosalind H. Williams, *Dream Worlds*, 3.

24. Bokhanov, *Burzhuaznaia pressa*. See also Fedinskii, "Material'nye usloviia"; Kiselev, "Reklama."

25. While many Western studies of advertising have also been ideological (for instance, Stewart Ewen's *Captains of Consciousness*), there has been a broad spectrum of approaches, including business, gender, and cultural history. The bibliography includes many of these titles. For a rich interpretation of American advertising as cultural history, see the works of T.J. Jackson Lears, especially *Fables of Abundance*.

26. See for example Anikst and Chernevich, *Russian Graphic Design*, which includes a beautifully illustrated section on commercial posters; Povelikhina and Kovtun, *Shop Signs*; Paltusova, *Torgovaia reklama*; Karas', *Uvlekatel'nyi mir*; Arkhangel'skaia, *Reklama*. Among other Russian publications that focus primarily on poster advertising, see Glinternik, "Nachalo Rossiiskoi reklamy"; Saveleva, "Kommertsiia v stile modern."

27. Uchenova and Starykh, *Istoriia reklamy*, 2 vols. This is the leading textbook on the history of Russian advertising.

28. Dubin, "Younger Generation." An early example of this focus is Roshchupkin, "Reklama kak fenomenon."

29. Karmalova, *Audiovizual'naia reklama*, 4.

30. In addition to the authors discussed in this passage, see also Kelly and Shepherd, *Constructing Russian Culture*.

31. A.A. Stepanov's recent work presents an overview of imperial newspaper advertising, with a plethora of illustrations. There is little analysis of the advertisements' content, however. *Istoriia ob"iavlenii*.

32. Burds, *Peasant Dreams*; Engel, *Between the Fields*.

33. On the "visual turn," see Peter Burke, *Eyewitnessing*. While analysis of visual culture is the mainstay of art history, until recently most historians have tended to privilege textual over visual sources. Two recent studies in the visual culture of imperial Russia are Stephen Norris, *War of Images*, and Kivelson and Neuberger, *Picturing Russia*.

34. Kivelson and Neuberger, *Picturing Russia*, 6.

35. McReynolds, *Russia at Play*; Stites, *Russian Popular Culture*.

36. Marjorie Hilton, "Commercial Cultures."

37. For the late imperial period, see especially Clements, Friedman, and Healey, *Russian Masculinities*.

38. Other, more scattered resources examined include an eclectic assortment of advertising material in personal archives or private collections; shop signs in the city museum of St. Petersburg; factory museums with memorabilia, including advertising, from their prerevolutionary incarnations. The factory museums rarely receive visitors and are not always easy to find. When, on the occasion of my trip to the former Treugol'nik rubber goods factory, the museum director retrieved the old visitors' book, I found myself signing my name only a few pages after an early "fellow traveler" of the

Soviet endeavor, Theodore Dreiser. My thanks to Volodia Nesterenko for arranging this visit, as well as one to the Skorokhod factory museum.

39. McReynolds, *News*; Bokhanov, Burzhuaznaia *pressa;* Cherepakhov and Fingerit, *Russkaia periodicheskaia pechat'*; Esin, *Russkaia dorevoliutsionnaia gazeta*. Jeffrey Burds notes that the largest circulation Moscow newspaper, *Russkoe slovo* (*Russian Word*), was also the most popular paper among peasants in the countryside of the Central Industrial Region. See *Peasant Dreams*, 178.

40. Burds notes a 1905 study of peasant reading that found 564 villages in Moscow province subscribed to 1,395 newspapers and journals, an average of 2.5 per village. The subscription rates were higher the further away the village was from Moscow itself. A contemporary noted, "Newspapers in the countryside rarely remain the property of just one person. Peasants love to read the newspaper aloud and often almost an entire village will gather to listen." *Peasant Dreams*, 176–77.

41. These particular weeks were selected as representative of advertising in "normal" times, i.e., avoiding the special advertisements for gift giving around Christmas and Easter, as well as the reduced urban population in the summers as some city residents left for the countryside.

42. *Russkoe slovo* reached a circulation of over one million by its demise. It regularly printed more advertisements and had more income from advertising than any other paper in late imperial Russia. The following years were missing from the holdings at the University of Illinois, Urbana-Champaign: 1900–1901; 1903–1904; 1908. *Gazeta-kopeika* attained the highest circulation in St. Petersburg (250,000 in 1909). Apart from the first six months of its run, all issues were available.

43. Neil Harris calls the introduction of the half-tone engraving process an "iconographic revolution." "Iconography and Intellectual History," 199.

44. Daniel Pope claims this as the major defining characteristic of modern advertising. *Making of Modern Advertising*, 8. This is not to say, of course, that traditional advertising did not contain elements of persuasion. For instance, store barkers' jobs depended on their ability to pressure and persuade. In print advertising, however, the tendency was simply to give out information. As Pope points out, the word "announcement" (or *ob"iavlenie* in Russian) could serve just as well as "advertisement" until the end of the nineteenth century. *Making of Modern Advertising*, 234.

45. The burgeoning Russian economy of the late nineteenth century experienced a crisis from 1900 to 1902 as a result of the western European monetary crisis. Recovery from 1903 to 1904 was curtailed by the Russo-Japanese War and the revolution of 1905, followed by a period of stagnation through 1908. The prosperity of 1909 to 1913, however, marked the peak of the imperial Russian economy. See Lyashchenko, *National Economy of Russia*, chaps. 32 and 33.

46. The entire collection of L. and E. Metzl advertising agency was not destroyed, as A.N. Bokhanov was led to believe during his research. Of twenty-four original files (*dela*), however, only four remain, and their contents provide little substantive information. See TsGIA SPb, f. 1584.

47. See Hower, *History of an Advertising Agency*. Also useful is the bibliographical essay in Marchand, *Advertising the American Dream*, 419–26.

48. Jib Fowles notes the extent to which, even today, advertising does not determine consumer behavior. He cites a statistic showing that ninety percent of new products failed in 1994 despite advertising. *Advertising and Popular Culture*, 19.

49. Ibid., 21.

50. Baudrillard, "Consumer Society."

1—THE DEVELOPMENT OF MODERN ADVERTISING IN RUSSIA

1. From the Latin *advertere*.

2. Povelikhina and Kovtun, *Shop Signs*, 13. For general histories of advertising in ancient times, see Wood, *Story of Advertising*, and Sampson, *History of Advertising*.

3. *Reklama* can mean "advertisement" or "advertising" in Russian. It is a borrowed term that accompanied the advent of modern advertising in the nineteenth century. The older Russian word *ob"iavlenie* originally meant only "notice" or "announcement" but came to be used for trade advertisements as well, with the expansion of the commercial press in the second half of the nineteenth century. The two terms are often used interchangeably, but whereas *reklama* can mean any kind of advertising, as well as the entire phenomenon of advertising, *ob"iavlenie* refers only to a print advertisement.

4. See Marjorie Hilton, "Commercial Cultures."

5. What makes modern advertising "modern," and when it becomes so, depends upon one's perspective and regional focus. Those who see modern advertising as a corollary of industrialization place its emergence in the mid- to late nineteenth century, part of the industrial revolution's second phase, as manufacturing began to emphasize consumer goods once the initial concentration on developing the machinery of production had succeeded. In Russia, as noted in the introduction, these two phases were largely simultaneous. See Nevett, *Advertising in Britain*. In contrast, those who stress modern advertising's persuasive rhetoric, as opposed to mere announcement of goods or services, reach further back into the late seventeenth century, at least for Great Britain, citing the prevalence of "puffery," or exaggerated advertising claims. By the late eighteenth century many British firms, such as the producers of Wedgwood pottery, had developed sophisticated marketing strategies. See McKendrick, Brewer, and Plumb, *Birth of a Consumer Society*. Despite the growing commercialization in eighteenth-century Britain, however, McKendrick concedes that it had not yet reached "the mature stage of a modern consumer society," ibid., 31. Fully fledged consumer societies, with their concomitant modern advertising, were phenomena of the second half of the nineteenth century across Europe and the United States. For a useful historiographical overview of literature on early British and American advertising, see Church, "Advertising Consumer Goods."

6. Povelikhina and Kovtun, *Shop Signs*, 17. In addition to historical background, this coffee-table book contains beautiful illustrations of shop signs over two centuries.

7. The oldest surviving example is a 1797 office sign for the Main Irkutsk Joint Russian-American Company, depicting the god of commerce, Mercury, among fish and fur traders. It is preserved in the Russian Museum in St. Petersburg. Povelikhina and Kovtun, *Shop Signs*, 23.

8. For a fuller assessment of these stereotypes, see Ruckman, *Moscow Business Elite*, 7–12.

9. Antonov, "Vyveski," 186.

10. Ibid.

11. In Paris a 1761 restriction banned shop signs from being suspended out from the store, due to the narrowness of the streets. On the history and cultural significance of shop signs in Paris, see Wrigley, "Street and Salon," 50–51.

12. Povelikhina and Kovtun, *Shop Signs*, 23.

13. "Peterburgskiia vyveski," 81.

14. Ibid.

15. In 1913 avant-garde artist David Burliuk wrote, "The people's genius for

painting found its only realization in shop signs . . . what a richness of subjects they encompass!" Povelikhina and Kovtun, *Shop Signs*, 186.

16. "Peterburgskiia vyveski," 81.

17. Gautier, *Voyage en Russie*, 44.

18. "Peterburgskiia vyveski," 82.

19. Ibid.

20. Ibid., 81.

21. Antonov, 186.

22. Ibid., 187.

23. Semeniuk, *Zhivopisets vyvesok*, 43.

24. Clark, *Petersburg*, 57–58.

25. RGIA, f. 23, op. 24, d. 1013, l. 558.

26. Ibid., l. 559.

27. Ibid., l. 552.

28. Povelikhina and Kovtun state that Larionov "is unimaginable without urban painted signs," *Shop Signs*, 62. Boris Kustodiev's admiration of signs is so clear, they go on to say, that "many of his characters and subjects seem to have been first viewed through the prism of painted signs." Ibid., 64.

29. Ibid., 74–75. The exhibition was part of Larionov's attempts not only to gain exposure for signs but to preserve them. Pictorial signs were gradually disappearing in favor of textual ones as the Russian population grew more literate by the turn of the century. Artists such as Larionov, Goncharova, and Burliuk attempted preservation by copying and photographing the signs. Others collected some originals that were being discarded. A few were placed in the Museum of Old St. Petersburg before the 1917 revolution and have survived until this day in the city museum.

30. Gray, *Russian Experiment in Art*, 37.

31. Povelikhina and Kovtun, *Shop Signs*, 78.

32. Cartoon by Aleksei Radakov, *Novyi satirikon* 9, 1914. Reproduced in Povelikhina and Kovtun, *Shop Signs*, 117.

33. Clark, *Petersburg*, 57.

34. Povelikhina and Kovtun, *Shop Signs*, 191. Quoted from *Zhizn' iskusstva*, November 12, 1920.

35. V.N. Davydov credits the initial introduction of poster columns in Moscow to a "notorious" entrepreneur, Taneev, who tried his hand at many projects in order to earn as much money as possible. *Rasskaz o proshlom*, 167.

36. Dokhman, *Raskleika*, 6. The 1897 census records a population of 54,000 in the Ukrainian city of Poltava. BE (St. Petersburg, 1906).

37. Okhochinskii, *Plakat*, 61.

38. *Mezhdunarodnaia vystavka khudozhestvennykh afish*.

39. Okhochinskii, *Plakat*, 65. On the development of Russian posters, see also Baburina, *Russkii plakat*.

40. Pliskii, *Reklama*, 118. An example is given of an unnamed St. Petersburg beer factory.

41. Ibid., 22.

42. On catalogs in Russia, see Ruane, *Empire's New Clothes*, 134–38.

43. On trade cards in the United States, see Laird, *Advertising Progress*, 77.

44. The oldest example I found was an 1849 booklet announcing a new shop for men's hats and toiletries, sent to the Botkin-Guchkov family. GIM, f. 122, d. 695, l. 117.

45. See Church and Clark, "Origins of Competitive Advantage," 108. The

authors cite tea producers as the first manufacturers of common dry goods to take up brand packaging in Britain.

46. McReynolds, *News*, appendix C.

47. PSZ, 2d ed., vol. 13, no. 10978, art. 21, February 16, 1838.

48. Kiselev, "Reklama," 29; Esin, *Russkaia dorevoliutsionnaia gazeta*, 34.

49. McReynolds, *News*, 23–4.

50. Ibid., see appendix B on statistical analysis of punishment by censorship.

51. Ibid., from appendix A, table 1 (source: *Ocherki po istorii Russkoi zhurnalistiki i kritiki* 2:449). These figures do not differentiate state-sponsored from independent publications. The area of growth, however, was in the latter category.

52. St. Petersburg's population grew from around 0.7 million to 2.2 million between 1870 and 1914. Bater, *St. Petersburg*, 308.

53. McReynolds, *News*, appendix A.

54. See Anthony Smith, *Newspaper*.

55. Bokhanov, *Burzhuaznaia pressa*, 30.

56. McReynolds, *News*, from appendix C.

57. The rates for the 1860s were taken from *Golos, Russkie vedomosti*, and *Birzhevye vedomosti*. Tracing the course of advertising rates is problematic. Publishers might define their fees differently at different times (per line or per character, for instance), as well as vary prices with the service. Front page advertisements were always more expensive than those after the text; publishing the same notice more than once involved a discount; larger scripts, illustrations, and borders cost extra; advertisements sent from abroad were sometimes charged more than domestic ones. To complicate matters, many newspapers stopped printing their rates at all at the end of the nineteenth century.

58. Fedinskii, "Material'nye usloviia," 26–29.

59. In the absence of archival records, Iu. I. Fedinskii attempted to assess the overall advertising income for a randomly chosen issue of *Gazeta-kopeika* (*Penny Gazette*)—May 16, 1910—by multiplying the number of lines of advertisements by the rate published on the front page. His method and conclusions are flawed, however, since commercial advertisers would often receive discounts, especially if they placed their advertisements through an agency. See Fedinskii, "Material'nye usloviia," 32.

60. The 1905 circulation of *Russkie vedomosti* was 50,000, compared with a circulation of 157,700 for *Russkoe slovo* during the same year. The latter's circulation rose to over a million during the First World War. McReynolds, *News*, appendix A, table 8.

61. It should also be noted that classified advertisements did not usually receive a discount unless they were printed more than once, so their quantity could go a long way toward making up for their cheap price.

62. Vol'fson, *Praktika gazetnogo izdatel'stva*, 25. This book was developed from a series of lectures given by the author in the summer of 1918 to the school of journalism, and is based on prerevolutionary practice, or as Vol'fson puts it in his conclusion, on "the conditions of normal times."

63. RGALI, f. 1666, op. 1, d. 11, reel 2, ll. 46 ob., 47.

64. Ibid., l. 61 ob.

65. Stephen Fox, *Mirror Makers*, 14.

66. Stepanov, *Istoriia ob"iavlenii*, 32. Nevertheless, celebrations were held in St. Petersburg in 2008 to commemorate the founding anniversary of the Metzl firm as Russia's first advertising agency.

67. RGIA, f. 23, op. 28, d. 1349, ll. 84–89.

68. Ibid., l. 33.

69. Ibid., ll. 84–89. Epshtein's investment was 5,000 rubles.

70. Ibid.

71. The number of advertising agents in Russia's capitals remained significantly smaller than in New York City, where they rose from 42 in 1869 to 288 in 1892. Laird, *Advertising Progress*, 157.

72. *Vsia Moskva*, 177.

73. Lears, "Some Versions of Fantasy," 358. See also Sivulka, *Ad Women*.

74. RGIA, f. 23, op. 11, d. 1126.

75. The historiography of the merchantry gives scant attention to women, who were relegated to domestic duties by the traditions of the *kupechestvo*, or merchant estate. See, for example, Rieber, *Merchants and Entrepreneurs*, and Owen, *Capitalism and Politics*. West and Petrov's collection of essays, *Merchant Moscow*, addresses women, but largely those of the merchant elite.

76. RGIA, f. 23, op. 11, d. 1126, l. 53.

77. Ibid., f. 1666, op. 1, d. 3, l. 69. Sources vary as to the firm's founding date, placing it in both 1880 and 1889.

78. Ibid., f. 23, op. 28, d. 1349, ll. 84–89.

79. On entrepreneurship and the modernization of Russian business, see Guroff and Carstensen, *Entrepreneurship in Imperial Russia*; Rieber, *Merchants and Entrepreneurs*; Owen, *Corporation under Russian Law*; Carstensen, *American Enterprise*; McKay, *Pioneers for Profit*.

80. McKay, *Pioneers for Profit*, 19.

81. RGIA, f. 1278, op. 5, d. 780, l. 5. On November 21, 1917 (N.S.), just two weeks after the Bolshevik Revolution, Lenin and Anatolii Lunacharskii (Commissar of Enlightenment in the new Soviet government) issued a "Decree on the Introduction of a State Monopoly on Advertising." In other words, advertising agencies were not closed but turned over to the state. Both leaders realized the potential of advertising to serve Soviet trade and industry and as a propaganda tool. See Okorokov, *Lenin o pechati*, 464–66; and Kanevskii, *Effekt reklamy*, 174.

82. RGALI, f. 1666, op. 1, d. 2.

83. Ibid., d. 11, reel 1, l. 46.

84. Ibid., f. 776. Only general advertising sheets were included in this count. Those requests that specialized in one type of product or service (for example, restaurants or books) were excluded.

85. Ibid., f. 595, op. 1, d. 16. Apparently this was not the only attempt to masquerade as an employee of *Russkoe slovo*. Along with records about Lissner's escapades is evidence of others claiming to be correspondents without the knowledge of the newspaper. In one particular case an anxious brother wrote to the editor to inquire about his new brother-in-law, who had impressed the family with his claims to journalism and taken his bride off to Italy on an "assignment." Having never seen the man's stories in print, the brother became suspicious, but too late. The editor informed him that his brother-in-law was totally unknown to the newspaper.

86. Laird, *Advertising Progress*, 6.

87. Ibid., 56, 70.

88. Tsyperovich, "Reklama," 191.

89. Chekhov, *Sochineniia*, 3: 90.

90. Lears, "Sherwood Anderson," 14.

91. RGIA, f. 776, op. 8, d. 2034. The journal does not seem to have material-

ized, since no copy exists in the Russian National Library.

92. The leaflets are part of the Russian National Library collection. This one is entitled *"Kaizer i Diadia Mikhei"* in *"Strashnaia byl',"* 1915 (37.80.2.70).

93. Dokhman, *Raskleika*, 4.

94. Bater, "Between Old and New."

95. Marjorie Hilton, "Commercial Cultures," 27–29.

96. On these tensions over changing retail practices, see also Ruane, "Clothes Shopping," 766–68.

97. On Sharapov, see Owen, *Capitalism and Politics*, 143.

98. Verigin, *Russkaia reklama*, 22.

99. However, Sharapov twice interjected personal footnotes lamenting the fact that, in his opinion, the Russian advertiser and reader had already accepted Western-style advertising. Ibid., 14, 18.

100. On the merchantry as an estate in the Russian context, see Rieber, *Merchants and Entrepreneurs*, xxii–xxv, and Ruckman, *Moscow Business Elite*, chap. 1. See also Gregory Freeze's reinterpretation of the concept of *soslovie* in historiography, *"Soslovie* (Estate) Paradigm."

101. I use the phrase "business community" in a broader sense than does Jo Ann Ruckman in her book on the Moscow business elite; she excludes the small traders from the *meshchanstvo* whereas I do not. My use of the word "merchantry," when it does appear, refers to the traditional Russian merchantry in the sense of a *soslovie*. The word "merchant" (*kupets*), however, is used more loosely to refer to anyone engaged in trade and sometimes as a general term for anyone in the field of trade or industry. This is in accordance with the Russian usage, since *kupsty* (plural of *kupets*) could legally manufacture as well as trade. See Owen, *Corporation under Russian Law*, 10, footnote 21. In contrast, my use of the word "manufacturer" excludes merchants who only engaged in trade.

102. See Rieber, *Merchants and Entrepreneurs*, chap. 6.

103. Ruckman, *Moscow Business Elite*, 15.

104. While the 1863 decree already cited had granted any individual the right to purchase a guild or merchant certificate, a new industrial tax law passed in 1898 replaced this personal certificate with a business certificate based on the enterprise rather than the individual, furthering the dissociation of industry and merchant *soslovie*. Rieber, *Merchants and Entrepreneurs*, 87.

105. Ibid., 88.

106. *Pervaia vseobshchaia perepis'*. The Moscow statistics are derived from volume 24, 326–27; St. Petersburg statistics come from volume 37, 242–43. Figures are rounded to the nearest percent.

107. Ruane, "Clothes Shopping," 766. For an in-depth study of the geography of trade in Moscow, see Gohstand, "Internal Geography."

108. Many, though not all, of the brochures and handbooks on advertising that were put out in the late imperial period were thinly veiled advertisements themselves, promoting the services of an advertising agency or publisher. The trade journals, in contrast, were didactic in nature, as is evident from the editors' expressed concern with commercial education and heightened ethical standards in trade. See, for example, in Odessa, *Torgovyi mir* (*Trade World*); in St. Petersburg, *Kupechestvo i promyshlennost'* (*Merchantry and Industry*); in Moscow, Zhurnal *kommercheskii mir* (*Commercial World Journal*), among others.

109. "Iz kupecheskoi praktiki," *Torgovyi mir* (August 1910): 15. References to

the "old ways" abound in this journal, which claimed to speak to an all-Russian, not just Odessan, mercantile audience. See also Mirles, *Iskusstvo*, 7–8.

110. Pliskii, *Reklama*, 20. On perceptions of the old-style merchant, see Ruckman, *Moscow Business Elite*, introduction; and Marjorie Hilton, "Commercial Cultures," chap. 1.

111. Mirles, *Iskusstvo*, 8.

112. This negative assessment of Russian merchants' ethical standards was not only accepted by contemporaries but by later historians as well. Thomas Owen blames the "relatively low level of business ethics among merchants, bankers and bureaucrats in St. Petersburg" on "centuries of Russian isolation from the European business world in the medieval and Early Modern period." *Corporation under Russian Law*, 49.

113. Fox, *Mirror Makers*, 19.

114. Ia., *Ob"iavleniia*, 4.

115. Pliskii, *Reklama*, 20.

116. "Torgovaia reklama," *Russkoe torgovoe delo* (Jan. 11, 1903): 93.

117. *Torgovo-promyshlennyi i kommissionnyi obozrevatel'* (April 1, 1907): 1. Published in St. Petersburg.

118. Ratner, *Tekhnika reklamy*, 5.

119. *Torgovyi mir* (February 1910): 22. The editor of *Sputnik pokupatelia, torgovo-spravochnyi zhurnal* made the same assertion in 1913 (Samara, no page numbers).

120. *Torgovyi mir* (September 1912): 8.

121. Ibid. (December 1910): 2.

122. *Uchites' reklamirovat' u amerikantsev* (Moscow: 1911), 6; and *Russkoe torgovoe delo* (January 11, 1903): 93.

123. *Russkoe torgovoe delo* (January 1903): 93.

124. *Torgovyi mir* (January 1910): 8–9.

125. Mirles, *Iskusstvo*, 8–9.

126. Tsyperovich, "Reklama," 181–82.

127. Verkhovoi *Reklama*, 8. See also Mirles, *Iskusstvo*, 9.

128. Dokhman, *Raskleika*, 2.

129. *Russkoe torgovoe delo* (January 1903): 93.

130. This slogan was widely used in the advertising industry in Western countries as well as Russia.

131. Shapiro, *Sputnik pokupatelia*, no. 1, 2. Published in Samara.

132. *Novye puti*, 2.

133. Laird, *Advertising Progress*, 7. U.S. retailers fell behind manufacturers in terms of innovation by the 1890s.

134. Ibid., 31.

135. Accountability was written into every corporation's charter, which was reviewed and approved by the government on an individual basis. This concessionary system of incorporation (as opposed to a more efficient system of simple registration) was a major obstacle to capitalist development in Russia and the repeated object of attempted reform. It was finally abolished under the Provisional Government in March 1917. See Owen, *Corporation under Russian Law*. The concessionary system did not apply to simple single-owner businesses or trading firms. The essential difference between these enterprises and corporations was the issue of liability. In corporations both owners and investors were granted limited liability; in trading firms owners (though not investors) were subject to full liability.

136. The number of trading firms (those companies not subject to governmen-

tal approval) rose from 1,625 in 1892, to 3,593 in 1905, 5,801 in 1911, and 9,202 in 1914. Owen, *Corporation under Russian Law*, 11, footnote 24.

137. In 1893 there were 648 joint stock companies; by 1900 their number had risen to 1,369. Ruckman, *Moscow Business Elite*, 1.

138. The liquor industry also advertised actively, but records are scarce for the major firms.

139. Originating in eighth-century Iraq, the Karaite sect rejects rabbinical and Talmudic teaching and accepts only the scriptures.

140. The Russian term for toiletries is *parfiumernye*, which includes perfumes, soaps, shampoos, and beauty products, as does the English word "toiletries."

141. In 1857 it became a trading firm. See Moskovskaia parfiumernaia fabrika "Svoboda," *K 40-letiiu Velikogo Oktiabria,*, 4. In 1897 Rallet was incorporated as a share partnership (*tovarishchestvo na paiakh*). RGIA, f. 23, op. 28, d. 1730. There were two main types of corporation, both of which could broadly be called joint stock. Owen clarifies the terminology, which was often confused in its Russian context and in subsequent historiography. In cases of fine distinctions, Owen uses the term "share partnership" for *tovarishchestvo na paiakh* and "joint-stock company" for *aktsionernye obshchestvo* or *kompaniia*. See *Corporation under Russian Law*, 12–13. In 1878 the Senate ruled that no legal difference existed between the two types of corporation. In effect, the share partnership was often used by families who wanted to provide their already established firms with limited liability. The share partnership tended to distribute larger, but fewer, shares to a chosen circle of family and friends. This form of corporation was most popular in Moscow because of the preference there for family firms. The joint stock company, in contrast, was generally used for newly formed large enterprises, selling many more shares at lower prices on the open market. This form flourished in St. Petersburg, where there was a more developed capital market (ibid., 51).

142. TsGIA g. Moskvy, f. 1098, op. 1, d. 66, ll. 109–10.

143. Ibid., d. 285, ll. 154–57.

144. Ibid., d. 7.

145. The chairman and one director were French; the second director, M.I. Proskuriakov, was a Russian who had served with the company since 1855.

146. TsGIA g. Moskvy, f. 1098, op. 1, d. 7, l. 30 ob.

147. Ibid., l. 36 ob.

148. Ibid., ll. 21 ob. and 22.

149. Although records are less complete for the Russian toiletry companies, it can be assumed that their directors played a similar hands-on role in advertising policies. Thomas Owen notes that Russian directors in general tended to take a more active role in managing their companies than did their counterparts in America. Owen, *Corporation under Russian Law*, 20, footnote 41.

150. TsGIA g. Moskvy, f. 429, op. 2, d. 5, l. 2.

151. *Zolotoi iubilei*. Photographs after text: no page number.

152. Chandler, *Visible Hand*, 1–6.

153. The I.M. Mashistov printing company, for example, listed each piece of work for some of its engravers, who were paid by the job in 1909. See TsGIA g. Moskvy, f. 877, op. 1, d. 21, l. 9. Other companies specialized in commercial labels and packaging.

154. Ibid., f. 429, op. 1, d. 4, l. 93 ob.

155. Emphasis here is on the business records of Moscow companies, due to the long-term inaccessibility of the St. Petersburg city archive.

156. The Chepelevetskii family maintained dominant control and sold shares only to two other families when the business became a share partnership in 1909. RGIA, f. 23, op. 28, d. 2413, ll. 5, 16.

157. TsGIA g. Moskvy, f. 1828, op. 1, d. 1, l. 125. Ostroumov reorganized his company as a share partnership in 1900, retaining management control and more than a quarter of the shares. He personally held 124 of 450 shares in 1903, and his family members held 55 more. See also RGIA, f. 23, op. 28, d. 1554, ll. 7–19, for a copy of the 1900 company charter.

158. According to a researcher in 1900, many merchants in the United States at the turn of the century considered from two-and-a-half to five percent of sales an appropriate advertising budget. Sherman, "Advertising in the United States," 36.

159. Schudson, *Advertising,* 17. The study mentioned is by Richard Schmalensee, *The Economics of Advertising* (Amsterdam: 1972).

160. For instance, the tobacco firm of Dukat estimated an advertising budget of 25,000 rubles for 1911, while the estimate for labels alone was set at 50,000 rubles. TsGIA g. Moskvy, f. 473, op. 1, d. 4, l. 21.

161. *Svod statisticheskikh dannykh*, 82, Table 2.

162. These were La Ferme, founded in St. Petersburg, 1852, by an Austrian; Gabai, founded in Moscow, mid-1850s; V.I. Asmolov, founded in Rostov-on-Don, 1856; A.N. Bogdanov, founded in St. Petersburg, 1864; A.N. Shaposhnikov, founded in St. Petersburg, 1872; Shapshal Brothers, founded in St. Petersburg, 1873; Kolobov and Bobrov, founded in St. Petersburg before 1880; Ottoman, founded in St. Petersburg, 1882; Dukat, founded in Moscow, 1891. For the available statistics on advertising expenditures for each of these firms, see Sally West, "Constructing Consumer Culture," chap. 3.

163. RGIA, f. 23, op. 24, d. 745, ll. 4, 5.

164. TsGIA g. Moskvy, f. 51, op. 10, d. 262, l. 9. The miscellaneous nature of the list of expenses suggests that the fence painting was maintenance, not advertising.

165. Ibid., f. 1171, op. 1, d. 21, l. 37.

166. Altundzhi, *Krupneishiia torgovo-promyshlennyia*, 49.

167. RGIA, f. 23, op. 24, d. 430, ll. 247–56.

168. TsGIA g. Moskvy, f. 473, op. 1, d. 44, l. 32. Most of the other major companies were compelled to join over the next year.

169. For La Ferme, see Shustov, *Sankt-Peterburgskoe kupechestvo*, part 1, 1. For Dukat see TsGIA g. Moskvy, f. 473, op. 1, d. 51, l. 16.

170. RGIA, f. 23, op. 28, d. 2425, l. 11.

171. Some liquor companies also went in for a variety of verses and stories, e.g., N.L. Shustov and Sons (see chap. 5).

172. BE, vol. 38, s.v. "chai." BSE, 1978 ed., s.v. "chai." Imports of tea almost doubled between the 1860s and 1870s, from an average of 762,000 to 1,498,000 *pudy* a year. (One pud is equal to 36 pounds.)

173. The company became a corporation in 1883. The Abrikosov family, which maintained a large interest, acquired most of their income from the Popov tea firm, even though they were famous for their own candy and confectionary business. Ruckman, *Moscow Business Elite*, 52.

174. TsGIA g. Moskvy, f. 766, op. 1, d. 1, l. 72.

175. Ibid., d. 2, ll. 90–91 ob.

176. *Torgovyi dom Vogau i Ko.*, 14. This firm was owned by the descendants of a German merchant, Maxim Wogau, who had settled in Moscow in the 1820s, taking

Russian citizenship shortly after his arrival. Ibid., 1.

177. *Otchet i balans.*

178. It remains unclear why the tea companies invested less in newspaper advertising than the other industries examined here. Their later transition to the individual retail market is surely a factor, and perhaps those companies such as Popov and Wogau that set up their own specialty shops gravitated more toward window and poster displays to attract attention. Several toiletry producers also boasted their own shops (e.g., Brocard), however, and they invested in both periodical and poster advertising.

179. TsGIA, f. 759, op. 1, dd. 14, 21, 23, 25.

180. Ibid., d. 21, l. 105 ob. The printer was Menert (previously Kirsten), but this is just one example among many.

181. Ibid., d. 2, ll. 89–90.

182. Verigin, *Russkaia reklama*, 4, 20. The fact that this article was published by a newspaper editor did not require him or the author to be apologists for advertising, since *Russkii trud* did not carry any.

2 — SEALS OF APPROVAL AND STAMPS OF CENSORSHIP

1. On the history and symbolism of the double-headed eagle, see Hellberg-Hirn, *Soil and Soul*, chap. 2. The eagle was originally adopted from Byzantium by Ivan III in 1472, on the occasion of his marriage to the niece of the last Byzantine emperor.

2. On this subject see Fitzpatrick, *Great Russian Fair*. In 1860 alone there were 5,653 trade fairs in Russia; most were small and of only a few days' duration. Only 102 had a turnover of more than 100,000 rubles. The Nizhnii Novgorod fair was one of only 23 with a turnover of over a million rubles. It assembled annually from mid-July through August. Ibid., 8–9.

3. Thomas Richards credits the Crystal Palace Exhibition with legitimizing capitalism by elevating mundane objects to the level of symbol and spectacle. See *Commodity Culture*, 3.

4. For example, Chicago in 1893 and Paris in 1878 and 1900.

5. BSE, vol. 9, 2nd ed., 1951, 493.

6. Pintner, *Russian Economic Policy*, 53.

7. PSZ, 2nd ed., vol. 3, art. 2367.

8. Pintner, *Russian Economic Policy*, 55.

9. Ibid., 103.

10. *Zhurnal manufaktur i torgovli* 5 (1829): 20–23. Cited in Pintner, *Russian Economic Policy*, 55.

11. PSZ, 2nd ed., vol. 3, article 2367.

12. Ibid.

13. BSE, 493.

14. PSZ, 2nd ed., vol. 11, 8755. Pintner, *Russian Economic Policy*, 103–4.

15. PSZ, 2nd ed., vol. 11, 9485.

16. Ibid., vol. 23, 21914.

17. Ibid.

18. Ibid.

19. Pintner, *Russian Economic Policy*, 100.

20. RGIA, f. 22, op. 1, d. 1136a, l. 12.

21. Ibid., f. 23, op. 17, d. 76, passim.

22. For example, advertisement of a Viennese exhibition was rejected just a few months later on the grounds that it was insufficiently industrial in nature. Ibid., d. 71, l. 25. Announcement of a Rome exhibition was refused in 1911 because the government had no information about it and it was feared that it might be confused with a concurrent exposition of the arts in the same city. Ibid., d. 184, l. 141.

23. It was apparently not illegal to stage unofficial exhibitions or to present prizes at them since both practices continued unhindered. However, the prizes would not be officially endorsed.

24. RGIA, f. 23, op. 17, d. 184, ll. 94, 98, 102, 144.

25. Ibid., ll. 5, 28.

26. Ibid., ll. 103, 108, 155, 175.

27. Ibid., ll. 62, 107.

28. Ibid., d. 288, passim.

29. PSZ, 2nd ed., vol. 51, pt. 1, 55996.

30. This, the fifteenth all-Russian industrial show, was the first to include fine art in the list of officially solicited exhibits. Consequently, it was titled the All-Russian Industry and Arts Exhibition. The 1896 exhibition in Nizhnii Novgorod again expanded the scope by including for the first time a display of industrial art ranging from printing to furniture design.

31. RGIA, f. 23, op. 17, d. 230, l. 2.

32. Ibid., d. 184, ll. 282, 294.

33. Ibid., l. 302.

34. Ibid., l. 3.

35. Ibid., d. 230, ll. 1–2. While the sheer volume of cases in 1911 regarding the illegitimate use of government awards was clearly in response to these government reports (which were probably sent to all governors), some cases predated them. It was almost certainly rival contentions among manufacturers that triggered official concern. Local authorities at times then responded overzealously. Many companies were required to present documentation of their awards without reason. The Riga city police even tried to revoke the rights to the state seal of the steamship company Kavkaz and Merkurii on the grounds that the honor had been granted in St. Petersburg and therefore could not be used in other towns—a ridiculous limitation for a transportation firm! Ibid., d. 184, l. 244. (A similar restriction did, however, apply to international companies; Russian awards won by entrepreneurs with property abroad as well as in Russia were accorded only to the Russian properties. Ibid., d. 184, l. 245.)

36. A first offense was punishable by a fine of no more than one hundred rubles. Subsequent offenses exacted two hundred rubles. *Svod Zakonov,* vol. 15 (1906), "Ulozhenie o Nakazaniiakh Ugolovnykh i Ispravitel'nykh," articles 1357–2 and 1357–3.

37. RGIA, f. 23, op. 17, d. 230, l. 2.

38. Ibid., d. 82, passim.

39. The questions included such details as complete patronymics, where those had been omitted, the origin of materials used, exact description of the goods, and so forth. Some nominees were excluded for various reasons of eligibility.

40. RGIA, f. 23, op. 17, d. 181, l. 2.

41. PSZ, 2nd ed., vol. 24, pt. 1, 22906. Some of the Ufa cases apparently did break the law by sending goods to other provinces and even abroad. The government, however, did not pursue the matter, despite the governor's various promptings.

42. Verstraete, *La Russie industrielle,* 313. See also Robert D. Warth, "Nizhnii Novgorod Exposition of 1896," MERSH 25: 26–28. Note that the title of this article

puts the exhibition in 1876, but that is a typographical error.

43. Verstraete, *La Russie industrielle*, i.

44. Manolov, *Sovremennyi ocherk*, 95–100; Warth, "Nizhnii Novgorod," 27. Warth cites a lack of popular entertainment in the first few weeks of the exhibition as one of the reasons for its failure to draw large crowds. Witte initially reacted with scorn to the idea that he should "enliven the exhibit with attractions for the visitor who has a penchant for amusements, restaurants and café singers." In his mind, the event was intended to educate, not entertain. Concessions to public tastes were subsequently made, however.

45. Manolov, *Sovremennyi ocherk*, 95.

46. *Svod Zakonov*, "Ustav o Promyshlennosti," articles 157–61. See also Von Laue, *Sergei Witte*, 96. For more on the history of trademarks in Russian commerce, see Uchenova and Starykh, *Istoriia reklamy, ili metamorfozy reklamnogo obraza*, 265–69.

47. For example, Ratner, *Tekhnika reklamy*, 13.

48. See Heald, *By Appointment*.

49. Opie, *Rule Britannia*, 8.

50. *Iubileiyny al'bom*, part 3, no page numbers.

51. Throughout the rest of the century, the Ministry of the Imperial Court took on additional areas, such as court ceremony and after 1893 the management of imperial appanages. Ministers of the Imperial Court held their posts with remarkable longevity in comparison with other, more politically volatile, ministries. There were only five ministers between 1826 and 1917. See L.E. Shepelev, "Ministries and Main Administrations," MERSH 22: 151.

52. This applied to each court location, i.e., there could be separate suppliers of tea to the emperor's court in Moscow and St. Petersburg.

53. The accession of Alexander II in 1855 caused a flurry of petitions from those who had been "Purveyors to the Court of His Highness the Tsarevich" to now be promoted to "Purveyors to the Court of His Imperial Majesty." RGIA, f. 472, op. 9, d. 1. Purveyors to the now deceased Nicholas I no longer had the right to the title.

54. In 1895 the empress requested that her personal purveyors thereafter be called "Purveyors to Her Imperial Majesty," rather than "Purveyors to the Imperial Court." RGIA, f. 472, op. 43, d. 16, l. 59.

55. Ibid., op. 9, d. 295, l. 97.

56. PSZ, 3rd ed., vol. 20, 19117.

57. RGIA, f. 472, op. 9, d. 179, ll. 62, 69.

58. Ibid., d. 250, l. 139.

59. Ibid., d. 114, ll. 1, 4. This petition was dated January 1857. The eagerness to flaunt royal favor manifested itself in other ways as well. For example, an expensive Moscow hotel whose restaurant exhibit the tsar and tsarina had visited while touring a 1902 fishing industry exposition in St. Petersburg, requested permission to keep the chairs and service used by the couple on permanent display behind a glass showcase in the foyer of the restaurant. In considering the request, the authorities weighed the declared motivation of patriotism and "loyal gratitude" with the potential to use (from their point of view, to misuse) the display for advertising purposes, to give the hotel a distinction lacking from other, equally worthy, competitors. Citing an 1893 precedent in which the Primorskaia railway put a plaque on a wagon used by the emperor, the Moscow hotel was allowed the display on condition that it posted a sign saying it was by permission of the Ministry of the Imperial Court. Ibid., op. 43, d. 178, passim.

60. Ibid., op. 9, d. 250, ll. 141, 158, 159.

61. For example, *Russkoe slovo*, June 2, 1913, front page. "The confectionary factory of A. Siou and Company was royally granted the title Purveyor to the Court of His Imperial Majesty on May 25, 1913."

62. Nevett, *Advertising in Britain*, 126–27.

63. The 1902 "Law against the Disfigurement of Regions with Exceptional Landscapes" applied to the Rhine valleys, but other states soon followed with similar legislation, and the laws expanded to protect cityscapes as well as countryside. See Repp, "Marketing, Modernity," 35.

64. Lears, "Some Versions of Fantasy," 366. See also Kenner, *Fight for Truth*.

65. See the works of Repin and Vasnetsov discussed in chap. 5. It was not only works of art but also famous people whom companies appropriated for commercial purposes. Nevett includes a reproduction of a British advertisement featuring the Pope drinking from a steaming cup of Bovril (used in part for its laxative properties). The inscription reads: "The Two Infallible Powers. The Pope and Bovril." Nevett, *Advertising in Britain*, 131.

66. *Svod Zakonov*, "Ustav o tsenzure i pechati," article 4, vol. 9 (1913), 82.

67. See Ruud, *Fighting Words*, for a full account of the 1865 reform and an English translation of the legislation. The exclusion of advertisements from the exemption from preliminary review was confirmed in 1885 by a decision of the Senate Criminal Cassation Department (Raz"iasneniia Kassatsionnago Ugolovnago Departamenta Pravitel'stvuiushchago Senata). Varadinov, *Sbornik uzakonenii*, 10–11.

68. *Svod Zakonov*, "Ustav o tsenzure i pechati," article 41. There were specified exceptions to this: advertisements for medicines and medical cures were submitted to the medical authorities for approval; those for foreign lotteries had to pass through the Ministry of Finance ("Ustav o tsenzure i pechati," articles 39, 40). In 1908 local medical authorities became additionally responsible for censorship of advertisements for cosmetic and hygienic preparations, health resorts, and medicinal or table waters (Varadinov, *Sbornik uzakonenii*, 16). In 1906 certain types of printed advertisements were exempted from censorship altogether. These included notices of a domestic nature, such as wedding invitations and apartment rentals, and commercial incidentals, such as labels and price lists ("Ustav o tsenzure i pechati," article 167).

69. RGIA, f. 776, op. 8, d. 1370, ll. 3, 4.

70. The inadequacy of these categories persisted into the Soviet period. For instance, Sredinskii used the term *melkie* to mean only classified, which was clearly not the way the prerevolutionary statute had been interpreted. See his *Gazetno-Izdatel'stvoe delo*, 31.

71. RGIA, f. 776, op. 8, d. 1370, l. 55.

72. It is possible that placers of onetime classified advertisements were simply unaware of the rules. Regular trade advertisers certainly did not approach the governor's office with their publications but either dealt directly with the periodicals or used the services of advertising agencies.

73. *Svod Zakonov*, "Ustav o tsenzure i pechati," article 167. Varadinov, *Sbornik uzakonenii*, 10–11. The punishment for printing an advertisement without preliminary censorship was a month's arrest or a fine of no higher than one hundred rubles. *Svod Zakonov*, "Ustav o nakazaniiakh nalagaemykh mirovymi sud'iami," article 34, vol. 15.

74. RGIA, f. 776, op. 8, d. 1370, l. 11.

75. Varadinov, *Sbornik uzakonenii*, 3.

76. RGIA, f. 776, op. 8, d. 1370, l. 55 ob.

77. Ibid.

78. Ibid., ll. 8–11.

79. Ibid., ll. 9–10.

80. Ibid., l. 10.

81. Ibid., ll. 21–22.

82. Ibid., ll. 24–25.

83. Ibid., ll. 1–2.

84. See Wortman, *Russian Legal Consciousness*.

85. RGIA, f. 776, op. 8, d. 1370, ll. 63–70.

86. Ibid., l. 59.

87. Ibid., ll. 75–76.

88. Ibid., l. 84.

89. Ibid., l. 85.

90. Ruud, *Fighting Words*, 220.

91. RGIA, f. 776, op. 8, d. 1370, ll. 95–98.

92. Ibid., f. 797, op. 81, d. 31, passim.

93. Ibid., f. 776, op. 10, d. 966, passim.

94. TsGIA g. Moskvy, f. 31, op. 3, d. 1376, passim.

95. Engelstein, *Keys to Happiness*, 360–71.

96. Varadinov, *Sbornik uzakonenii*, 11–12.

97. Article 1001 in 1845 was based on legislation from Hungary, Belgium, and France. See Paul W. Goldschmidt, "Article 242," 469.

98. Varadinov, *Sbornik uzakonenii*, 4–10. The other countries were Germany, Austria-Hungary, Belgium, Brazil, Denmark, Spain, the United States, France, Great Britain, Italy, the Netherlands, Portugal, and Switzerland. The official name of the agreement is the Paris Convention on the Suppression of the Traffic in Obscene Publications.

99. *Svod Zakonov*, "Ulozhenie o nakazaniiakh ugolovnykh i ispravitel'nykh," article 1001, vol. 15 (izdanie 1895 g., po prodolzh. 1906 g.).

100. RGIA, f. 776, op. 21, part 1, d. 537, ll. 1, 10, 18.

101. On censoring of medical advertising, see Varadinov, *Sbornik uzakonenii*, 15–24.

102. Varadinov, *Sbornik uzakonenii*, 21.

103. RGIA, f. 776, op. 10, d. 387, ll. 1, 25–70.

104. These included: *Novoe vremia, Peterburgskaia gazeta, Peterburgskii listok, Rech', Gazeta-kopeika, Vsemirnaia panorama, Zemshchina, Birzhevye vedomosti, Ogonek, Rodina*, and *Sinii zhurnal*. Ibid., l. 3.

105. *Svod Zakonov*, "Ustav o nakazankiiakh nalagaemnykh mirovymi sud"iami," article 34, and "Ulozhenie o nakazaniiakh ugolovnykh i ispravitel'nykh," article 1001, in vol. 15 (izdanie 1885 g., po prodolzh. 1906 g.). The St. Petersburg rule was enacted in 1909 by order of the city governor, Drachevskii. Varadinov, *Sbornik uzakonenii*, 24.

106. RGIA, f. 776, op. 10, d. 387, ll. 19–20. *Gazeta-kopeika* also enjoyed the biggest circulation in St. Petersburg.

107. Ibid., ll. 22–23.

108. Ferenczi, "Freedom of the Press," 199. For this information, Ferenczi cites the research of Rigberg, "Tsarist Censorship Operations."

109. Ferenczi, "Freedom of the Press," 201.

110. Goldschmidt, "Article 242," 460.

111. "K voprosu o rasprodazhakh," *Torgovo-promyshlennaia gazeta*, November 12, 1899.

112. RGIA, f. 23, op. 24, d. 1013, l. 3.

113. According to their findings, Canada, Norway, the Netherlands, and Sweden were all without any advertising legislation at this time. Ibid., ll. 9–10.

114. Ibid., d. 101, l. 413. Quotations from a petition sent to the Kharkov governor, signed by sixty local merchants, November 1911. Anti-Semitism was added to the furor over this issue in some of the press treatment. In 1903 *Our Time* (*Nashe vremia*), a weekly supplement to *Peterburgskaia gazeta*, printed a cartoon depicting a two-faced, hook-nosed "Itsak Shel'menzon" selling the same bolt of cloth from one hand as part of a reopening sale and from the other as a final closing sale. *Nashe vremia*, March 13, 1903.

115. It was not clear whether these new customers would receive a free trinket or a discount with their coupons. Practice probably varied.

116. RGIA, f. 23, op. 24, d. 1013, ll. 533–540.

117. Ibid., l. 579.

118. The popular image of eleventh-century English king Canute is of a ruler so enamored of his power that he believed his orders could and should control nature (he is said to have ordered the waves to stop). However, his act was intended to demonstrate the limits of monarchical power. Intentionally or not, this was also the effect of the tsarist policy in censoring advertising.

119. On the treatment of state seals in the revolution, see Figes and Kolonitskii, *Interpreting the Revolution*; Stites, "Iconoclastic Currents."

3—CLASSROOM FOR CONSUMERS

1. Hamm, *City*, 2–3.

2. Bradley, "Moscow," 13.

3. Bater, *St. Petersburg*, 309–10.

4. Louise McReynolds notes that the political orientation of newspapers grew more blurred as the publications came to be regarded as businesses. "News became merchandise, which reporters found, bought, or sold without regard for . . . editorial positions." *News*, 155.

5. Ibid., 120.

6. Marchand, *Advertising the American Dream*, 1. Most scholarship on consumer culture explicitly connects it with various aspects of modernity. Some works that focus particularly on advertising, in addition to Marchand, include Laird, *Advertising Progress*; Richards, *Commodity Culture*; Pope, *Making of Modern Advertising*.

7. Owen, *Capitalism and Politics*; Rieber, *Merchants and Entrepreneurs*; Ruckman, *Moscow Business Elite*.

8. Owen, *Capitalism and Politics*, ix.

9. Owen, *Corporation under Russian Law*, chap. 4.

10. Clark, *Petersburg*, 57.

11. Boym, *Common Places*, 40.

12. Ibid., 29. Theorists Iurii M. Lotman and Boris A. Uspenskii trace this dichotomy and Russian culture's difficulty in finding neutral moral ground for the profane to medieval Orthodoxy. See their essay "Role of Dual Models." See also Kelly, "*Byt*." Kelly notes the various uses of the term *byt* over time, including the neutral meaning, "way of life." However, she concedes that "detestation" of *byt* was a self-defining myth of late nineteenth- and early twentieth-century intellectual culture.

13. Kelly, *Refining Russia*, 119.

14. Steinberg, *Proletarian Imagination*, 35.

15. Stephen P. Frank, "Confronting the Domestic Other," 76.

16. T. J. Jackson Lears notes that, despite disparate calls for market segmentation, belief in this practice remained the "minority view" among American advertisers into the 1920s. The standardized, homogenous audience was middle class, with little attention paid to the working class. See "Some Versions of Fantasy," 381.

17. Timothy Burke, *Lifebuoy Men*, 20.

18. See, for instance, Tian-Shanskaia, *Village Life*; Slanskaia, "House Calls."

19. For instance, one peasant superstition told that sickness would not leave if infected rags from the patient were burned. Slanskaia, "House Calls," 197.

20. *Zolotoi iubilei*. Other companies also published flattering histories of their own businesses, for instance, P.A. Smirnov (liquor) in 1896, V. Perlov and Sons (tea) in 1898, and A. Siou (confectionary and cosmetics) in 1905. This practice was continued under the Soviets.

21. Ibid., 15.

22. Ibid., picture appears after page 18.

23. *Russkoe slovo*, May 16, 1909. Many of the newspaper advertisements cited throughout this book appeared multiple times in various daily papers. Only one reference is given for each.

24. Beer, "'Microbes of the Mind,'" 539–40.

25. Harvey, *Consciousness*, 250–51.

26. Ibid.

27. Zelnik, *Radical Worker*, 7.

28. Ibid.

29. Steinberg, *Proletarian Imagination*; see especially chap. 4.

30. *Russkoe slovo*, October 21, 1907.

31. Ibid., November 27, 1907.

32. Burds, *Peasant Dreams*, 151.

33. *Russkoe slovo*, September 10, 1911.

34. Ibid., October 2, 1911.

35. Georg Simmel, "Tendencies in German Life and Thought since 1870," *International Monthly* 5 (1902): 95. Quoted in Frisby, *Fragments of Modernity*, 42.

36. *Russkoe slovo*, August 12, 1910.

37. Ibid., December 12, 1909.

38. On the popularity of flight among the Russian public, see Palmer, *Dictatorship of the Air*, 22; and Wohl, *Passion for Wings*, chaps. 5 and 6.

39. *Gazeta-kopeika*, August 6, 1911.

40. Ibid., January 30, 1910.

41. Pamela Walker Laird notes that, along with the forerunner of branded goods, patent medicines, the first industries in America to invest heavily in brand-name packaging were tobacco, alcohol, and cosmetics because they needed to sell their products in small, consumer-sized units, rather than in bulk. *Advertising Progress*, 18–19.

42. Jib Fowles, *Advertising and Popular Culture*, 35–37.

43. Calinescu, *Five Faces of Modernity*, 3. Contemporary critics who focused on this aspect of modernity include Charles Baudelaire, Georg Simmel, and Walter Benjamin.

44. Frisby, *Fragments of Modernity*, 254–56.

45. On this tendency in Victorian British advertising, see Loeb, *Consuming Angels*.

46. Laird, *Advertising Progress*, 96–97.

47. Leo Marx has noted the tendency of Western industrialists to disseminate the "progressive world view" through "the mere appearance of the new instruments of power." "Railroad-in-the-Landscape." Quoted in Laird, *Advertising Progress*, 129.

48. TsGIA g. Moskvy, f. 51, op. 10, d. 1289, l. 38 (1916).

49. Anikst and Chernevich, *Russian Graphic Design*, 106.

50. *Moskovskii listok*, May 9, 1897. Emphasis is in the original. The advertisement was for Fru-Fru brand cigarettes.

51. *Russkoe slovo*, September 28, 1913.

52. Ibid., July 25, 1907.

53. Pallot, "Women's Domestic Industries," 175.

54. Hellberg-Hirn, *Soil and Soul*, 96.

55. Ewen and Ewen, *Channels of Desire*, 173.

56. Buck-Morss, "Dream World," 310–11.

57. See Romaniello and Starks, "Tabak: An Introduction," in *Tobacco in Russian History*, 1–2.

58. Klioutchkine, "'I Smoke,'" 85.

59. Ibid., 91.

60. Ibid., 94.

61. Tobacco was a booming industry in late imperial Russia, with 272 factories throughout the Russian empire in 1897 producing 3.5 million *puds* of loose tobacco, over 181 million cigars, and more than 6 billion large, Russian-style cigarettes (*papirosy*), as well as other tobacco products such as snuff, altogether worth over 31 million rubles. *Svod dannykh fabrichno-zavodskoi promyshlennosti*, 159. By 1908, although the number of factories had decreased to 241, the number of cigarettes manufactured had risen to 10.4 billion, and the total worth of production had almost doubled to 58 million rubles. Clearly, many Russians smoked, and the market was expanding, particularly in the demand for modern, machine-made cigarettes. Ibid., tables 2 and 21, pages 5–6 and 25–26.

62. Frank, "Confronting the Domestic Other," 86–87.

63. Rosenberg, "Representing Workers," 249.

64. *Gazeta-kopeika*, March 14, 1913.

65. S.A. Smith, "Masculinity in Transition," 102.

66. *Gazeta-kopeika*, September 18, 1910.

67. *Russkoe slovo*, February 26, 1910.

68. The same principle often applied with the naming of slaves. Olaudah Equiano, for instance, whose famous autobiography of eighteenth-century slavery (*The Interesting Narrative of the Life of Olaudah Equiano*, 1791) played an important part in the abolitionist cause, was named by his slave owner after the Swedish king, Gustavus Vassa.

69. *Gazeta-kopeika*, October 27, 1911.

70. Russian State Library poster collection. No date, but probably 1910s.

71. On the persistence of workplace paternalism, see Steinberg, *Moral Communities*. On the worker intelligentsia, see Zelnik, *Radical Worker*, and Steinberg, *Proletarian Imagination*.

72. *Gazeta-kopeika*, June 9, 1913.

73. A form of folklore that emerged in the late nineteenth century, the *chastushka* was usually a four-lined, rhymed verse, "widely popular at the points of contact between village and city." These verses were often impromptu improvisations, ranging

in content from the lyrical to the satirical and the witty insult. Smith and Kelly, "Commercial Culture," 128.

74. Although the current translation of *mashinka* is "typewriter," the literal translation "little machine" was more likely the intended one in 1910. It may refer to the increasing mechanization of tobacco production, which the industry so proudly touted. My thanks to Tricia Starks for bringing this possibility to my attention.

75. *Gazeta-kopeika*, April 16–17, 1910.

76. Frank, "Confronting the Domestic Other," 74–75. See also Engelstein, *Keys to Happiness*, 6; Neuberger, *Hooliganism*.

77. *Gazeta-kopeika*, October 31, 1911.

78. Shiryaeva, "Poetic Features," 76.

79. *Gazeta-kopeika*, May 10, 1911.

80. Ibid., April 21, 1911.

81. *Russkoe slovo*, April 18, 1910.

82. *Gazeta-kopeika,* June 8, 1913.

83. Foucault, *History of Sexuality*, 1:127.

84. Geldern, "Life In-Between," 382.

85. Brooks, *When Russia Learned to Read*.

86. Steinberg, *Proletarian Imagination*, 65.

87. Corrigan, *Sociology of Consumption*, 4.

88. Fowles, *Advertising and Popular Culture*, 30.

89. Anderson, *Imagined Communities*, 6.

90. Buck-Morss, "Dream World," 332.

91. *Russkoe slovo*, October 9, 1911.

92. Ibid., January 3, 1910.

93. See Kelly, *Refining Russia*, 130, n. 134. Kelly cites Mariamna Davydoff, *On the Estate: Memoirs of Russia before the Revolution* (London: 1986), 139. Also see Alison Smith's discussion of the development of cookbooks and cooking columns in nineteenth-century Russia, showing how these texts focused on "perfecting" and educating housewives. *Recipes for Russia*, 148.

94. *Russkoe slovo*, March 8, 1914.

95. Ibid., September 21, 1912. Advertisement for the Gramophone Company.

96. Ibid., October 30, 1911. Advertisement for the shop of I.F. Müller in Moscow.

97. Ibid., January 4, 1909.

98. Ibid., May 16, 1909.

99. Ibid., September 11, 1909.

100. *Gazeta-kopeika*, December 11, 1911.

101. Robert Bocock defines consumerism as "the active ideology that the meaning of life is to be found in buying things and pre-packaged experiences." See *Consumption*, 50. The term "consumerism" was coined in the post–World War II era in response to what was seen as a developing ideology of consumption and planned obsolescence.

102. *Russkoe slovo*, January 18, 1912.

103. Ibid., September 17, 1909.

104. Ibid., February 25, 1907.

105. Ibid., December 17, 1899.

106. Ibid., December 28, 1912.

107. *Gazeta-kopeika*, October 17, 1909.

108. *Russkoe slovo*, November 5, 1911.

109. Ibid., February 15, 1912.

110. *Zolotoi iubilei,* after p. 62.

111. *Russkoe slovo,* November 21, 1912.

112. Ibid., April 8, 1912.

113. Ibid., November 29, 1912.

114. Ibid., December 28,1913.

115. Ibid., December 24, 1913.

116. For more on the medical literature and its relationship to advertising, see Morrissey, "Economy of Nerves," 658–65.

117. *Russkoe slovo,* September 19, 1912 ("No. 4711" eau de cologne).

118. *Gazeta-kopeika,* June 10, 1912.

119. Ibid., January 11, 1909. See chap. 4 for analysis of cure-alls for gender-based maladies.

120. *Russkoe slovo,* January 17, 1910.

121. Ibid., November 25, 1909.

122. By one estimate the suicide rate in St. Petersburg jumped from 903 in 1906 to 3,196 in 1910. The city had become one of the "suicide capitals of Europe." Morrissey, *Suicide,* 314–16.

123. Ibid., 314.

124. *Russkoe slovo,* June 20, 1913.

125. *Gazeta-kopeika,* January 25, 1909.

126. On the renovations of the trading rows, see Marjorie Hilton, "Commercial Cultures," ch. 3.

127. *Russkoe slovo,* February 8, 1905.

128. Ibid., January 10, 1906.

129. See Owen, *Capitalism and Politics,* chap. 7; Rieber, *Merchants and Entrepreneurs,* chaps. 7 and 8.

130. *Russkoe slovo,* February 23, 1907.

131. The title contains a play on the words *duma* (parliament) and *umnyi* (clever). Its double meaning may be translated as "Parliamentary/clever advice." *Gazeta-kopeika,* November 9, 1912. The terms "Trudovik" and "Kadet" refer to two of the political parties that emerged in 1905.

132. The zemstvo reform of 1864 instituted limited local self-government in the provinces. Many zemstvo activists staffed provincial schools, clinics, and other projects to benefit the rural population.

133. *Russkoe slovo,* January 31, 1907.

134. Schudson, *Advertising,* 214.

135. Burds, *Peasant Dreams,* 152.

4—BEAUTY AND BRAVADO

1. Written in 1889 and first published in 1891.

2. See, for instance, Loeb, *Consuming Angels.*

3. On the prevalent association between women and clothes shopping in late imperial Russia, see Ruane, "Clothes Shopping."

4. In 1897 St. Petersburg, for instance, there were 121 men for every 100 women. S.A. Smith, "Masculinity in Transition," 95, 109.

5. More work has been done recently in this field for the Soviet and post-Soviet periods, but Clements, Friedman, and Healy's *Russian Masculinities in History*

and Culture is an excellent collection of essays spanning the Muscovite through the Soviet periods.

6. See Engel, *Mothers and Daughters*, 8.

7. For a useful overview of the development of these associations, see Grazia, introduction to pt. 1, in *Sex of Things*.

8. See Marjorie Hilton's survey of memoir literature on this issue. "Commercial Cultures," 90–92.

9. One of the best historical treatments of the impact of department stores on women's ability to shop freely is in Rosalind Williams, *Dream Worlds*. As Christine Ruane correctly notes, however, fixed-price shopping could be intimidating for lower-class women, who felt unwelcome in stores with goods priced beyond their range. See "Clothes Shopping," 769.

10. Christopher Breward points out that contemporary perceptions and subsequent scholarship emphasized department stores as the focal points of early consumer culture, thus obscuring much male shopping activity that took place in smaller establishments such as outfitters and hosiers. *Hidden Consumer*, 101. Geoffrey Crossick and Serge Jaumain note that department stores constituted a small proportion of retail establishments in the West by 1910 (only 2–3 percent in Britain and Germany and less than one percent in the United States), in contrast to the extensive critical and scholarly attention paid to them. See *Cathedrals of Consumption*, 5–6. Moscow only boasted one department store at that time (Miur and Mirrielees), although shopping arcades were more common (about ten existed in downtown Moscow). See Gohstand, "Internal Geography," 612–18. See also Matthew Hilton, "Class, Consumption," 659.

11. Ruane, "Clothes Shopping," 770.

12. Kuchta, "Self-Made Man." Kuchta places the origin of the trend toward simplicity in male dress with the late seventeenth-century English aristocracy, who were responding to the more modest styles of William and Mary after the Glorious Revolution. A century later the middle class began to appropriate "sartorial restraint" as their own sign of moral virtue. For the later period, see Breward, *Hidden Consumer*, 24.

13. Men's vicarious acquisition of status through their wives' consumption was a major point of Thorstein Veblen's *Theory of the Leisure Class*. Leora Auslander encapsulates the point nicely by showing that the bourgeois home, the quintessence of the domestic sphere, was in reality fully part of the outside world because it constructed the family's identity for that world. See "Gendering of Consumer Practices," 83.

14. For an elaboration of the argument for empowerment that goes against the general feminist critique of consumer culture, see the study of the cosmetics industry by Peiss, *Hope in a Jar*. See also Scott, *Fresh Lipstick*.

15. As Mary Douglas and Baron Isherwood put it, "Goods are neutral; their uses are social." *World of Goods*, xv.

16. Ibid., 49.

17. See Ruane's discussion of social commentator Iulii Elets's 1914 diatribe against women's obsession with shopping. "Clothes Shopping," 773–75.

18. Felski, *Gender of Modernity*, 19.

19. Ibid., 62.

20. Ibid.

21. Some scholars of eighteenth- and nineteenth-century Britain have also begun to question the assumed predominance of women in consumption. See Breward, *Hidden Consumer*; and Finn, "Men's Things," 133–55.

22. Loeb, *Consuming Angels*, 11–12.

23. "The Appeal to Women," *Advertising World* (February 1913): 208. Cited in Loeb, *Consuming Angels*, 8–9.

24. Glickman, *Russian Factory Women*, 111.

25. See Engel, *Mothers and Daughters*, 7; Wagner, "Trojan Mare."

26. *Russkoe slovo*, March 3, 1909. The ad first appeared in February.

27. Ibid., March 10, 1909.

28. Even tea, one of the items listed, had been a luxury item in Russia until the late nineteenth century. Smith and Christian, *Bread and Salt*, 234–35.

29. *Russkoe slovo*, March 11, 1907.

30. Olga Vainshtein, "Russian Dandyism," 59.

31. Ibid., 60. Vainshtein notes that western European dandies disdained uniforms as a suppression of their individuality, and she suggests that the level of governmental control in Russia may have intensified the "semiotic code" imbued by Russian men into the details of their dress. Ibid., 64.

32. Ibid., 70–71.

33. Skilled metalworkers in 1908 St. Petersburg spent over fifteen percent of their income on clothing and footwear. S. A. Smith, "Masculinity in Transition," 107.

34. *Russkoe slovo*, April 6, 1907. For some workers there was pride in dressing according to one's class. The peaked cap, for instance, was part of the unofficial workers' "uniform," which some fashion-conscious men rejected in favor of hats. S.A. Smith, "Masculinity in Transition," 107.

35. In addition to department stores and arcades, by 1911 Moscow could boast 267 individual stores that sold ready-made clothing. Ruane, "Clothes Shopping," 766.

36. Steinberg, "Workers in Suits," 132.

37. *Russkoe slovo*, March 17, 1907.

38. Ibid., March 10, 1910.

39. Ibid., March 11, 1914.

40. *Gazeta-kopeika*, August 19, 1909.

41. *Russkoe slovo*, November 12, 1913.

42. Russian State Library poster collection.

43. *Russkoe slovo*, February 16, 1914. La Ferme's No. 6 brand.

44. Ibid., April 18, 1907.

45. *Russkoe slovo*, November 6, 1907.

46. Goffman, *Gender Advertisements*, 25, 43–45.

47. *Russkoe slovo*, December 4, 1912.

48. Engel, "Transformation Versus Tradition," 138.

49. Evgeniia Tur, *Plemiannitsa*, cited in Tovrov, "Mother-Child Relationships," 37.

50. *Peterburgskaia gazeta*, May 9, 1892.

51. Ibid., May 6, 1903.

52. Russian State Library poster collection.

53. *Russkoe slovo*, November 28, 1910.

54. *Gazeta-kopeika*, August 10, 1911.

55. Kelly, "'Better Halves'?"

56. Cited in Bisha and others, *Russian Women*, 58.

57. *Gazeta-kopeika*, February 29, 1912.

58. Ibid., August 3, 1912.

59. Bobroff, "Russian Working Women," 213–14.

60. *Russkoe slovo,* November 18, 1911.

61. Examples of such poems included "Betrayal" (*Izmena*), *Gazeta-kopeika,* April 12, 1912, and "Serenade," *Gazeta-kopeika,* December 25, 1911.

62. Bobroff, "Russian Working Women," 224. In contrast, folk songs demanded exclusive love from a woman, no matter how fickle or abusive her husband.

63. *Gazeta-kopeika,* March 30, 1912.

64. Ibid., August 26, 1910. The poem reads: "If the mother-in-law is pressuring you, / Everything in the house is flying topsy-turvy, / If since morning washing soda / Is already filling your home, / Then friends, don't despair, / Smile, sneeze your fill, / Smoke Iar and then / The rest is trivial." Iar means "ravine," but it was also the name of a popular restaurant in Moscow.

65. Ibid., January 12, 1911.

66. See Kelly, "'Better Halves'?" and Bobroff, "Russian Working Women."

67. *Russkoe slovo,* November 23, 1907.

68. For an example of the rheumatism ads, see *Gazeta-kopeika,* June 6, 1911.

69. See Transchel, *Under the Influence.*

70. *Russkoe slovo,* October 7, 1912.

71. One ad from 1914, for instance, showed a man raising his fist to his cowering wife, with the testimony that thanks to the remedy his "inclination for alcohol stopped." Ibid., May 3, 1914.

72. Although alcoholism among women was far less common than among men, nonetheless it did exist. Approximately 6.5% of all people treated for alcoholism in the early 1900s were women. See Mendel'son, *Lechenie alkogolizma,* 25. My thanks to Kate Transchel for this reference.

73. *Gazeta-kopeika,* October, 14, 1912. Shapshal's Kumir brand.

74. Ibid., March 25, 1912.

75. *Russkoe slovo,* January 20, 1912.

76. Ibid., March 8, 1909. Bogdanov's Roskosh (luxury) brand.

77. *Gazeta-kopeika,* May 3, 1912. "A surprising discovery for weak, nervous men."

78. Kelly, *Refining Russia,* 176. Susan K. Morrissey emphasizes the similarities between medical advice literature and advertising in her article, "Economy of Nerves," 663.

79. *Gazeta-kopeika,* October 23, 1912.

80. *Moskovskii listok,* May 5, 1902.

81. *Gazeta-kopeika,* September 3, 1911.

82. *Russkoe slovo,* July 8, 1907.

83. Ibid., October 21, 1917.

84. *Nashe vremia,* May 1, 1903.

85. *Russkoe slovo,* March 7, 1910.

86. Ibid., March 1, 1907.

87. *Peterburgskii listok,* October 27, 1911.

88. *Russkoe slovo,* August 14, 1911. "Jeanne Grenier's method."

89. Ibid., January 13, 1913. "Metamorphosis of the bust."

90. Ibid., August 14, 1911.

91. *Gazeta-kopeika,* December 2, 1912.

92. *Russkoe slovo,* August 15, 1913. "A magnificent bust guaranteed within a month."

93. One of the major contentions of the Russian women's movement in the late nineteenth century was that women should be educated for more than the fulfillment of domestic duties. See Stites, *Women's Liberation,* pts. 2 and 3.

94. Tovrov, "Mother-Child Relationships," 38.

95. Bobroff, "Russian Working Women," 206–27.

96. Stites, *Women's Liberation*, 7.

97. *Gazeta-kopeika*, February 10, 1913. "Sexual hunger. Are you numbered among these people?"

98. See Lutz, *American Nervousness*, and Lears, "From Salvation to Self-Realization." On neurasthenia in Russia, see Morrissey, "Economy of Nerves." Morrissey also discusses the Spermin advertisements, noting that the product was derived from the testicles of bulls and stallions ("Economy of Nerves," 666).

99. *Moskovskii listok*, May 6, 1907.

100. A euphemism commonly used in patent medicine advertisements.

101. Engelstein, *Keys to Happiness*, 222. The quotation is from a 1905 work on prostitution and venereal disease by Voronezh physician and medical editor Anatolii Sabinin.

102. *Gazeta-kopeika*, October 23, 1912.

103. Ibid., October 27, 1913.

104. *Russkoe slovo*, October 7, 1911.

105. Ibid., March 13, 1914. "Men, here is an example for you!"

106. *Gazeta-kopeika*, October 27, 1913.

107. Ibid., January 9, 1911. "To men—a word of truth."

108. Ibid., February 8, 1909.

109. *Russkoe slovo*, May 3 1907. On Krafft-Ebing, see Engelstein, *Keys to Happiness*, 131–32.

110. *Gazeta-kopeika*, March 13, 1912.

111. Ibid., March 20, 1912. The word *bogatyr* (a medieval folk hero) is also used in association with athletic champions.

112. *Russkoe slovo*, October 29, 1909. Advertisement for the Shaposhnikov factory.

113. McReynolds, *Russia at Play*, 132–33. McReynolds discusses the world champion wrestler Ivan Poddubnyi as an example of the masculine ideal suited to industrial society.

114. Worobec, "Masculinity," 82.

115. McReynolds, "Visualizing Masculinity," 134.

116. *Russkoe slovo*, April 29, 1914.

117. Russian State Library poster collection. The copywriter, Sergei Korotkii, often portrayed himself in his tobacco advertisements and pamphlets.

5—MODERNITY THROUGH TRADITION

1. The inclusion of the Shustov factory comes at the end of a long list of Moscow's claims to fame, here translated only in part. *Gazeta-kopeika*, December 3, 1911.

2. Charles Baudelaire's oft-cited definition states: "Modernity is the transient, the fleeting, the contingent; it is one half of art, the other being the eternal and the immoveable." From "Painter of Modern Life," 403.

3. On the relatively recent creation of many traditions usually assumed to be centuries old, see Hobsbawm and Ranger, *Invention of Tradition*.

4. Lotman and Uspenskii, "Role of Dual Models," 28.

5. Boym, *Common Places*, 30.

6. Ibid., 5.

7. The notion of culturally constructed, "imagined" communities goes back to Benedict Anderson's analysis of modern nationalism, but his widely adopted phrase is often appropriate in other contexts of cultural construction. See his *Imagined Communities*.

8. Renan, "What is a Nation?" 145.

9. Twitchell, *Adcult USA*, 43.

10. Hughes, "Monuments and Identity," 171.

11. Stuart Hall, "For Allon White," 294.

12. Ibid., 292.

13. Hughes, "Monuments and Identity," 172.

14. Johnson, *Peasant and Proletarian*, 31.

15. Bater, *St. Petersburg*, 254.

16. See especially Burds, *Peasant Dreams*, 128–31; and Steinberg, *Proletarian Imagination*, 196.

17. Russian State Library poster collection.

18. Ibid., no date.

19. Brooks, *When Russia Learned to Read*, chap. 3.

20. Burds, *Peasant Dreams*, 24.

21. *Russkoe slovo*, April 17, 1914.

22. Burds, *Peasant Dreams*, 178.

23. Shapshal Brothers Tobacco Company, "'Kumir' v pesniakh," 11. The story was also printed without illustration in *Gazeta-kopeika*, August 26, 1912.

24. Bailey and Ivanova, *Russian Folk Epics*, 293–306.

25. See Burke, *Popular Culture*, chap. 1, "Discovery of the People."

26. Letter from artist Elena Polenova to P.D. Antipova, 1885. Quoted in Alison Hilton, "Russian Folk Art," 237.

27. Alison Hilton, "Russian Folk Art," 237.

28. Gray, *Russian Experiment in Art*, 10.

29. Brown, "Native Song," 78. Brown points out, however, that folk influences in Russian composition had a long tradition, going back well into the eighteenth century.

30. One of the many tensions of Tolstoy's life was the pride he continued to feel in his aristocratic heritage, alongside his impulses toward the simple peasant life. In between his affinities for both the aristocracy and the peasantry, however, he felt little comprehension for those in the middle of society, especially his petty bourgeois compatriots. He noted that he could no more understand what a shopkeeper feels "as he invites people to buy braces and ties" than he could understand "what a cow thinks when it is being milked." Quoted in Nikolai Tolstoy, *Tolstoys*, 271.

31. *Russkoe slovo*, May 7, 1905.

32. Some of Vasnetsov's subjects were too mythical to suit his fellow Wanderers' taste for realism, but he is nevertheless considered a member of this circle of artists.

33. Bailey and Ivanova, *Russian Folk Epics*, xx.

34. Sokolov, *Russian Folklore*, 291. Emphasis on the heroic Russian people carries overtones of the Stalinist period during which this book was originally written.

35. For a discussion of Vasnetsov's creation of this painting, see Galerkina, *Vasnetsov*, 84–86.

36. Goscilo, "Viktor Vasnetsov's Bogatyrs."

37. Russian State Library poster collection. No date.

38. Goscilo, "Viktor Vasnetsov's Bogatyrs," 250.

39. Douglas, "Jokes," 295–96.

40. Russian State Library poster collection. No date.

41. Benjamin, *Illuminations*, 221.

42. Dégh, *American Folklore*, 1.

43. Ibid., 2.

44. Ibid., 37.

45. Ibid., 53.

46. For a critical overview of Orthodoxy's essentialized treatment in much of Russian historiography, see the introduction to Kivelson and Greene, *Orthodox Russia*.

47. *Russkoe slovo*, March 19, 1909. The Einem Company. This advertisement was repeated over several years.

48. Ibid., April 10, 1913. Nikolai Ivanovich Kazakov, baker and confectioner.

49. In general, the Orthodox church had more religious holidays than Western churches. Burds, *Peasant Dreams*, 121–22.

50. On department store holiday displays, see Majorie Hilton, "Commercial Cultures," 124.

51. *Russkoe slovo*, April 8, 1905. This advertisement is just one example of egg-shaped Easter packaging, which was common among toiletries firms. On the Lilies of the Valley egg, see Forbes, *Fabergé Eggs*, 54–55. My thanks to Julia DeLancey for pointing out the ad's imitation of this particular Fabergé egg.

52. *Russkoe slovo*, March 28, 1914.

53. Fraser, *House by the Dvina*, 147–48. Of mixed Russian and Scottish parentage, the author grew up in a merchant family in Archangel from 1905 to 1920. Note that in British English, "fancy dress ball" means "costume ball," which corresponds more closely to the imagery in fig. 5.9.

54. Sokolov, *Russian Folklore*, 187.

55. *Russkoe slovo*, February 7, 1906.

56. Buck-Morss, *Dialectics*, 81–82.

57. Buck-Morss, "Dream World of Mass Culture," 318.

58. Lears, *Fables of Abundance*, 9.

59. Hubbs, *Mother Russia*, xv.

60. Ivanits, *Russian Folk Belief*, 15.

61. Hubbs, *Mother Russia*, xiv.

62. Hellberg-Hirn, *Soil and Soul*, 112.

63. P. Ostashov, Moscow, 1884. From the Russian State Library collection, Moscow. Also reproduced in Anikst and Chernevich, *Russian Graphic Design*, 93.

64. A broad and varied array of female images throughout the centuries has been interpreted by some scholars as representations of Mother Russia. Hellberg-Hirn, for instance, sees her in guises as diverse as the popular tourist souvenir nesting doll (*matrioshka*) and the fierce female patriot in World War II posters, urging her compatriots to fight (*Soil and Soul*, 116–20).

65. *Russkoe slovo*, September 8, 1905.

66. Russian State Library poster collection, Moscow.

67. See for example Naremore and Brantlinger, *Modernity and Mass Culture*, 5; and Rosalind Williams, *Dream Worlds*, chap. 1.

68. On Singer's advertising strategies, see Coffin, *Politics of Women's Work*, chap. 3; Ruane, *Empire's New Clothes*, 58–61, 138–43; Carstensen, *American Enterprise*.

69. On attitudes to commercialization as "foreign," see Smith and Kelly, "Commercial Culture," 136.

70. Franklin and Widdis, *National Identity*, xii.

71. For instance, consider Vissarion Belinskii's words: "Everything human is European, and everything European is human. . . . Peter acted entirely within the national spirit when he brought his native land into closer contact with Europe." From his article "On I.I. Golikov's Work, *The Deeds of Peter the Great*," 1841, excerpted in Vernadsky, *Source Book*, 2:568.

72. Slavophile Konstantin Aksakov, for one, expressed these ideas in the 1850s.

For example: "All European states are formed by conquest. Their fundamental principle is enmity. . . . The Russian state, on the contrary, was founded, not by conquest, but by a *voluntary invitation* to govern. Hence, its basis is not hatred but peace and harmony." From his manucript "Concerning the Fundamental Principles of Russian History." On the necessary foreignness of the state, consider the following from his manuscript "Short Historical Sketch of the Zemskii Sobor": "Recognizing the state as a necessary, unavoidable evil, regarding it merely as an extraneous means, and not the goal, not the ideal of their national existence, the Slavs (in Russia) did not transform themselves into a state . . . but summoned the state from overseas, from outside, from an alien place, as an alien phenomenon." Excerpted in Vernadsky, *Source Book*, 577–79.

73. Wortman, *Scenarios of Power*, 1:5. The last two tsars turned to overt identification with Russianness, favoring the pre-Petrine past. Nicholas II's sense of sanctified autocracy and mystical union with his people ran counter not only to the tumultuous politics of Russian society in the last decades of tsarist rule (see ibid., 2:366) but also to the realities of modernizing commerce and culture.

74. On the geographical separation between Russian and foreign retailing in Moscow, see Marjorie Hilton, "Commercial Cultures," and Ruane, "Clothes Shopping."

75. Tolz, *Russia*. For her larger discussion of the perception of the Russian empire as a nation-state, see all of chap. 5.

76. Ibid., 178.

77. Boym, *Common Places*, 24.

78. Hellberg-Hirn, *Soil and Soul*, 37.

79. *Russkoe slovo*, December 6, 1912. On the late nineteenth-century increase in awareness of public monuments due to the greater ease of travel and wider dissemination of tourist information, see Hughes, "Monuments and Identity," 180.

80. This particular example is from *Gazeta-kopeika*, January 9, 1910, but the advertisement was long-lived and widespread.

81. Hughes, "Monuments and Identity," 178.

82. TsGIA g. Moskvy, f. 473, op. 1, d. 11, l. 42.

83. *Russkoe slovo*, January 26, 1907.

84. On the tsar's commemoration, see Wortman, *Scenarios of Power*, vol. 2, chap. 12.

85. *Gazeta-kopeika*, November 4, 1910.

86. See Stephen Norris, *War of Images*, 13–19.

87. *Russkoe slovo*, February 14, 1912.

88. Ibid., September 27, 1912.

89. Ibid., December 17, 1911. For photographs of Napoleon-themed commercial packaging in 1912 from the collection of the State Historical Museum in Moscow, see *Torgovai reklama*, 59, 62–63.

90. See Wortman, *Scenarios of Power*, vol. 2, chap. 13; and Clark, *Petersburg*, chap. 2.

91. *Russkoe slovo*, May 25, 1913.

92. Poster reproduced in Anikst and Chernevich, *Russian Graphic Design*, 97.

93. *Russkoe slovo*, March 3, 1913.

94. Wortman, *Scenarios of Power*, 2:440–42.

95. Ibid., 2:443.

96. Ibid., 2:445.

97. Produced from at least 1905 on.

98. *Russkoe slovo*, February 2, 1905.

99. *Gazeta-kopeika*, November 24, 1911.

100. Ibid., November 21, 1911.

101. Boym, *Common Places*, 5.

102. Brooks, "Russian Nationalism," 315.

103. See McReynolds and Neuberger, *Imitations of Life*. Beth Holmgren also discusses the blurring of divisions between popular and classical literature as the late imperial press facilitated the expansion of the literary market. See "Gendering the Icon."

104. Brooks, *When Russia Learned to Read*, 325. See also McReynolds on the impact of the press: *News*.

105. Brooks, "Russian Nationalism," 316.

106. Ibid., 322.

107. Ibid., 325. For example, by 1895 Suvorin had printed 3.8 million copies of his "Inexpensive Library."

108. Ibid., 329.

109. GIM, f. 37, op. 1, d. 556, l. 132. Those featured are: Zhukovskii, Glinka, Krylov, Derzhavin, Goncharov, Nekrasov, Lermontov, Griboedov, and Gogol'. Pushkin was also part of this series.

110. Even though education was not mandatory in imperial Russia, by the early twentieth century primary school education was spreading. In 1911 roughly forty-eight percent of eight- to eleven-year-olds were in school empire-wide. Urban children were more likely to be in school than rural (seventy-five percent of urban boys and fifty-nine percent of girls). See Eklof, *Russian Peasant Schools*, 293.

111. Levine, *Highbrow/Lowbrow*, 4.

112. Translation by John Fennel, in *Pushkin* (Baltimore, MD: Penguin Books, 1964), 235–36.

113. *Peterburgskaia gazeta*, May 9, 1912.

114. I have been unable to find any archival records for the Shustov liquor company, so it is not clear who wrote its advertising copy. The consistently irreverent tone suggests a single author—or perhaps the guiding spirit of the owner.

115. Moeller-Sally, "Parallel Lives," 78.

116. *Gazeta-kopeika*, January 26, 1912.

117. Ibid., November 19, 1911.

118. Ibid., December 12, 1911.

119. Steve Smith and Catriona Kelly assert that the Russian elite were more "condescending" to their noneducated countrymen than the elite of any nation in late nineteenth-century Europe. See "Commercial Culture," 154. On popular entertainment see also McReynolds, *Russia at Play*; Stites, *Russian Popular Culture*; Geldern and McReynolds, *Entertaining Tsarist Russia*.

120. Douglas, "Jokes," 297, 301.

121. *Gazeta-kopeika*, June 19, 1912.

122. Steinberg, *Proletarian Imagination*, 90.

123. Shustov ads never disclosed price, but they did occasionally mention that this cognac was cheaper than (and just as good as) foreign brands. We can assume that it was accessible to many poorer pockets, or the sustained focus on *Gazeta-kopeika's* readership would have made no business sense.

124. Wicke, *Advertising Fictions*, 11. Wicke argues for the symbiotic rise of Western advertising and the modern novel.

125. *Gazeta-kopeika*, November 5, 1911.

126. Ibid., April 6, 1912.

127. Stites, *Russian Popular Culture*, 22.

128. Lears, "Some Versions of Fantasy," 349.

BIBLIOGRAPHY

PRIMARY SOURCES

Periodicals

Gazeta-kopeika
Kommivoiazher torgovo-promyshlennyi zhurnal
Kupechestvo i promyshlennost'
Moskovskii listok
Niva
Peterburgskaia gazeta
Reklamist
Russkie vedomosti
Russkoe slovo
Russkoe torgovoe delo
Torgovlia
Torgovlia i sovremennaia tekhnika
Torgovlia i zhizn'
Torgovlia, promyshlennost' i tekhnika
Torgovo-promyshlennoe obozrenie
Torgovo-promyshlennyi i kommissionyi obozrevatel'
Torgovo promyshlennyi mir
Torgovyi mir
Ves' Peterburg
Vsia Moskva
Zhurnal kommercheskii mir

Archival Materials

GIM:
f. 1   Bakhrushin (1673–1917)
f. 37   Simoni, Pavel Konstantinovich
f. 122   Botkiny-Guchkovy
f. 195   Stromilov, N.S.
f. 402   Muzei staroi Moskvy

ORRGB:
f. 10   D.N. Anuchin (pk. 29: Otcheti gazety *Russkie vedomosti*)
f. 251   V.A. Rozenberg (pk. 27: Otcheti gazety *Russkie vedomosti*)
f. 259   *Russkoe slovo*

RGALI:
f. 191   Efremov, Petr Aleksandrovich
f. 595   *Russkoe slovo*
f. 598   *Kur'er*
f. 880   Taneevy, S.I. i V.I.
f. 912   Shaliapin, F.I.

f. 1657 Khudekov, Sergei Nikolaevich
f. 1666 *Rech'*
f. 1701 *Russkie vedomosti*
f. 2085 Glier, Reingol'd Moritsevich
f. 2430 Kollekstiia Rabinovicha, L'va Il'icha

RGIA:
f. 20 Departament torgovli i manufaktur
f. 22 Tsentral'nye uchrezhdeniia Ministerstva Finansov po chasti torgovli i promyshlennosti
f. 23 Ministerstvo torgovli i promyshlennosti
f. 472 Kantseliariia Ministerstva imperatorskago dvora
f. 564 Redaktsiia periodicheskikh izdanii Ministerstva Finansov
f. 776 Kantseliariia glavnago upravleniia po delam pechati
f. 1278 Gosudarstvennaia duma
f. 1409 Sobstvennoi ego imperatorskago velichestva kantseliarii

TsGIA g. Moskvy:
f. 16 Kantseliariia moskovskogo general-gubernatora
f. 31 Moskovskii tsenzurnyi komitet po delam pechati
f. 51 Moskovskaia kazennaia palata
f. 429 Tovarishchestvo parfiumernogo proizvodstva "Brokar i Ko."
f. 473 Tovarishchestvo tabachnoi fabriki "Dukat"
f. 639 Rossiiskoe vzaimnoe obshchestvo kuptsov, fabrikantov i zavodchikov dlia sodeistviia razvitiia torgovykh snoshenii i oborotov, 1911–1914
f. 759 Tovarishchestvo chainoi torgovli Vysotskogo i Ko.
f. 766 Tovarishchestvo chainoi torgovli i skladov "Brat'ia K. i S. Popovy"
f. 877 Tovarishchestvo tipo-litografiia I.M. Mashistova v Moskve
f. 1098 Tovarishchestvo vysshei parfiumerii Ralle i Ko.
f. 1171 Tovarishchestvo tabachnoi fabriki S. Gabai
f. 1828 Tovarishchestvo parfiumernoi fabriki A.M. Ostroumova

TsGIA SPb:
f. 1584 Torgovyi dom "L. i E. Mettsl' i Ko." Kontora ob"iavlenii

Books, Articles, and Other Primary Sources

Abramovich, N. Ia. "Russkoe slovo." Petrograd: K-vo "Pamflet," 1916.

Altundzhi, Petr. *Krupneishiia torgovo-promyshlennyia i tekhnicheskiia firmy gor. Rostova na Donu.* Rostov-on-Don: 1910.

Baudelaire, Charles. "The Painter of Modern Life." In *Selected Writings on Art and Literature.* Translated by P. E. Charvet. London: Penguin, 1992.

Beable, William Henry. *Commercial Russia.* London: Constable & Co., 1918.

Blau, A. A., comp. *Torgovo-promyshlennaia Rossiia.* St. Petersburg: Novoe Vremia, 1899.

Bobrov, S. P. "Osnovy novoi Russkoi zhivopisi." *Trudy vserossiiskago s"ezda khudozhnikov v Petrograde* 1 (December 1911–January 1912): 41–46.

Burshtein, M. I., comp. *Kommercheskii spravochnik i ezhegodnik n 1912 god.* Odessa: Knigoizdatel'stvo Biblioteka kommercheskikh znanii, 1912.

Buryshkin, Pavel Afanas'evich. *Moskva kupecheskaia.* Moscow: Izdatel'stvo Vysshaia shkola, 1991.

Chai. Proisvodstvo chaia. Torgovlia chaem v Rossii i v drugikh stranakh. Moscow: Izdanie T-va Karavan, 19—.

Chekhov, A.P. *Sochineniia.* Berlin: Slovo, 1921.

Chto vami sdelano . . . ot sluzhashchikh khoziaevam v chest' piatidesiatiletiia torgovago doma A. Siou i Ko. Moscow: 1905.

Dokhman, I. A. *Raskleika i raznoska reklam.* Poltava: 1904.

Engels, Friedrich. *The Condition of the Working Class in England.* 1845. Oxford: Oxford University Press, 1999.

Fraser, Eugenie. *The House by the Dvina: A Russian Childhood.* 1984. London: Corgi Books, 1993.

Gautier, Théophile. *Voyage en Russie.* Paris: 1961.

Guliaev, A. I. *Spravochnaia kniga po torgovopromyshlennomu zakonodatel'stvu i torgovoi praktike.* St. Petersburg: Izdanie T-vo Knizhnoe Delo, 1912.

Ia., S. *Ob"iavleniia i drugiia sredstva reklamy.* Moscow: 1904.

Ipatov, A. D. *Bylye gody. Vospominaniia starykh rabochikh tabachnykh fabrik g. Saratova.* Saratov: Saratovskoi oblastnoe izdatel'stvo, 1937.

Iskusstvo prodavat'. Odessa: Torgovoe delo, 1911.

Iskusstvo rasprostranit' svoi tovar. Soviety sdaiushchim ob"iavelniia. Moscow: T-vo tipografii A.I. Mamontova, 1913.

Istoricheskii ocherk firmy postavshchika dvora ego imperatorskago velichestva vysochaish utverzhdennago tovarishchestva Petra Arsen'evicha Smirnova. Moscow: Tipografiia M.G. Volchaninova, 1896.

Iubileiyny al'bom postavshchikov dvora ego imperatorskago velichestva i velikoknizheskikh dvorov. St. Petersburg: 191–.

Korotkii, Sergei Apollonovich. *Diadia Mikhei za granitsei.* St. Petersburg: 1905.

———. "Tabachnoe zelie" na Rusi. St. Petersburg: 1907.

———. *Puteshestvie za tabakami na vostok, 1903–1904 gg.* Petrograd: 1915.

Kra––vskii, A. *Mozhno li v Moskve torgovat' chestno?* Moscow: 1886.

Manolov, I.U. *Sovremennyi ocherk torgovli i promyshlennosti Rossiiskoi imperii.* St. Petersburg, 1897.

Mendel'son, A.L. *Lechenie alkogolizma v ambulatoriiakh S.-Peterburgskago gorodskogo popechitel'stva o narodnoi trezvosti, 1903–1909 gg.* St. Petersburg: 1910.

Mezhdunarodnaia vystavka khudozhestvennykh afish. Katalog. St. Petersburg: 1897.

Mirles, A. *Iskusstvo reklamirovat'sia.* Vladimir-Volynsk: 1901.

Moskva v eia proshlom i nastoiashchem. Moscow: Moskovskoe T-vo Obrazovanie, 1909.

Nikolaev, Ivan K. *K voprosu o gazetnykh publikatsiiakh.* Moscow: Russkoe bibliograficheskoe obshchestvo pri imperatorskom Moskovskom universitete, 1907.

Novye puti dlia reklamy. Moscow: 1913.

Ogir, M. *Reklama, kak factor vnusheniia v obshchestvennoi zhizni.* Riga: 1913.

Okhochinskii, V. K. *Plakat.* Leningrad: 1926.

Okunev, V.N. *Sovremennaia bor'ba s fal'sifikatsiei i torgovym obmanom.* Petrograd: Tipografiia Petrogradskoi tiur'my, 1915.

Otchet i balans tovarishchestva chainoi torgovli Petra Botkina Synov'ia c 1-go okt. 1907, po 1-oe okt. 1908. Moscow: 1909.

Otchet obshchestva torgovtsev tabachnymi izdeliiami za 1909 god. St. Petersburg: 1910.

———. . . . za 1910 god. St. Petersburg, 1911.

———. . . . za 1912 god. St. Petersburg, 1913.

Pamiati Genrikha Afanas'evicha Brokar. Moscow: 1901.

Pekarskii, V.F. *Torgovaia reklama, konkurentsiia i potrebitel'skiia obshchestva.* Petrograd: Izdatel'stvo T-vo kooperativnykh Soiuzov "kooperatsiia," 1918.

Pervaia vseobshchaia perepis' naseleniia Rossiisskoi Imperii, 1897 g., 50 vols. St. Petersburg: 1897.

"Peterburgskiia vyveski." *Illiustratsiia* 30 (1848): 81–82.

Plavuchaia vystavka Russkikh tovarov, 1909–1910. Moscow: 1911.

Pliskii, N. *Reklama: Eia znachenie, proiskhozhdenie i istoriia.* St. Petersburg: Izdanie F.V. Shchepanskii, 1894.

Ratner, A. *Tekhnika reklamy ob"iavleniiami.* St. Petersburg: 1908.

Reklama est' dvigatel' torgovli. Kazan: Izdanie Iv. Ivanova, 1900.

Roin-Bobrov, A.G. *Torgovlia i promyshlennost' skvoz' prizmu opyta.* Warsaw: Izdanie fabrichno-promyshlennago i torgovago doma Aron Biber, 1913.

Rossiiskoe vzaimnoe obshchestva kuptsov, fabrikantov i zavodchikov: Nastol'naia spravochnaia kniga dlia kommersantov. Moscow: 1912.

Rowell, George P. *Forty Years an Advertising Agent, 1865–1905.* New York: Printer's Ink, 1906.

Rukovodstvo reklamirovat'. Odessa: Kommercheskaia biblioteka, no. 1, 1911.

Semeniuk, A. *Zhivopisets vyvesok.* Petrograd: 1916.

Shapiro, A.N., ed. *Sputnik pokupatelia, torgovo-spravochnyi zhurnal.* Samara: 1913.

Shaposhnikov Tobacco Company. *V tumane merknut dni Stambula.* Petrograd: 1915.

Shapshal Brothers Tobacco Company. *Zabavnoe povestvovanie.* St. Petersburg: 1911.

———. *Liubimitsa publiki papirosa "Kumir" v pesniakh, skazkakh i pribautkakh.* 3rd ed. St. Petersburg: 1913.

———. *Boevaia povest' Markel i "Kumir."* Petrograd: 1915.

Sherman, Sidney A. "Advertising in the United States." *Journal of the American Statistical Association* 7 (December 1900): 120–62.

Shustov, A.S. *Sankt-Peterburgskoe kupechestvo i torgovo-promyshlennyia predpriiatiia goroda k 200-letnemu iubileiu stolitsy.* St. Petersburg: 1903.

Slonimskii, L.Z. "Periodicheskaia pechat' i kapitalizm." *Vestnik Evropy* 7 (1910): 286–95.

Snegirev, N. *Lubochnyia kartinki russkago naroda v Moskovskom mire.* Moscow: 1861.

Sokolov, N.V. *Ekonomicheskie voprosy i zhurnal'noe delo.* St. Petersburg, 1866.

Sputnik pokupatelia. Samara: Izdatel'stvo Sotrudnik Torgovli, 1913.

Sredinskii, S. *Gazetno-Izdatel'stvoe delo.* Moscow: 1924.

Stolpianskii, P.N. *Zhizn' i byt peterburgskoi fabriki za 210 let ee sushchestvovaniia, 1704–1914 gg.* Leningrad: Izdanie Leningradskogo Gubernskogo Soveta Professional'nykh Soiuza, 1925.

Svedeniia o torgovykh domakh, deistvovavshikh v Rossii v 1892 godu. St. Petersburg: 1893.

Svod dannykh fabrichno-zavodskoi promyshlennosti v Rossii za 1897 god. St. Petersburg: Ministry of Finance, 1900.

Svod statisticheskikh dannykh po fabrichno-zavodskoi promyshlennosti s 1887 po 1926 god. Moscow: Gosudarstvennoe Izdatel'stvo, 1929.

Svod Zakonov. Izdanie 1893 g., po prod. 1906, 1908, 1909 i 1910 gg.

Tarasov, I. *Roman Kniaz Smurskii (v stikakh): marshruty tramvaev g. SPB., kalendar' i ob"iavleniia.* St. Petersburg: 1909.

Tikhomirov, L. *Zakony o pechati.* St. Petersburg: 1909.

Torgovyi dom Vogau i Ko.: Istoricheskii ocherk deiatel'nosti s 1840 po 1916. Moscow: 1916.

Tsyperovich, G. "Reklama." *Sovremennyi Mir* (January 1911): 179–214.

———. *Sindikaty i tresty v Rossii.* St. Petersburg: 1918.

Uchites' reklamirovat' u amerikantsev. Moscow: 1911.

Umanskii, V. Ia. *Pravila o tovarnykh znakakh.* Odessa: 1896.

Uspeshnaia reklama i kak eiu pol'zovat'sia. Kiev: Izdanie kontory ob"iavlenii "Reklama," 1913.

Varadinov, N.N., comp. *Sbornik uzakonenii i rasporiazhenii pravitel'stva o poriadke pechataniia ob"iavlenii.* St. Petersburg: 1912.

Veblen, Thorstein. *Theory of the Leisure Class.* New York: Mentor Books, 1952.

Verigin, Aleksei. *Russkaia reklama.* St. Petersburg: Izdanie redaktora gazety "Russkii Trud," 1898.

Verkhovoi, N. *Reklama v XX veke kak neobkhodimost'.* Iaroslavl': 1902.

———. *Raskleika i raznoska reklam.* Poltava: Elektro-pechatnia I.A. Dokhmana, 1904.

Vernadsky, George, ed. *A Source Book for Russian History from Early Times to 1917,* vol. 2. (New Haven, CT: Yale University Press, 1972).

Verstraete, Maurice. *La Russie industrielle: Étude sur l'exposition de Nijni-Novgorod.* Paris: 1897.

Vol'fson, I.V. *Praktika gazetnogo izdatel'stva. Kratkoe rukovodstvo.* Petrograd: 1919.

———. *Adresnaia i spravochnaia kniga gazetnyi mir.* 2nd ed. St. Petersburg: 1913.

Vsia Moskva na 1896 g. Moscow: Izdanie A.S. Suvorina.

Zelnik, Reginald, ed. *A Radical Worker in Tsarist Russia: The Autobiography of Semen Ivanovich Kanatchikov.* Stanford, CA: Stanford University Press, 1986.

Zhurnal sostoiavshagosia 24 fevralia—8 marta 1914 g. pri glavnom upravlenii neokladnykh sborov i kazennoi prodazhi pitei soveshchaniia po voprosu o vliianii tabachnago ustava na tabakovodstvo i fabrikatsiiu tabaka. St. Petersburg: 1914.

Zolotoi iubilei parfiumernago proizvodstva tovarishchestva Brokar i Ko. v Moskve, 1864–1914. Moscow: 1915.

SECONDARY SOURCES

Anderson, Benedict. *Imagined Communities,* rev. ed. London: Verso, 1991.

Anikst, Mikhail, and Elena Chernevich. *Russian Graphic Design, 1880–1917.* New York: Abbeville, 1990.

Annenberg, Maurice. *Advertising 3000 B.C–1900 A.D.* Baltimore: Maran Printing Services, 1969.

Antonov, P. "Vyveski." *Neva* 4 (1986): 183–88.

Appadurai, Arjun, ed. *The Social Life of Things: Commodities in Cultural Perspective.* Cambridge: Cambridge University Press, 1986.

Arkhangel'skaia, I.D. *Reklama v starye dobrye vremena: konets XIX—nachalo XX veka* (Moscow: Izdatel'stvo Oktopus, 2009).

Auslander, Leora. "The Gendering of Consumer Practices in Nineteenth-Century France." In *The Sex of Things: Gender and Consumption in Historical Perspective,* edited by Victoria de Grazia and Ellen Furlough, 79–112. Berkeley: University of California Press, 1996.

Baburina, N.I. *Russkii plakat.* Leningrad: 1988.

Bailey, James, and Tatyana Ivanova. *An Anthology of Russian Folk Epics.* Armonk, NY: M.E. Sharpe, 1998.

Bakhrushin, S.V., ed. *Moskovskii krai v ego proshlom: Ocherki po sotsial'noi i ekonomicheskoi istorii XVI—XIX vekov.* Moscow: 1928.

Bakhtin, Mikhail. *Rabelais and His World.* Translated by Hélène Iswolsky. Bloomington: Indiana University Press, 1984.

Barkin, Kenneth D. "The Crisis of Modernity, 1887–1902." In *Imagining Modern*

German Culture, 1889–1910, Studies in the History of Art, edited by Françoise Forster-Hahn. No. 53, Symposium Papers 31. Hanover, NH: University Press of New England, 1996.

Barnard, Malcolm. "Advertising: The Rhetorical Imperative." In *Visual Culture*, edited by Chris Jenks, 26–41. London: Routledge, 1995.

Barthes, Roland. *Mythologies*. Translated by Annette Lavers. New York: Farrar, Straus and Giroux, 1972.

Bater, James. *St. Petersburg: Industrialization and Change*. London: Edward Arnold, 1976.

———. "Between Old and New: St. Petersburg in the Late Imperial Era." In *The City in Late Imperial Russia*, edited by Michael F. Hamm, 43–78. Bloomington: Indiana University Press, 1986.

Baudrillard, Jean. "Consumer Society." In *Jean Baudrillard: Selected Writings*, edited by Mark Poster, 29–56. Stanford, CA: Stanford University Press, 1988.

Beer, Daniel. "'Microbes of the Mind': Moral Contagion in Late Imperial Russia," *Journal of Modern History* 79 (September 2007): 531–71.

Benjamin, Walter. *Illuminations: Essays and Reflections*. 1955. Translated by Harry Zohn. New York: Shocken, 1968.

Berger, John. *Ways of Seeing*. London: Penguin, 1972.

Berman, Marshall. *All That Is Solid Melts into Air: The Experience of Modernity*. New York: Penguin, 1988.

Bisha, Robin, Jehanne M. Gheith, Christine Holden, and William G. Wagner, eds. *Russian Women, 1698–1917: Experience and Expression, An Anthology of Sources*. Bloomington: Indiana University Press, 2002.

Blackbourn, David. *The Long Nineteenth Century: A History of Germany, 1780–1918*. Oxford: Oxford University Press, 1997.

Bobroff, Anne. "Russian Working Women: Sexuality in Bonding Patterns and the Politics of Daily Life." In *Powers of Desire: The Politics of Sexuality*, edited by Ann Snitow, Christine Stansell, and Sharon Thompson, 206–27. New York: Monthly Review Press, 1983.

Bochacher, M.N. *Gazetnoe khoziaistvo: Opyt posobiia po gazetno-izdatel'skomu delu*. Moscow: Gosudarstvennoe izdatel'stvo, 1929.

Bocock, Robert. *Consumption*. London: Routledge, 1993.

Bokhanov, Aleksandr Nikolaevich. *Burzhuaznaia pressa Rossii i krupnyi kapital konets XIX v–1914 g*. Moscow: Izdatel'stvo Nauka, 1984.

Boym, Svetlana. *Common Places: Mythologies of Everyday Life in Russia*. Cambridge, MA: Harvard University Press, 1994.

Bradley, Joseph. *Muzhik and Muscovite: Urbanization in Late Imperial Russia*. Berkeley: University of California Press, 1985.

———. "Moscow: From Big Village to Metropolis." In *The City in Late Imperial Russia*, edited by Michael F. Hamm, 9–41. Bloomington: Indiana University Press, 1986.

Brantlinger, Patrick. "Mass Media and Culture in Fin-de-Siècle Europe." In *Fin-de-Siècle and Its Legacy*, edited by Mikulas Teich and Roy Porter, 98–114. Cambridge: Cambridge University Press, 1990.

Breward, Christopher. *The Hidden Consumer: Masculinities, Fashion and City Life, 1860–1914*. Manchester, UK: Manchester University Press, 1999.

Bronner, Simon J., ed. *Consuming Visions: Accumulation and Display of Goods in America, 1880–1920*. New York: W. W. Norton, 1989.

Brooks, Jeffrey. "Russian Nationalism and Russian Literature: The Canonization of the

Classics." In *Nation and Ideology: Essays in Honor of Wayne S. Vucinich,* edited by Ivo Banac, John G. Ackerman, and Roman Szporluk, 315–34. New York: Columbia University Press, 1981.

———. *When Russia Learned to Read: Literacy and Popular Literature, 1861–1917.* Princeton, NJ: Princeton University Press, 1985.

Brower, Daniel R. *The Russian City between Tradition and Modernity, 1850–1900.* Berkeley: University of California Press, 1990.

———. "The Penny Press and Its Readers." In *Cultures in Flux: Lower-Class Values, Practices, and Resistance in Late Imperial Russia,* edited by Stephen P. Frank and Mark D. Steinberg, 147–67. Princeton, NJ: Princeton University Press, 1994.

Brown, Malcolm Hamrick. "Native Song and National Consciousness in Nineteenth-Century Russian Music." In *Art and Culture in Nineteenth-Century Russia,* edited by Theofanis George Stavrou, 57–84. Bloomington: Indiana University Press, 1983.

Bruttini, Adriano. "Advertising and the Industrial Revolution." *Economic Notes* 4, no. 2–3 (1975): 90–116.

Buck-Morss, Susan. *The Dialectics of Seeing: Walter Benjamin and the Arcades Project.* Cambridge, MA: MIT Press, 1989.

———. "Dream World of Mass Culture: Walter Benjamin's Theory of Modernity and the Dialectics of Seeing." In *Modernity and the Hegemony of Vision,* edited by David Michael Levin, 309–38. Berkeley: University of California Press, 1993.

Burds, Jeffrey. *Peasant Dreams and Market Politics: Labor Migration and the Russian Village, 1861–1905.* Pittsburgh, PA: University of Pittsburgh Press, 1998.

Burke, Peter. *Popular Culture in Early Modern Europe.* New York: New York University Press, 1978.

———. *Eyewitnessing: The Uses of Images as Historical Evidence.* Ithaca, NY: Cornell University Press, 2001.

Burke, Timothy. *Lifebuoy Men, Lux Women: Commodification, Consumption, and Cleanliness in Modern Zimbabwe.* Durham, NC: Duke University Press, 1996.

Calinescu, Matei. *Five Faces of Modernity.* Durham, NC: Duke University Press, 1987.

Carstensen, Fred V. *American Enterprise in Foreign Markets: Studies of Singer and International Harvester in Imperial Russia.* Chapel Hill: University of North Carolina Press, 1984.

Certeau, Michel de. *The Practice of Everyday Life.* Translated by Steven Rendell. Berkeley: University of California Press, 1984.

Chandler, Jr., Alfred D. *The Visible Hand: The Managerial Revolution in American Business.* Cambridge, MA: Belknap Press of Harvard University Press, 1977.

Chartier, Roger. "Culture as Appropriation: Popular Cultural Uses in Early Modern France." In *Understanding Popular Culture: Europe from the Middle Ages to the Nineteenth Century,* edited by Steven L. Kaplan, 229–53. New York: Mouton, 1984.

Cherepakhov, M.S., and E.M. Fingerit. *Russkaia periodicheskaia pechat' 1895–1917 gg.* 2 vols. Moscow: 1957.

Cherniavsky, Michael, ed. *The Structure of Russian History.* New York: Random House, 1970.

Church, Roy. "Advertising Consumer Goods in Nineteenth-Century Britain: Reinterpretations." *Economic History Review* 53, no. 4 (November 2000): 621–45.

Church, Roy, and Christine Clark. "The Origins of Competitive Advantage in the Marketing of Branded Packaged Consumer Goods: Colman's and Reckitt's in Early Victorian Britain." *Journal of Industrial History* 3, no. 2 (2000): 98–119.

Clark, Katerina. *Petersburg: Crucible of Cultural Revolution.* Cambridge, MA: Harvard University Press, 1995.

Clements, Barbara Evans, Barbara Alpern Engel, and Christine D. Worobec, eds. *Russia's Women: Accommodation, Resistance, Transformation.* Berkeley: University of California Press, 1991.

Clements, Barbara Evans, Rebecca Friedman, and Dan Healey, eds., *Russian Masculinities in History and Culture* (New York: Palgrave, 2002).

Clowes, Edith W., Samuel D. Kassow, and James L. West. *Between Tsar and People: Educated Society and the Quest for Public Identity in Late Imperial Russia.* Princeton, NJ: Princeton University Press, 1991.

Clyman, Toby W., and Judith Vowles. *Russia through Women's Eyes: Autobiographies from Tsarist Russia.* New Haven, CT: Yale University Press, 1996.

Coffin, Judith G. *The Politics of Women's Work: The Paris Garment Trades, 1750-1915.* Princeton, NJ: Princeton University Press, 1996.

Cooper, Frederick. *Colonialism in Question: Theory, Knowledge, History.* Berkeley: University of California Press, 2005.

Corrigan, Peter. *The Sociology of Consumption.* London: Sage Publications, 1997.

Cox, Randi Barnes. "The Creation of the Socialist Consumer: Advertising, Citizenship and NEP." PhD diss., Indiana University, 2000.

———. "All This Can Be Yours!: Soviet Commercial Advertising and the Social Construction of Space, 1928-1956." In *The Landscape of Stalinism: The Art and Ideology of Soviet Space,* edited by Evgeny Dobrenko and Eric Naiman, 125-62. Seattle: University of Washington Press, 2003.

———. "'NEP Without Nepmen!' Soviet Advertising and the Transition to Socialism." In *Everyday Life in Early Soviet Russia,* edited by Christina Kiaer and Eric Naiman, 119-52. Bloomington: Indiana University Press, 2006.

Crisp, Olga, and Linda Edmondson, eds. *Civil Rights in Imperial Russia.* Oxford: Clarendon Press, 1989.

Crossick, Geoffrey, and Serge Jaumain, eds. *Cathedrals of Consumption: The European Department Store, 1850-1939.* Aldershot, UK: Ashgate, 1999.

Crossley, Nick, and John Michael Roberts, eds. *After Habermas: New Perspectives on the Public Sphere.* Oxford: Blackwell Publishing, 2004.

Czikszentmihalyi, Mihaly, and Eugene Rochberg-Halton. *The Meaning of Things: Domestic Symbols and the Self.* Cambridge: Cambridge University Press, 1981.

Danna, Sammy R., ed. *Advertising and Popular Culture: Studies in Variety and Versatility.* Bowling Green, OH: Bowling Green State University Popular Press, 1992.

Davydov, V.N. *Rasskaz o proshlom.* Leningrad/Moscow: Izdatel'stvo Iskusstvo, 1962.

Dégh, Linda. *American Folklore and the Mass Media.* Bloomington: Indiana University Press, 1994.

Douglas, Mary. "Jokes." In *Rethinking Popular Culture: Contemporary Perspectives in Cultural Studies,* edited by Chandra Mukerji and Michael Schudson, 291-310. Berkeley: University of California Press, 1991.

Douglas, Mary, and Baron Isherwood. *The World of Goods: Towards an Anthropology of Consumption.* 1979. New York: Routledge, 1996.

Dubin, Boris. "The Younger Generation of Culture Scholars and Culture-Studies in Russia Today." *Studies in East European Thought* 55 (March 2003): 27-36.

Edmondson, Linda Harriet. *Feminism in Russia, 1900-1917.* London: Heinemann Educational Books, 1984.

———, ed. *Women and Society in Russia and the Soviet Union.* Cambridge: Cambridge University Press, 1992.

Eklof, Ben. *Russian Peasant Schools: Officialdom, Village Culture, and Popular Pedagogy, 1861–1914*. Berkeley: University of California Press, 1986.

Elias, Norbert. *The Civilizing Process*, rev. ed. Oxford: Blackwell Publishers, 2000.

Engel, Barbara Alpern. *Mothers and Daughters: Women of the Intelligentsia in Nineteenth-Century Russia*. Cambridge: Cambridge University Press, 1983.

———. "Transformation Versus Tradition." In *Russia's Women: Accommodation, Resistance, Transformation*, edited by Barbara Evans Clements, Barbara Alpern Engel, and Christine D. Worobec, 135–47. Berkeley: University of California Press, 1991.

———. *Between the Fields and the City: Women, Work, and Family in Russia, 1861–1914*. Cambridge: Cambridge University Press, 1996.

Engelstein, Laura. *The Keys to Happiness: Sex and the Search for Modernity in Fin-de-Siècle Russia*. Ithaca, NY: Cornell University Press, 1992.

Esin, B.I. *Russkaia dorevoliutsionnaia gazeta, 1702–1917 gg., kraktii ocherk*. Moscow: Izdatel'stvo Moskovskogo Universiteta, 1971.

Ewen, Stuart. *Captains of Consciousness: Advertising and the Social Roots of the Consumer Culture*. New York: McGraw-Hill, 1976.

Ewen, Stuart, and Elizabeth Ewen. *Channels of Desire: Mass Images and the Shaping of American Conşciousness*. New York: McGraw-Hill, 1982.

Fedinskii, Iu. I. "Material'nye usloviia izdanii russkoi burzhuaznoi gazet." *Vestnik MGU: Zhurnalistika* 2 (1980): 25–32.

Felski, Rita. *The Gender of Modernity*. Cambridge, MA: Harvard University Press, 1995.

Ferenczi, Caspar. "Freedom of the Press under the Old Regime, 1905–1914." In *Civil Rights in Imperial Russia*, edited by Olga Crisp and Linda Edmondson, 191–214. Oxford: Clarendon Press, 1989.

Figes, Orlando, and Boris Kolonitskii. *Interpreting the Revolution: The Language and Symbols of 1917*. New Haven, CT: Yale University Press, 1999.

Finn, Margot. "Men's Things: Masculine Possession in the Consumer Revolution." *Social History* 25, no. 2 (May 2000): 133–55.

Fitzpatrick, Anne Lincoln. *The Great Russian Fair: Nizhnii Novgorod, 1840–1890*. New York: St. Martin's Press, 1990.

Flugel, J.C. *The Psychology of Clothes*. London: Hogarth Press, 1966.

Forbes, Christopher. *Fabergé Eggs: Imperial Russian Fantasies*. New York: Harry N. Abrams, 1980.

Foucault, Michel. *The History of Sexuality*, vol. 1. New York: Vintage, 1990.

Fowles, Jib. *Advertising and Popular Culture*. Thousand Oaks, CA: Sage Publications, 1996.

Fox, Richard Wightman, and T.J. Jackson Lears, eds. *The Culture of Consumption*. New York: Pantheon, 1983.

Fox, Stephen. *The Mirror Makers: A History of American Advertising and Its Creators*. New York: Vintage, 1985.

Frank, Stephen P. "Confronting the Domestic Other: Rural Popular Culture and its Enemies in Fin-de-Siècle Russia." In *Cultures in Flux: Lower-Class Values, Practices, and Resistance in Late Imperial Russia*, edited by Stephen P. Frank and Mark D. Steinberg, 74–107. Princeton, NJ: Princeton University Press, 1994.

Frank, Stephen P., and Mark D. Steinberg, eds. *Cultures in Flux: Lower-Class Values, Practices, and Resistance in Late Imperial Russia*. Princeton, NJ: Princeton University Press, 1994.

Franklin, Simon, and Emma Widdis, eds. *National Identity in Russian Culture*. Cambridge: Cambridge University Press, 2004.

Fraser, W. Hamish. *The Coming of the Mass Market, 1850–1914*. Hamden, CT: Archon Books, 1981.

Freeze, Gregory. "The *Soslovie* (Estate) Paradigm and Russian Social History." *American Historical Review* 91, no. 1 (February 1986): 11–36.

Fridman, R.A. *Parfiumeriia.* 2nd ed. Moscow: Pishchepromizat, 1955.

Frisby, David. *Fragments of Modernity: Theories of Modernity in the Work of Simmel, Kracauer and Benjamin.* Cambridge, MA: MIT Press, 1986.

Galerkina, O. *Khudozhnik Viktor Vasnetsov.* Leningrad: Detgiz, 1957.

Geldern, James von. "Life In-Between: Migration and Popular Culture in Late Imperial Russia." *Russian Review* 55 (July 1996): 365–83.

Geldern, James von, and Louise McReynolds, eds. *Entertaining Tsarist Russia: Tales, Songs, Plays, Movies, Jokes, Ads, and Images from Russian Urban Life, 1779–1917.* Bloomington: Indiana University Press, 1998.

Gifford, Don. *The Farther Shore: A Natural History of Perception, 1798–1984.* New York: Atlantic Monthly Press, 1990.

Glickman, Rose. *Russian Factory Women: Workplace and Society, 1880–1914.* Berkeley: University of California Press, 1984.

Glinternik, Eleanora. "Nachalo Rossiiskoi reklamy." *Nashe nasledie* 56 (2001): 223–34.

Goffman, Erving. *Gender Advertisements.* New York: Harper and Row, 1979.

Gohstand, Robert. "The Internal Geography of Trade in Moscow from the Mid-Nineteenth Century to the First World War." PhD diss., University of California, Berkeley, 1973.

Goldschmidt, Paul W. "Article 242: Past, Present, and Future." In *Eros and Pornography in Russian Culture*, edited by M. Levitt and A. Toporkov, 459–538. Moscow: Publishing House Ladomir, 1999.

Goscilo, Helena. "Viktor Vasnetsov's Bogatyrs: Mythic Heroes and Sacrosanct Borders Go to Market." In *Picturing Russia: Explorations in Visual Culture*, edited by Valerie A. Kivelson and Joan Neuberger, 248–53. New Haven, CT: Yale University Press, 2008.

Gosudarstvennyi muzei izobrazitel'nykh iskusstv imeni A. S. Puskhina, *Moskva-Parizh, 1900–1930.* Moscow: 1981.

Gray, Camilla. *The Russian Experiment in Art, 1863–1922.* 1962. London: Thames and Hudson, 1986.

Grazia, Victoria de, and Ellen Furlough, eds. *The Sex of Things: Gender and Consumption in Historical Perspective.* Berkeley: University of California Press, 1996.

Gregory, Paul R. *Before Command: An Economic History of Russia from Emancipation to the First Five-Year Plan.* Princeton, NJ: Princeton University Press, 1994.

Gunn, Simon. "The Public Sphere, Modernity and Consumption: New Perspectives on the History of the English Middle Class." In *Gender, Civic Culture and Consumerism: Middle-Class Identity in Britain, 1800–1940*, edited by Alan Kidd and David Nicholls, 12–29. Manchester: Manchester University Press, 1999.

Guroff, Gregory, and Fred V. Carstensen, eds. *Entrepreneurship in Imperial Russia and the Soviet Union.* Princeton, NJ: Princeton University Press, 1983.

Habermas, Jürgen. *The Structural Transformation of the Public Sphere: An Inquiry into a Category of Bourgeois Society.* Translated by Thomas Burger. Cambridge, MA: MIT Press, 1989.

Hall, Edward T. *Beyond Culture.* Garden City, NY: Doubleday, 1976.

Hall, Lesley A. *Hidden Anxieties: Male Sexuality, 1900–1950.* Cambridge: Polity Press, 1991.

Hall, Stuart. "For Allon White: Metaphors of Transformation." In *Stuart Hall: Critical Dialogues in Cultural Studies*, edited by David Morley and Kuan-Shing Chen, 287–308. London: Routledge, 1996.

Hamm, Michael F., ed. *The City in Late Imperial Russia*. Bloomington: Indiana University Press, 1986.

Harris, Neil. "Iconography and Intellectual History: The Half-Tone Effect." In *New Directions in American Intellectual History*, edited by John Higham and Paul K. Conkin, 196–211. Baltimore, MD: Johns Hopkins University Press, 1979.

Harvey, David. *Consciousness and the Urban Experience*. Oxford: Basil Blackwell, 1985.

Heald, Tim. *By Appointment: 150 Years of the Royal Warrant and Its Holders*. London: Queen Anne Press, 1989.

Hellberg-Hirn, Elena. *Soil and Soul: The Symbolic World of Russianness*. Aldershot, UK: Ashgate, 1998.

Henriksson, Anders. "Nationalism, Assimilation and Identity in Late Imperial Russia: The St. Petersburg Germans, 1906–1914." *Russian Review* 52 (July 1993): 341–53.

Herlihy, Patricia. "Strategies of Sobriety: Temperance Movements in Russia, 1880–1914." *Kennan Institute for Advanced Russian Studies*. Occasional Paper 238 (1990).

Higham, John, and Paul K. Conkin, eds. *New Directions in American Intellectual History*. Baltimore, MD: Johns Hopkins University Press, 1979.

Hilton, Alison. "Russian Folk Art and 'High' Art in the Early Nineteenth Century." In *Art and Culture in Nineteenth-Century Russia*, edited by Theofanis George Stavrou, 237–54. Bloomington: Indiana University Press, 1983.

Hilton, Marjorie Louise. "Commercial Cultures: Modernity in Russia and the Soviet Union, 1880–1930." PhD diss., University of Illinois, Urbana-Champaign, 2003.

Hilton, Matthew. "Class, Consumption and the Public Sphere." *Journal of Contemporary History* 35, no. 4 (Oct. 2000): 655–66.

Hobsbawm, Eric, and Terence Ranger, eds. *The Invention of Tradition*. Cambridge: Cambridge University Press, 1983.

Hoffmann, David L., and Yanni Kotsonis, eds. *Russian Modernity: Politics, Knowledge, Practices*. New York: St. Martin's Press, 2000.

Holmgren, Beth. "Gendering the Icon: Marketing Women Writers in Fin-de-Siècle Russia." In *Russia, Women, Culture*, edited by Helena Goscilo and Beth Holmgren, 321–46. Bloomington: Indiana University Press, 1996.

Horkheimer, Max, and Theodor Adorno. *Dialectic of Enlightenment*. New York: Continuum, 1988.

Hower, Ralph M. *The History of an Advertising Agency: N. W. Ayer & Son at Work, 1869–1939*. 1939. New York: Arno Press, 1978.

Hubbs, Joanna. *Mother Russia: The Feminine Myth in Russian Culture*. Bloomington: Indiana University Press, 1988.

Hughes, Lindsey. "Monuments and Identity." In *National Identity in Russian Culture*, edited by Simon Franklin and Emma Widdis, 171–96. Cambridge: Cambridge University Press, 2004.

Ivanits, Linda. *Russian Folk Belief*. Armonk, NY: M.E. Sharpe, 1987.

Johnson, Robert Eugene. *Peasant and Proletarian: The Working Class of Moscow in the Late Nineteenth Century*. New Brunswick, NJ: Rutgers University Press, 1979.

Joyce, Patrick. *Democratic Subjects: The Self and the Social in Nineteenth-Century England*. Cambridge: Cambridge University Press, 1994.

———, ed. *Class*. Oxford: Oxford University Press, 1995.

Kamenka, Eugene, ed. *The Portable Karl Marx*. London: Penguin, 1983.

Kanevskii, E.M. *Effekt reklamy*. Moscow: Izdatel'stvo Ekonomika, 1980.

Kaplan, Steven L., ed. *Understanding Popular Culture: Europe from the Middle Ages to the Nineteenth Century*. New York: Mouton, 1984.

Karas', N.M. *Uvlekatel'nyi mir moskovskoi reklamy XIX—nachala XX veka.* Moscow: Museum of the History of the City of Moscow, 1996.

Karmalova, Elena Iur'evna. *Audiovizual'naia reklama v kontekste kul'tury: mif, literatura, kinematograf.* St. Petersburg: SPbGU, 2008.

Kelly, Catriona. "'Better Halves'? Representations of Women in Russian Urban Popular Entertainments, 1870–1910." In *Women and Society in Russia and the Soviet Union*, edited by Linda Edmondson, 5–31. Cambridge: Cambridge University Press, 1992.

———. *Refining Russia: Advice Literature, Polite Culture, and Gender from Catherine to Yeltsin.* Oxford: Oxford University Press, 2001.

———. *"Byt*: Identity and Everyday Life." In *National Identity in Russian Culture*, edited by Simon Franklin and Emma Widdis, 149–67. Cambridge: Cambridge University Press, 2004.

Kelly, Catriona, and David Shepherd, eds. *Constructing Russian Culture in the Age of Revolution: 1881–1940.* Oxford: Oxford University Press, 1998.

Kenner, H.J. *The Fight for Truth in Advertising.* 1936. New York: Garland, 1985.

Kidd, Alan, and David Nicholls. *Gender, Civic Culture and Consumerism: Middle-Class Identity in Britain, 1800–1940.* Manchester: Manchester University Press, 1999.

Kiselev, A.P. "Reklama v dorevoliutsionnoi gazette." *Vestnik MGU: Zhurnalistika* Series 10, no. 4 (1990): 28–34.

Kivelson, Valerie A., and Robert H. Greene, eds. *Orthodox Russia: Belief and Practice under the Tsars.* University Park: Pennsylvania State University Press, 2003.

Kivelson, Valerie A., and Joan Neuberger, eds. *Picturing Russia: Explorations in Visual Culture.* New Haven, CT: Yale University Press, 2008.

Klioutchkine, Konstantine. "'I Smoke Therefore I Think': Tobacco as Liberation in Nineteenth-Century Literature and Culture." In *Tobacco in Russian History and Culture from the Seventeenth Century to the Present*, edited by Matthew P. Romaniello and Tricia Starks, 83–101. New York: Routledge, 2009.

Koenker, Diane. *Moscow Workers and the 1917 Revolution.* Princeton, NJ: Princeton University Press, 1981.

Kuchta, David. "The Making of the Self-Made Man: Class, Clothing, and English Masculinity, 1688–1832." In *The Sex of Things: Gender and Consumption in Historical Perspective*, edited by Victoria de Grazia and Ellen Furlough, 54–78. Berkeley: University of California Press, 1996.

Laird, Pamela Walker. *Advertising Progress: American Business and the Rise of Consumer Marketing.* Baltimore, MD: Johns Hopkins University Press, 1998.

Landauer, Bella. "Literary Allusions in American Advertising." *New York Historical Society Quarterly* 31, no. 3 (July 1947): 148–219.

Laverychev, V. Ia. "Russkie kapitalisty i periodicheskaia pechat' vtoroi poloviny XIX v." *Istoriia SSSR* 1 (1972): 26–47.

Lears, T.J. Jackson. *No Place of Grace: Antimodernism and the Transformation of American Culture, 1880–1920.* Chicago: University of Chicago Press, 1981.

———. "From Salvation to Self-Realization: Advertising and the Therapeutic Roots of the Consumer Culture, 1880–1930." In *The Culture of Consumption*, edited by Richard Wightman Fox and T.J. Jackson Lears, 1–38. New York: Pantheon, 1983.

———. "Some Versions of Fantasy: Toward a Cultural History of American Advertising, 1880–1930." In *Prospects*, no. 9. New York: Cambridge University Press, 1984: 349–405.

———. "Sherwood Anderson: Looking for the White Spot." In *The Power of Culture: Critical Essays in American History*, edited by Richard Wightman Fox and T.J. Jackson Lears, 13–37. Chicago: University of Chicago Press, 1993.

———. *Fables of Abundance: A Cultural History of Advertising in America*. New York: Basic Books, 1994.

Leiss, William, Stephen Kline, and Sut Jhally. *Social Communication in Advertising: Persons, Products, and Images of Well-Being*. Toronto: Methuen, 1986.

Levin, David Michael, ed. *Modernity and the Hegemony of Vision*. Berkeley: University of California Press, 1993.

Levine, Lawrence. *Highbrow/Lowbrow: The Emergence of Cultural History in America*. Cambridge, MA: Harvard University Press, 1988.

———. "The Folklore of Industrial Society: Popular Culture and Its Audiences." *American Historical Review* 97, no. 5 (December 1992): 1369–99.

Loeb, Lori Anne. *Consuming Angels: Advertising and Victorian Women*. New York: Oxford University Press, 1994.

Lotman, Iurii M., and Boris A. Uspenskii. "The Role of Dual Models in the Dynamics of Russian Culture." In *The Semiotics of Russian Culture*, edited by Ann Shukman, 3–35. Ann Arbor: University of Michigan Press, 1984.

Lutz, Tom. *American Nervousness, 1903: An Anecdotal History*. Ithaca, NY: Cornell University Press, 1991.

Lyashchenko, Peter I. *History of the National Economy of Russia to the 1917 Revolution*. New York: Macmillan, 1949.

Maltby, Richard, ed. *Passing Parade: A History of Popular Culture in the Twentieth Century*. Oxford: Oxford University Press, 1988.

Marchand, Roland. *Advertising the American Dream: Making Way for Modernity, 1920–1940*. Berkeley: University of California Press, 1985.

Marx, Leo. "The Railroad-in-the-Landscape: An Iconological Reading of an Icon in American Art." In *The Railroad in American Art: Representations of Technological Change*, edited by Susan Danly and Leo Marx, 183–208. Cambridge, MA: MIT Press, 1988.

McKay, John P. *Pioneers for Profit: Foreign Entrepreneurship and Russian Industrialization, 1885–1913*. Chicago: University of Chicago Press, 1970.

McKendrick, Neil, John Brewer, and J.H. Plumb. *The Birth of a Consumer Society: The Commercialization of Eighteenth-Century England*. Bloomington: Indiana University Press, 1982.

McLuhan, Marshall. *The Mechanical Bride: Folklore of Industrial Man*. Boston: Beacon Press, 1951.

McReynolds, Louise. *The News under Russia's Old Regime: The Development of a Mass-Circulation Press*. Princeton, NJ: Princeton University Press, 1991.

———. *Russia at Play: Leisure Activities at the End of the Tsarist Era*. Ithaca, NY: Cornell University Press, 2003.

———. "Visualizing Masculinity: The Male Sex That Was Not One in Fin-de-Siècle Russia." In *Picturing Russia: Explorations in Visual Culture*, edited by Valerie A. Kivelson and Joan Neuberger, 133–38. New Haven, CT: Yale University Press, 2008.

McReynolds, Louise, and Joan Neuberger, eds. *Imitations of Life: Two Centuries of Melodrama in Russia*. Durham, NC: Duke University Press, 2002.

Miller, Michael B. *The Bon Marché: Bourgeois Culture and the Department Store, 1869–1920*. Princeton, NJ: Princeton University Press, 1981.

Moeller-Sally, Stephen. "Parallel Lives: Gogol''s Biography and Mass Readership in Late Imperial Russia." *Slavic Review* 54, no. 1 (Spring 1995): 62–79.

Morrissey, Susan K. *Suicide and the Body Politic in Imperial Russia.* Cambridge: Cambridge University Press, 2006.

———. "The Economy of Nerves: Health, Commercial Culture, and the Self in Late Imperial Russia." *Slavic Review* 69, no. 3 (Fall 2010): 645–75.

Moskovskaia parfiumernaia fabrika "Svoboda." *K 40-letiiu Velikogo Oktiabria 1917–1957.* Moscow: Mosgorsovnarkhoz, 1957.

Naremore, James, and Patrick Brantlinger, eds. *Modernity and Mass Culture.* Bloomington: Indiana University Press, 1991.

Neuberger, Joan. *Hooliganism: Crime, Culture, and Power in St. Petersburg, 1900–1914.* Berkeley: University of California Press, 1993.

Nevett, T.R. *Advertising in Britain: A History.* London: Heinemann, 1982.

Norris, James D. *Advertising and the Transformation of American Society, 1865–1920.* New York: Greenwood Press, 1990.

Norris, Stephen M. *A War of Images: Russian Popular Prints, Wartime Culture, and National Identity, 1812–1945.* DeKalb: Northern Illinois University Press, 2006.

Ocherki istorii Leningrada, vol. 3. Moscow: Izdatel'stvo Akademii Nauk SSSR, 1956.

Okorokov, A.Z., comp. *V.I. Lenin o pechati.* Moscow: Izdatel'stvo Politicheskoi Literatury, 1974.

Opie, Robert. *Rule Britannia: Trading on the British Image.* New York: Viking Penguin, 1985.

Oram, Hugh. *The Advertising Book: The History of Advertising in Ireland.* Dublin: M.O. Bokks, 1986.

Owen, Thomas C. "The Moscow Merchants and the Public Press, 1858–1868." *Jahrbücher für Geschichte Osteuropas* 1 (1975): 26–38.

———. *Capitalism and Politics in Russia: A Social History of the Moscow Merchants, 1855–1905.* Cambridge: Cambridge University Press, 1981.

———. *The Corporation under Russian Law, 1800–1917: A Study in Tsarist Economic Policy.* Cambridge: Cambridge University Press, 1991.

———. "Impediments to a Bourgeois Consciousness in Russia, 1880–1905: The Estate Structure, Ethnic Diversity, and Economic Regionalism." In *Between Tsar and People: Educated Society and the Quest for Public Identity in Late Imperial Russia,* edited by Edith Clowes, Samuel D. Kassow, and James L. West, 75–89. Princeton, NJ: Princeton University Press, 1991.

Pallot, Judith. "Women's Domestic Industries in Moscow Province, 1880–1900." In *Russia's Women: Accommodation, Resistance, Transformation,* edited by Barbara Evans Clement, Barbara Alpern Engel, and Christine D. Worobec, 163–84. Berkeley: University of California Press, 1991.

Palmer, Scott. *Dictatorship of the Air: Aviation Culture and the Fate of Modern Russia.* Cambridge: Cambridge University Press, 2006.

Paltusova, Irina N. *Torgovaia reklama i upakovka v Rossii XIX–XX vv.* Moscow: State Historical Museum, 1993.

Peiss, Kathy. *Hope in a Jar: The Making of America's Beauty Culture.* New York: Henry Holt, 1999.

Pintner, Walter McKenzie. *Russian Economic Policy under Nicholas I.* Ithaca, NY: Cornell University Press, 1967.

Pollay, Richard W., ed. *Information Sources in Advertising History.* Westport: Greenwood Press, 1979.

Pope, Daniel. *The Making of Modern Advertising.* New York: Basic Books, 1983.

Porter, Patrick G. "Advertising in the Early Cigarette Industry: W. Duke, Sons & Company of Durham." *North Carolina Historical Review* 48, no. 1 (1971): 31–43.

Povelikhina, Alla, and Evgeny Kovtun. *Russian Painted Shop Signs and Avant-garde Artists*. Leningrad: Aurora Art Publishers, 1991.

Presbrey, Frank. *The History and Development of Advertising*. Garden City: Doubleday, Doran, 1929.

Ransel, David L. *The Family in Imperial Russia*. Urbana: University of Illinois Press, 1978.

Renan, Ernst. "What is a Nation?" In *The Nationalism Reader,* edited by Omar Dahbour and Micheline R. Ishay, 143–55. Atlantic Highlands, NJ: Humanities Press, 1995.

Repp, Kevin. "Marketing, Modernity, and the German People's Soul: Advertising and Its Enemies in Late Imperial Germany, 1896–1914." In *Selling Modernity: Advertising in Twentieth-Century Germany*, edited by Pamela E. Swett, Jonathan Wiesen, and Jonathan R. Zatlin, 27–51. Durham, NC: Duke University Press, 2007.

Richards, Thomas. *The Commodity Culture of Victorian England: Advertising and Spectacle, 1851–1914*. Stanford, CA: Stanford University Press, 1990.

Rieber, Alfred J. *Merchants and Entrepreneurs in Imperial Russia*. Chapel Hill: University of North Carolina Press, 1982.

Rigberg, B. "Efficacy of Tsarist Censorship Operations," *Jahrbücher für Geschichte Osteuropas* 14 (1966): 327–46.

Rivosh, Ia. N. *Vremia i veshchi: ocherki po istorii material'noi kul'tury v Rossii nachala XX veka*. Moscow: Iskusstvo, 1990.

Romaniello, Matthew P., and Tricia Starks, eds. *Tobacco in Russian History and Culture: From the Seventeenth Century to the Present*. New York: Routledge, 2009.

Rosenberg, William G. "Representing Workers and the Liberal Narrative of Modernity." *Slavic Review* 55, no. 2 (Summer 1996): 245–69.

Roshchupkin, S.N. "Reklama kak fenomenon kul'tury." *Kul'turologiia* 2 (1997): 81–88.

Rothstein, Robert A. "Death of the Folk Song?" In *Cultures in Flux: Lower-Class Values, Practices, and Resistance in Late Imperial Russia*, edited by Stephen P. Frank and Mark D. Steinberg, 108–20. Princeton, NJ: Princeton University Press, 1994.

Ruane, Christine. "Clothes Shopping in Imperial Russia: The Development of a Consumer Culture." *Journal of Social History* 28, no. 4 (Summer 1995): 765–82.

———. *The Empire's New Clothes: A History of the Russian Fashion Industry, 1700–1917*. New Haven, CT: Yale University Press, 2009.

Ruckman, Jo Ann. *The Moscow Business Elite: A Social and Cultural Portrait of Two Generations, 1840–1905*. DeKalb: Northern Illinois University Press, 1984.

Ruud, Charles A. *Fighting Words: Imperial Censorship and the Russian Press, 1804–1906*. Toronto: University of Toronto Press, 1982.

Sampson, Henry. *A History of Advertising from the Earliest Times*. London: Chatto and Windus, 1874.

Saveleva, Olga Olegovna. "Kommertsiia v stile modern." *Chelovek* 5 (2002): 54–75.

Schudson, Michael. *Advertising, the Uneasy Persuasion: Its Dubious Impact on American Society*. New York: Basic Books, 1984.

Schwartz, Vanessa R. *Spectacular Realities: Early Mass Culture in Fin-de-Siècle Paris*. Berkeley: University of California Press, 1998.

Scott, Linda M. *Fresh Lipstick: Redressing Fashion and Feminism*. New York: Palgrave MacMillan, 2005.

Sergienko, M. "K biografii reklamy." *Reklama* 3 (1971): 22–24.

Shepelev, L.E. *Akstionernye kompanii v Rossii*. Leningrad: Izdatel'stvo Nauka, 1973.

Shiryaeva, P.G. "Poetic Features and Genre Characteristics of the Songs of Russian

Workers." *Soviet Anthropology and Archeology* (Summer/Fall 1975): 71–95.

Silverman, Debora L. *Art Nouveau in Fin-de-Siècle France: Politics, Psychology and Style.* Berkeley: University of California Press, 1989.

Simon, Richard. "Advertising as Literature: The Utopian Fiction of the American Marketplace." *Texas Studies in Literature and Language* 22, no. 2 (Summer 1980): 154–74.

Sivulka, Juliann. *Ad Women: How They Impact What We Need, Want, and Buy.* New York: Prometheus, 2009.

Slanskaia, Ekaterina. "House Calls: A Day in the Practice of a Duma Woman Doctor in St. Petersburg." In *Russia through Women's Eyes: Autobiographies from Tsarist Russia*, edited by Toby W. Clyman and Judith Vowles, 186–216. New Haven, CT: Yale University Press, 1996.

Smith, Alison. *Recipes for Russia: Food and Nationhood under the Tsars.* DeKalb: Northern Illinois University Press, 2008.

Smith, Anthony. *The Newspaper: An International History.* London: Thames and Hudson, 1979.

Smith, Bonnie G. *Ladies of the Leisure Class: The Bourgeoises of Northern France in the Nineteenth Century.* Princeton, NJ: Princeton University Press, 1981.

Smith, R.E.F., and David Christian. *Bread and Salt: A Social and Economic History of Food and Drink in Russia.* Cambridge: Cambridge University Press, 1984.

Smith, S.A. "Masculinity in Transition: Peasant Migrants to Late-Imperial St. Petersburg." In *Russian Masculinities in History and Culture*, edited by Barbara Evans Clements, Rebecca Friedman, and Dan Healey, 94–112. New York: Palgrave, 2002.

Smith, Steve, and Catriona Kelly. "Commercial Culture and Consumerism." In *Constructing Russian Culture in the Age of Revolution, 1881–1940*, edited by Catriona Kelly and David Shepherd, 106–64. Oxford: Oxford University Press, 1998.

Snitow, Ann, Christine Stansell, and Sharon Thompson, eds. *Powers of Desire: The Politics of Sexuality.* New York: Monthly Review Press, 1983.

Sokolov, Yuri M. *Russian Folklore.* 1938. Detroit, MI: Folklore Associates, 1971.

Solomon, Susan Gross, and John F. Hutchinson, eds. *Health and Society in Revolutionary Russia.* Bloomington: Indiana University Press, 1990.

Stavrou, Theofanis George, ed. *Art and Culture in Nineteenth-Century Russia.* Bloominton: Indiana University Press, 1983.

Steinberg, Mark D. *Moral Communities: The Culture of Class Relations in the Russian Printing Industry, 1867–1907.* Berkeley: University of California Press, 1992.

———. *Proletarian Imagination: Self, Modernity, and the Sacred in Russia, 1910–1925.* Ithaca, NY: Cornell University Press, 2002.

———. "Workers in Suits: Performing the Self." In *Picturing Russia: Explorations in Visual Culture*, edited by Valerie A. Kivelson and Joan Neuberger, 128–32. New Haven, CT: Yale University Press, 2008.

Stepanov, A. A. *Istoriia ob"iavlenii: gazetnaia reklama v Rossii XVIII–XX vv.* St. Petersburg: RIAL—Pronto-Peterburg, 2007.

Stites, Richard. *The Women's Liberation Movement in Russia: Feminism, Nihilism, and Bolshevism, 1860–1930.* Princeton, NJ: Princeton University Press, 1978.

———. "Iconoclastic Currents in the Russian Revolution: Destroying and Preserving the Past." In *Bolshevik Culture: Experiment and Order in the Russian Revolution*, edited by Abbott Gleason, Peter Kenez, and Richard Stites, 1–24. Bloomington: University of Indiana Press, 1985.

———. *Revolutionary Dreams: Utopian Vision and Experimental Life in the Russian*

Revolution. New York: Oxford University Press, 1989.

———. *Russian Popular Culture: Entertainment and Society since 1900.* Cambridge: Cambridge University Press, 1992.

Swett, Pamela E., Jonathan Wiesen, and Jonathan R. Zatlin, eds. *Selling Modernity: Advertising in Twentieth-Century Germany.* Durham, NC: Duke University Press, 2007.

Swingewood, Alan. *Cultural Theory and the Problem of Modernity.* New York: St. Martin's Press, 1998.

Taylor, Charles. "Two Theories of Modernity." *The Hastings Center Report* 25, no. 2 (March-April 1995): 24–33.

Tian-Shanskaia, Olga Semenova. *Village Life in Late Tsarist Russia.* Edited, translated, and with notes by David L. Ransel. Bloomington: Indiana University Press, 1993.

Tiersten, Lisa. "Redefining Consumer Culture: Recent Literature on Consumption and the Bourgeoisie in Western Europe." *Radical History Review* 57 (Fall 1993): 116–59.

———. *Marianne in the Market: Envisioning Consumer Society in Fin-de-Siècle France.* Berkeley: University of California Press, 2001.

Tolstoy, Nikolai. *The Tolstoys: Twenty-Four Generations of Russian History.* New York: William Morrow, 1983.

Tolz, Vera. *Russia: Inventing the Nation.* London: Arnold, 2001.

Tovrov, Jessica. "Mother-Child Relationships among the Russian Nobility." In *The Family in Imperial Russia: New Lines of Historical Research,* edited by David L. Ransel, 15–43. Urbana: University of Illinois Press, 1978.

Transchel, Kate. *Under the Influence: Working-Class Drinking, Temperance, and Cultural Revolution in Russia, 1895–1932.* Pittsburgh, PA: University of Pittsburgh Press, 2006.

Tugenkhol'd, Ia. "Plakat." *Gazetnyi i knizhny mir* 2 (1926): 325–51.

Twitchell, James. *Adcult USA: The Triumph of Advertising in American Culture.* New York: Columbia University Press, 1996.

Uchenova, V.V., and N.V. Starykh. *Istoriia reklamy, ili metamorfoza reklamnogo obraza.* Moscow: Iuniti-Dana, 1999.

———. *Istoriia reklamy,* 2 vols. St. Petersburg: 2002.

Vainshtein, Olga. "Russian Dandyism: Constructing a Man of Fashion." In *Russian Masculinities in History and Culture,* edited by Barbara Evans Clements, Rebecca Friedman, and Dan Healey, 51–75. New York: Palgrave, 2002.

Volkov, Solomon. *St. Petersburg: A Cultural History.* New York: Free Press, 1995.

Von Laue, Theodore. *Sergei Witte and the Industrialization of Russia.* New York: Atheneum, 1973.

Wagner, William G. "The Trojan Mare: Women's Rights and Civil Rights in Late Imperial Russia." In *Civil Rights in Imperial Russia,* edited by Olga Crisp and Linda Edmondson, 65–84. Oxford: Clarendon Press, 1989.

Walkowitz, Judith R. *City of Dreadful Delight: Narratives of Sexual Danger in Late-Victorian London.* Chicago: University of Chicago Press, 1992.

Wandel, Torbjörn. "Too Late for Modernity." *Journal of Historical Sociology* 18, no. 3 (September 2005): 255–68.

West, James L., and Iurii A. Petrov, eds. *Merchant Moscow: Images of Russia's Vanished Bourgeoisie.* Princeton, NJ: Princeton University Press, 1998.

West, Sally. "Constructing Consumer Culture: Advertising in Imperial Russia to 1914."

PhD diss., University of Illinois, Urbana-Champaign, 1995.

———. "The Material Promised Land: Advertising's Modern Agenda in Late Imperial Russia." *Russian Review* 57, no. 3 (July 1998): 345–63.

———. "Smokescreens: Tobacco Manufacturers' Projections of Class and Gender in Late Imperial Russian Advertising." In *Tobacco in Russian History and Culture: From the Seventeenth Century to the Present*, edited by Matthew P. Romaniello and Tricia Starks, 102–19. New York: Routledge, 2009.

Wicke, Jennifer. *Advertising Fictions: Literature, Advertisement, and Social Reading.* New York: Columbia University Press, 1988.

Williams, Raymond. *Keywords: A Vocabulary of Culture and Society*, rev. ed. New York: Oxford University Press, 1983.

Williams, Rosalind H. *Dream Worlds: Mass Consumption in Late Nineteenth-Century France.* Berkeley: University of California Press, 1982.

Williamson, Judith. *Decoding Advertisements: Ideology and Meaning in Advertising.* London: Marion Boyars, 1978.

Wirtschafter, Elise Kimerling. *Structures of Society: Imperial Russia's 'People of Various Ranks.'* DeKalb: Northern Illinois University Press, 1994.

Wohl, Robert. *A Passion for Wings: Aviation and the Western Imagination, 1908–1918.* New Haven, CT: Yale University Press, 1994.

Wood, James Playsted. *The Story of Advertising.* New York: Ronald Press, 1958.

Worobec, Christine. "Masculinity in Late-Imperial Russian Peasant Society." In *Russian Masculinities in History and Culture*, edited by Barbara Evans Clements, Rebecca Friedman, and Dan Healey, 76–93. New York: Palgrave, 2002.

Wortman, Richard. *The Development of a Russian Legal Consciousness.* Chicago: University of Chicago Press, 1976.

———. *Scenarios of Power: Myth and Ceremony in Russian Monarchy*, vol. 1, *From Peter the Great to the Death of Nicholas I.* Princeton, NJ: Princeton University Press, 1995.

———. *Scenarios of Power: Myth and Ceremony in Russian Monarchy*, vol. 2, *From Alexander II to the Abdication of Nicholas II.* Princeton, NJ: Princeton University Press, 2000.

Wrigley, Richard. "Between the Street and the Salon: Parisian Shop Signs and the Spaces of Professionalism in the Eighteenth and Early Nineteenth Centuries." *Oxford Art Journal* 21, no. 1 (1998): 45–67.

INDEX